Henry James and
the Experimental Novel

Henry James and the Experimental Novel

Sergio Perosa

University Press of Virginia
Charlottesville

THE UNIVERSITY PRESS OF VIRGINIA
Copyright © 1978 by the Rector and Visitors
of the University of Virginia

First published 1978

Library of Congress Cataloging in Publication Data

Perosa, Sergio.
  Henry James and the experimental novel.

  Includes index.
  1. James, Henry, 1843–1916—Criticism and interpretation. I. Title.
PS2124.P37   813'.4   77-16487   ISBN 0-8139-0727-6

Printed in the United States of America

Contents

Preface

This book grows out of an interest of many years in Henry James. It would not have been completed without the support and the assistance of many friends and colleagues. Four in particular I wish to thank here: Alastair Fowler, John Guthrie, A. Walton Litz, and Peter Shaw. On various occasions they read drafts of the book, offered advice and encouragement, and told me to persevere. I am glad I followed their advice.

Parts of the book are based on two essays of mine, which appeared in Italian in my *Le vie della narrativa americana* (Milan, 1965) and in *Studi americani*, 12 (1966). For permission to rewrite and expand them in a totally different context in this study, I am grateful to Ugo Mursia Editore and to Agostino Lombardo. An American Council of Learned Societies Advanced Fellowship allowed me to consult and check primary and secondary sources, including unpublished material, during a year's stay in the United States, mainly at Princeton University, Harvard University, and the University of Virginia. I owe a great debt of gratitude to these institutions, their libraries, and the ACLS. Grateful acknowledgment is also made to the Italian Consiglio Nazionale delle Ricerche, whose contribution helped to defray in part editorial expenses.

Like all James scholars, I owe much to the work and the example of Leon Edel. On two occasions I experienced his exquisite kindness. Given the wealth, indeed the proliferation, of James criticism, notes have been kept (comparatively speaking) to a minimum. Had all possible references been given, the book would have been twice as long. Even so, they are an integral part of the argument.

The University of Venice, Ca' Foscari, 1976

Introduction

Introduction

MORE than any other nineteenth-century novelist Henry James deserves consideration as an experimental writer—for the wealth of revolutionary principles and technical innovations he bestowed on twentieth-century fiction and for the intrinsically experimental quality of most of his novels. His long career as a writer was marked and sustained by a continuous and tireless search for the new. Every step of his achievement was a move forward, an attempt at probing the possibilities of fiction. This is true of his novels and short stories, as well as of his criticism, and can be said of every really great writer. In James, however, this aspiration became a daily struggle with the angel of inspiration and the phantom of reality, an unabated trial of strength with the available or unsuspected potentialities of expression. It became a driving force, an unrelenting challenge to language—a determination, one might say, that informed and supported every moment of his lifelong striving toward renewal and achievement. "Every attempt," as T. S. Eliot put it, is "a wholly new start": a breakthrough and a new beginning that sums up and makes the most of previous achievements, while experimenting with new subjects, forms, and methods.

This tendency became of paramount importance in that group of novels and short stories that marked the transition to James's later manner, from the novels culminating in *The Portrait of a Lady* (1881) to the novels of the major phase, which significantly coincided with the beginning of our century. In this twenty-year-long middle period, divided into two distinct but complementary stages by the theatrical experiences of his "dramatic years" (1889–95), this experimental tendency was clearly determined by an avowed need for renewal and by an unremitting exploration of the nature and possibilities of fiction writing. James's early novels had taken up the challenge and explored the possibilities of the "international theme," but he had kept within the framework of available and traditional techniques. Although he anticipated here and there his later use of the limited point of view and of the center of consciousness, his books wavered between the completeness of pictorial illustration and the revealing intensity of great dramatic moments, moving from long descriptive and analytical passages to the resolution provided by "big scenes" in a manner clearly reminiscent of nineteenth-century models— Dickens, George Eliot, Nathaniel Hawthorne.

To reach the thematic complexity and the balanced precision of dramatic structure of *The Wings of the Dove* (1902), *The Ambassadors* (1903), and *The Golden Bowl* (1904), James had to test the themes and the varied narrative techniques that were to contribute to the greatness of these last novels: the tendency toward painstaking and self-conscious experimentation, the increased attention to detail and groundwork, began to gather momentum. Hence the slow unwinding of a long process of tests and trials, the gradual focusing on problems of technique and presentation that not only prepared James for the achievement of his major phase but provided twentieth-century fiction with advanced and refined means of expression.

The path followed by James in his middle phase did not of course lead to artistic achievement only in his later novels. It was marked at every stage by notable achievements in their own right or by serious attempts that make this period one of the richest for the outstanding originality of his work. It is true that here one finds the premises or the germs of James's "mannerism." Giorgio Melchiori has pointed out that in order to endow his novels with depth and amplitude James had to choose the most devious methods and to adopt "undulating and serpentine" lines of development.[1] But it is also true that the attention he paid to stylistic and technical problems enabled him to fashion the most appropriate instruments to

[1] *The Tightrope Walkers: Essay on Mannerism in Modern English Literature* (London, 1956), pp. 13–33.

express, then and later, the world of forms and values he was gradually to claim as his own, to test in joy and torment the literary techniques which were already at his disposal or which he was in the process of discovering and perfecting for the enrichment of the novel.

I have chosen to examine the novels of James's middle period from the point of view of their experimental aspects. If a further distinction within this group may be made, then the novels written *before* his "dramatic years" (*The Bostonians*, 1886, *The Princess Casamassima*, 1886, *The Reverberator*, 1888, and *The Tragic Muse*, 1890) can be considered as more typically transitional novels, while the five novels written after his disappointing theatrical experience (*The Other House*, 1896, *The Spoils of Poynton*, 1896, *What Maisie Knew*, 1897, *The Awkward Age*, 1899, and *The Sacred Fount*, 1901) appear as more strictly and avowedly experimental in a technical sense. In the former James seemed to be testing new subjects and themes rather than new techniques, even though the new thematic concerns inevitably turned him to new narrative forms. In the latter his tireless activity led him to experiment openly with new methods, forms, and techniques suited to the new themes ("being 'very artistic,' I have a constant impulse to try experiments of form," he had written as early as 1878 to his brother William)[2] to the extent, one might say, of working out new forms to determine new contents, or even raising the formal elaboration itself to thematic dignity (as in the case of *The Sacred Fount*).

This distinction within James's middle period will show that the latter group of novels, experimental in the strict sense, depended heavily for their methodological and technical premises on his theatrical experience, while the theoretical premises stated in 1884 in *The Art of Fiction* inform more specifically the novels of the earlier group. There is a widespread tendency to see in this well-known essay of James a kind of poetics of his middle period, on which he drew inspiration for

[2] *The Letters of Henry James*, ed. Percy Lubbock, 2 vols. (New York, 1920), I, 66.

most of the works immediately preceding his major phase. In fact, only the earlier novels were motivated by the application of those principles; the others were basically the result of the stimulus and the drive provided by the application of strictly dramatic methods to fiction. The principles of *The Art of Fiction*, which informed the earlier group of novels, served the purpose, as it were, of freeing James from his youthful adherence to traditional methods of presentation and turning him toward an illustrative treatment of "naturalistic" themes. The dramatic method and the insistence on the limited point of view applied to the second group of novels, on the other hand, besides endowing them with an unmistakable novelty and intensity of presentation, opened up for the artist an altogether new perspective for attempting the more ambitious novels of the major phase.

In a valuable study of these novels, Walter Isle has remarked that their pattern of development "seemed to reflect in miniature many of the general changes from nineteenth century to twentieth century fiction, or rather vaguely, from 'Victorian' to 'Modern' ".[3] This idea underlies most of the pages that follow. And one has only to look at *The Sacred Fount*, that extraordinarily "modern" novel James published in 1901 (the date is significant), at the very end of the experimental period, to realize how relevant such a contention can be. So much has already been written on that novel—the typical puzzle to excite contemporary criticism—that one feels somewhat uneasy in writing about it once more. But it holds a crucial position, both in terms of James's development and in terms of contemporary fiction, and it must be regarded as the culmination of the experimental period, especially if I am right in detecting in it a possible opening and a perspective on the way that was to lead to the French *nouveau roman*.

---

[3] *Experiments in Form: Henry James's Novels, 1896–1901* (Cambridge, Mass., 1968), p. vii. Donald David Stone, in his *Novelists in a Changing World: Meredith, James, and the Transformation of English Fiction in the 1880's* (Cambridge, Mass., 1972), claims almost as much for the novels of the earlier group.

After this baffling attempt James came into his own with the great novels of the major phase, where twentieth-century fiction is already on its way. Experimentation then had to find byways and secondary paths, retrace its steps, look for disregarded nooks. It is surprising to find James in 1906 collaborating with eleven other writers, almost all of them second-rate, on the novel *The Whole Family*. It is less surprising to see, as it were, in vitro how the application of his by now perfected method could distinguish him from the other writers while bringing them—and the novel itself—almost to a standstill. In *The Whole Family* one seems to be watching the coils and tendrils of James's method and James's prose enwrap and entangle the narrative structure itself, reach out in all directions, push off opponents and collaborators alike from a field that was by then recognizable as his own.

Finally, in the two unfinished novels of his old age, *The Sense of the Past* and *The Ivory Tower* (both published posthumously in 1917), James was again in the process of full-scale experimentation, all the more so as their unfinished state allows the reader to penetrate into the very secrets of their composition. In the former, a revolutionary application of the limited point of view in terms of past, present, and future awareness on the part of the center of consciousness formed the basis for a thorough reconsideration of James's attitude toward past and present, Europe and America. In the latter, experimentation was once more (as in the early novels of the middle period) mainly related to the exploration of new subjects and themes—coming to grips for the first time in a novel with the world, and the fictional possibilities, of American business and American wealth, with the "home scene," which James had revisited with expectation and dismay in 1904. The wheel of experimentation had gone full circle, back to where it had appropriately started: to a reconsideration of America as such—unrelated, that is to Europe, as in the case of *The Bostonians*—but enhanced now by the full mastery of a peculiar and perfected technique. James's search for the new and his endless struggle with the possible ways and means of expression found here their culmination.

PART ONE

Art lives upon discussion, upon experiment,
upon curiosity, upon variety of attempt,
upon the exchange of views and the comparison
of standpoints. . . . Art derives a
considerable part of its beneficial exercise
from flying in the face of presumptions.
The Art of Fiction

I. Middle Period: (1) Experimental Themes

1

In *The Art of Fiction*, taking his cue from a lecture by Walter Besant, James laid out a conception of fiction that stressed its artistic aim ("fiction is one of the *fine* arts"—"it is at once as free and as serious a branch of literature as any other" [pp. 6, 8]) and opposed the prevailing concept of the naif novel, devoid of any theory, conviction, or consciousness of its own.[1] Besant's lecture, delivered in April 1884 and immediately printed, was called in England "Fiction as One of the Fine Arts," and it stressed the value of the story against a "new school" of fiction with which it was easy for James to identify himself. Besant also emphasized that the novel was "governed and directed by general laws" that could be laid down and taught with precision and exactness and that it was almost always started "with a conscious moral purpose." Besant added that the novel must be "the result of personal experience and observation"; and although James was ready to accept that, and Besant's plea for workmanship and style, he felt compelled to take exception to the idea of the "general laws" and of the "moral purpose" of fiction.

[1] *The Art of Fiction*, originally in *Longman's Magazine* (September 1884); reprinted, with some revisions, in *Partial Portraits* (1888), ed. Leon Edel (Ann Arbor, Mich., 1970), pp. 375–408, in *The Future of the Novel*, ed. Leon Edel (New York, 1956), pp. 3–27, and in *The House of Fiction*, ed. Leon Edel (London, 1957), pp. 23–45. In this chapter, page references in the text are to the reprint in *The Future of the Novel*. The 1884 version is available in *Henry James and Robert Louis Stevenson: A Record of Friendship and Criticism*, ed. J. A. Smith (London, 1948), pp. 53–84, together with Stevenson's "A Humble Remonstrance," which may have led James to make some of the changes.—See Stone, *Novelists in a Changing World*, p. 244, and John Goode, "The Art of Fiction: Walter Besant and Henry James," in *Tradition and Tolerance in Nineteenth-Century Fiction*, ed. David Howard, John Lucas, and John Goode (London 1966), pp. 243–81.

In his reply, accordingly, James did not go so far as to put forth a theory of his own. He insisted instead on the necessity of allowing the novelist a far-ranging freedom of choice ("the only obligation to which in advance we may hold a novel . . . is that of being interesting" [p. 9]) as well as on the widest possibilities open to him in terms of themes and techniques. But even in the midst of his repeated affirmation of the innumerable ways of fiction, which were "not to be marked out or fenced in by prescription"—"The advantage, the luxury, as well as the torment and the responsibility of the novelist, is that there is no limit to what he may attempt as an executant—no limit to his possible experiments, efforts, discoveries, successes" (p. 10)—James emphasized some fundamental principles that we later find applied in large measure precisely in the first group of novels of his middle period.

He started out by underlining the fact that "the only reason for the existence of the novel is that it does attempt to represent life" ([p. 5]; or, as he put it in the original version, "that it *does* compete with life"). Fiction, however, was not to limit itself to make-believe, as had been the case, for instance, with Anthony Trollope. Trollope's admission that he was only "making believe" seemed to James "a betrayal of a sacred office," "a terrible crime." Fiction ought to aspire instead to reach such an "air of reality," such "solidity of specification," as to enable the novelist to compete in his creation with life itself: "it is here in very truth that he competes with life" (p. 14), James wrote.

In this respect there was a complete analogy between the painter's task and the novelist's. Although James also stressed, in an eighteenth-century manner reminiscent of Fielding, a possible parallel between the novel and history—" As the picture is reality, so the novel is history. That is the only general description (which does it justice) that we may give of the novel. . . . To represent and illustrate the past, the actions of men, is the task of either writer" (p. 5, 6)[2]— and between the

[2] See *English Theories of the Novel, II: Eighteenth Century*, ed. Walter F. Greiner (Tübingen, 1970) for a collection of relevant texts

novelist and the philosopher, he insisted particularly on equating fiction with painting: "the analogy between the art of the painter and the art of the novelist is, so far as I am able to see, complete. Their inspiration is the same, their process (allowing for the different quality of the vehicle) is the same, their success is the same." (p. 5). "[The novelist] competes with his brother the painter in *his* attempt to render the look of things, the look that conveys their meaning, to catch the color, the relief, the expression, the surface, the substance of the human spectacle" (p. 14).[3]

This led him on the one hand to conceive of the novel as "a personal, a direct impression of life," whose artistic value was "greater or less according to the intensity of the impression" (p. 9). On the other hand, the concept of the novel as picture would inevitably lead him to the narrative principle of the so-called illustrative method, which implied an adherence to realistic and, indeed, naturalistic modes of presentation.

The first formulation, later repeated in his 1888 essay on Maupassant and in his 1889 letter on "The Great Form" ("Any point of view is interesting that is a direct impression of life . . . . make that into a picture, a picture framed by your own personal wisdom")[4], embodied the premises—or perhaps

by eighteenth-century writers, including Fielding. Also Ioan Williams, ed., *Novel and Romance, 1700–1800: A Documentary Record* (New York, 1970).

[3] The statement is repeated, but with further qualifications, in *Essays in London and Elsewhere* (New York, 1893), p. 197: "The novelist competes with the painter and the painter with the novelist, in the treatment of the aspect and figure of things; but what a happy tact each of them needs to keep his course straight, without poaching on the other's preserves!"; and p. 220: "Of course the general truth remains that if you wish to compete with the painter prose is a roundabout vehicle and it is simpler to adopt the painter's tools." And in *Picture and Text* (New York, 1893), p. 65: "The forms are different, though with analogies; but the field is the same—the immense field of contemporary life observed for an artistic purpose."

[4] *Partial Portraits*, p. 246, and *The Future of the Novel*, pp. 28–29. "We agreed that the laws imposed upon novelists by aesthetics resolve themselves into this: to give a personal impression of life," Paul Bourget wrote in 1884 in a book of his he inscribed to James (quoted in Leon Edel, *Henry James: The Middle Years* [Philadelphia, 1962], p. 115).

an echo—of narrative impressionism. In a well-known statement James had objected to the impressionist painters: "The
beautiful, to them, is what the supernatural is to the Positivists—
a metaphysical notion, which can only get one into a muddle
and is to be severely let alone. . . . None of its [the group's]
members show signs of possessing first-rate talent, and indeed
the 'Impressionist' doctrines strike me as incompatible, in an
artist's mind, with the existence of first-rate talent." But his
later insistence on "indirect vision" was bound to qualify him
as a supporter and practitioner of impressionistic fiction.[5] He
was well aware of the possibilities inherent in such a principle,
as is shown by a passage in his *Notebooks,* where he relates how
he was to make *The Coxon Fund* "an *Impression*—as one of
Sargent's pictures is an impression. That is, I must do it from
my own point of view—that of an imagined observer, partici-
pator, chronicler. I must picture it, summarize it, impres-
sionize it, in a word—compress and confine it by making it the
picture of what I see. That was the great advantage, which
perhaps after all would have been an imperative necessity, of
rendering the picture of Saltram an implied and suggested
thing."[6]

As the second half of the quotation indicates, James's
impressionism is, however, to be related to his later preoccupation with foreshortening and dramatic compression,
and in this sense it has more to do with his "scenic method"
than with his pictorial awareness. As I shall try to show later
on, although often complementary in his fiction, the pictorial
and the scenic methods represent two distinct and even
opposed principles in James's development. His equating fiction with painting, the novel with the picture (to go back to

[5] *The Painter's Eye: Notes and Essays on the Pictorial Arts,* ed. John L.
Sweeney (Cambridge, Mass., 1956), pp. 114–15. James was to alter his views
of the impressionists in a considerable way; see *The American Scene,* ed.
Leon Edel (Bloomington, Ind., 1968), pp. 45–46. For James's insistence on
"indirect vision," see *The Art of the Novel: Critical Prefaces,* ed. R. P.
Blackmur (New York, 1953), and Edel, *The Middle Years,* p. 263.

[6] *The Notebooks of Henry James,* ed. F. O. Matthiessen and Kenneth
B. Murdock (New York, 1955), p. 160 (25 April 1894).

The Art of Fiction), was bound to lead him at this stage to conceive of the novel as a historical or social fresco, a wide panorama of the actions of men against their social and historical background, in which the principles of full-fledged realism—or indeed the very tenets of naturalism—play a remarkable part.

Although being a living organism beyond the reach of any theoretical codification, the novel was to be above all "truthful" and "sincere," requiring as its sole condition to be "as complete as possible." These and other casual remarks in James's essay show that he was leaning toward an acceptance of the kind of realism that was being warmly debated and consistently practiced in France at the time. This can be seen all the more clearly when one notices how even some of his characteristic statements were colored by an explicit adherence to the principle of inclusiveness: "Art is essentially selection, but it is a selection whose main care is to be typical, to be inclusive. . . . the province of art is all life, all feeling, all observation, all vision" (p. 20).

Faithful to his personal form of psychological realism, James stressed the fact that "a psychological reason is, to my imagination, an object adorably pictorial; . . . I feel as if that idea might inspire one to Titianesque efforts" (p. 23)—thus keeping the door open for the subtleties of psychological analysis. But the reference to Titian seems to me revealing, since even for psychological renderings he was evidently to rely on the pictorial, illustrative method, which appears as the key concept of the essay. Furthermore, in the final part of the essay, taking up an idea he developed in various letters of this period, James claimed for the novel the right and indeed the duty to deal openly with every aspect of life, even those regarded as taboo in the Victorian Age. There was to be no withdrawing in the face of prurient and delicate topics; the moral blackmail of the "young readers" was to be ignored, because "the essence of moral energy is to survey the whole field" (p. 25).

"To survey the whole field" meant for the novelist taking

sides with the battle waged in France by the younger writers. In *The Art of Fiction* there was more than an echo of the proto-naturalistic manifesto launched by the brothers Goncourt in their Preface to *Germinie Lacerteux* (1864). This is how Emond and Jules de Goncourt had put their case:

Vivant au XIX⁰ siècle, dans un temps de suffrage universel, de démocratie, de libéralisme, nous nous sommes demandé si ce qu'on appelle "les basses classes" n'avait pas droit au Roman; si ce monde sous un monde, le peuple, devait rester sous le coup de l'interdit littéraire et des dédains d'auteurs, qui ont fait jusqu'ici le silence sur l'âme et le coeur qu'il peut avoir.

     . . . . .

Aujourd'hui que le Roman s'élargit et grandit, qu'il commence à être la grande forme sérieuse, passionée, vivante de l'étude littéraire et de l'enquête sociale, qu'il devient, par l'analyse et par la recherche psychologique, l'Histoire morale contemporaine; aujourd'hui que le Roman s'est imposé les études et les devoirs de la science, il peut en revendiquer les libertés et les franchises. Et qu'il cherche l'Art et la Verité.[7]

James had reviewed *Germinie Lacerteux,* and in a letter on Daudet's *Sappho* he showed himself perfectly aware of the implications of their "creed."[8] A plea for realistic fiction as it was practiced in France underlay most of the argument against moral allegory and symbolic elusiveness in his controversial book *Hawthorne* (1879). But that is not all. In the impassioned

---

[7] *Anthologie des préfaces de romans français du XIX⁰ siècle,* ed. Herbert S. Gershman and Kernan B. Whitworth, Jr. (Paris, 1964), p. 223. "Nothing else they [the Goncourts] have written has an equal ability with 'Germinie Lacerteux,' " James was to write in his essay on Pierre Loti (1888) (*Essays in London and Elsewhere,* p. 159).

[8] *Letters,* I, 108–9. For his early views on French writers, see *French Poets and Novelists* (1878), ed. Leon Edel (New York, 1964); *Partial Portraits* (1888); *Notes and Reviews,* ed. Pierre de Chaignon La Rose (1921; rpt. Freeport, N.Y., 1968); *Literary Reviews and Essays,* ed. Albert Mordell (New York, 1957); *Selected Literary Criticism,* ed. Morris Shapira (New York, 1964). Ezra Pound maintained that "all James would seem but a corollary to one passage in a Goncourt preface" ("Henry James" [1918], in *Literary Essays of Ezra Pound,* ed. T. S. Eliot [London, 1954], p. 309).

conclusion to *The Art of Fiction*—a song of praise to the magnificence of the "open form" of the novel and the complete freedom of the artist—James openly referred to Zola as the novelist "to whose solid and serious work no explorer of the capacity of the novel can allude without respect" (p. 27).

This is not so surprising if one remembers that James had frequently referred to Zola in terms of praise in the letters of this period. "*Il n'y a que Zola!*"—he had written in 1879—"I admire him more than you. . . . Zola's Naturalism is ugly and dirty, but he seems to me to be *doing something*—which surely (in the imaginative line) no one in England and the U.S. is, and no one else here."[9] And in 1884, the year of *The Art of Fiction*: "I have been seeing something of Daudet, Goncourt and Zola; and there is nothing more interesting to me now than the effort and experiment of this little group, with its truly infernal intelligence of art, form, manner."[10] Naturalism was the cry in France in the 1880s, and it was infiltrating England in the same period. James, who was to support Zola in the Dreyfus case, was aware of Zola's proclamations in "Le Roman expérimental" (1880), with its stress on the laws of heredity and environmental determinism which the novelist was to trace and illustrate with scientific detachment in his work.[11] No wonder, again, especially if we keep in mind that Zola considered the novel "une expérience 'pour voir' " (a concept that must have appealed to James) and was by no means unaware of the need for psychological illustration as well: a work of art was for him "un coin de la création vu à travers un tempérament." "J'estime que la question d'hérédité a une grande

---

[9] Virginia Harlow, *Thomas Sargeant Perry: A Biography* (Durham, N.C., 1950), with letters from the James brothers, pp. 304. ("Zola has his faults and his merits; and it doesn't seem to me important to talk of the faults. The merits are rare, valuable, extremely solid" (1881, p. 309).

[10] *Letters*, I, 104. For a more balanced view of Zola, see his later essay in *Notes on Novelists* (New York, 1914), pp. 26–64.

[11] See Leon Edel, *Henry James: The Treacherous Years* (Philadelphia, 1969), p. 274.

influence dans les manifestations intellectuelles et pas-
sionelles de l'homme. Je donne aussi une importance con-
sidérable au milieu," Zola had written. But he also added:
"Et c'est là ce qui constitue le roman expérimental: posséder
des phénomènes chez l'homme, montrer les rouages des
manifestations intellectuelles et sensuelles telles que la
physiologie nous les expliquera, sous les influences de
l'hérédité et des circonstances ambientes, puis montrer
l'homme vivant dans le milieu social qu'il a produit lui-
même, qu'il modifie tous les jours, et au sein duquel il
éprouve à son tour une transformation continue."[12]

Lyall H. Powers has called this period James's "naturalistic" period and has convincingly analyzed it in detail. He
has shown how James's "cultural background," so steeped
in French literature, had acquainted him at an early stage
with Taine and Comte, Flaubert and Zola. Americans like
Oliver Wendell Holmes and William Dean Howells had
supported this interest. It took James some time, however,
to move from the hardly disguised mistrust of the 1860s and
1870s (based mainly on moral grounds) to the gradual
acceptance of Zola, Daudet, Maupassant, and the Gon-
courts in the 1880s, which coincided with his growing
interest in forms of illustrative realism. Philip Grover has
in turn shown how the early lesson of Balzac combined
with the influence of Flaubert's style, and of Flaubert's way
of "seeing things" in an artistic way, to lead James to an
acceptance of the main principles of French realism.[13]
James went even farther: for some time, at least, he felt at
heart, and was in his fictional practice, a full-fledged,
scientific "naturalist" in the sense that Zola had given to
those terms.

[12] Anthologie des préfaces de romans français du XIXᵉ siècle, pp. 272–73.

[13] See Powers, "Henry James and Zola's Roman Expérimental," University of
Toronto Quarterly, 30 (1960), 16–30, where he sees The Art of Fiction "shot
through with theoretical attitudes of the cercle Flaubert" (p. 17); his book
Henry James and the Naturalist Movement (East Lansing, Mich., 1971); and
Grover, Henry James and the French Novel: A Study in Inspiration (London,
1973).

One would not want to emphasize James's dependence on French naturalism too much, but the conception of the novel as illustrative picture expressed in *The Art of Fiction* brought James to the appropriation of themes and techniques that bear a decided resemblance to, or imply a striking coincidence with, naturalistic modes. The premise of the novel as picture led naturally to the principle of pictorial illustration (applied to the psychological realm as well).[14] From here it was but a short step to a concern with themes and to a consistent application of modes of presentation that can be best described as "experimental" in the sense of Zola—marked, that is, by an awareness of social and environmental problems and by a reliance on the principle of full documentary exposition. James was inspired by these principles in the early novels of his middle period. The laborious, minute, and exciting technical experimentation that marked James's break with nineteenth-century fiction and opened the way for the twentieth-century novel was yet to come. At this point experimentation lay mainly in the "open" attitude of the writer toward the themes offered or suggested by contemporary reality; in his conscious adherence to historical and social, rather than merely moral or psychological, problems; in his methodical application of a "pictorial," "illustrative" mode of presentation. The refinements and complexities of presentation and treatment came later; they broke and renewed from the inside a fictional world and a narrative method whose main characteristic was a reliance on "solidity of specification."

[14] Philip Grover shows how the French "realists" were influenced in their fiction by their interest in pictures and paintings (*Henry James and the French Novel*, pp. 122–24, 151, and passim). For a different treatment, see Viola Hopkins Winner, "Pictorialism in James's Theory of the Novel," *Criticism*, 9 (1967), 204–27.

2

Each of the novels of the 1880s, as has often been observed, is characterized by the presence of a well-defined social or historical problem. The relationship between the individual and society, the difficulties and aberrations in such a relationship, the invasions of the private domain by society, were—and were to remain—typical Jamesian themes. But here they are analyzed and illustrated in historically defined contexts and with direct reference to contemporary circumstances. The individual experiences of the characters serve to define and exemplify problems and concerns that have a distinct social and historical interest, and they are in turn characterized or defined by the wider social context or by their particular milieu. *The Bostonians* offers an analysis and an illustration of the negative implications of the feminist movement and the perversion of the New England reformist impulse. *The Princess Casamassima* is a searching examination of the dangers, both private and public, of contemporary anarchism. With a lighter touch, *The Reverberator* sets out to deal with the threatening power of the press on private lives. *The Tragic Muse* is concerned with the relationship between political and diplomatic interests, on one side, and the world of artistic endeavor on the other.

In each case social themes bring to light and to a climax the moral and psychological motivations of individual behavior, while moral or psychological problems acquire depth and complexity, "solidity of specification" and greater significance by being constantly referred to a wider background of sociohistorical definition and illustration. James seems to have reached a compromise between his typical preoccupation with the fate of the individual and a wish to present that destiny in the framework of an almost documentary view of the historical circumstances and the social setting. The naturalistic principles are not followed out to their extreme conclusion, but rather accepted and foreshadowed as the occasion demands or the inspiration dictates. They never become a tenet and are seldom fully applied. But they are at work under the surface, and their presence is sufficient indication, for the moment, of James's early experimental urge in the direction of realism.

The Bostonians (serialized in the Century Magazine in 1885–86) set out to be "as local, as American as possible, and as full of Boston," and was to vie in "*pictorial* quality" with Daudet's Evangéliste. Dealing with the history of "one of those friendships between women which are so common in New England," it was to be "a tale very characteristic of our conditions . . . . the situation of women, the decline of the sentiment of sex, the agitation on their behalf."[15] The original psychological motif—the conflict in the mind of the heroine, Verena Tarrant—soon developed, however, into a peculiar, almost psychoanalytical theme: the morbid friendship linking the puritanical spinster Olive Chancellor to her protégée. This was meant to expose the negative implications of the feminist movement in its early manifestations of public activism and equivocal reforming protest. A "committed" work, of great breadth and ranging interests, in which Lionel Trilling rightly detects an "explicit awareness of history, of the grosser movements of society and civilization,"[16] The Bostonians differs sharply from the novels dealing with the international theme and achieves its desired "pictorial quality" through a detailed description of the New England world of which Olive's hysteria is both illustration and product. James was doubtless mindful of the care for realistic detail to be found in Dickens and of Hawthorne's Blithedale Romance, with its mild satire of the ambiguities of social reform.[17] But he went further than

[15] Notebooks, pp. 46–47 (8 April 1883). James made it clear that "Daudet's Evangéliste [1883] has given me the idea of this thing. If I could only do something with that *pictorial* quality!" (p. 47).

[16] Lionel Trilling, Introduction, The Bostonians (London, 1952), now in The Opposing Self (New York, 1959), pp. 104–17.

[17] According to F. R. Leavis, "He gives us Martin Chuzzlewit redone by an enormously more intelligent and better educated mind" (The Great Tradition [Garden City, N.Y., 1954], p. 165); and "The Bostonians is

both in his wide-ranging analysis of psychological motivations and social ambiguities, giving us in the end what might be defined as a treatise on the psychological distortions of certain American women (and men) and, at the same time, a full picture of the social world that determined and reflected those distortions.

A great number of minor characters appear in the novel. But their main purpose is not so much to define the personality and behavior of the protagonist (as for instance in *Roderick Hudson* or *The Portrait of a Lady*) as to give substance to the social framework and milieu that bring about those aberrations. The novel cannot properly be called a *roman à thèse* only because James did not provide it with the dialectical pole of the "positive character." Basil Ransom too, who is in conflict with Olive for the possession of Verena and violently opposed to feminism, is subjected to criticism and denunciation on account of his reactionary traditionalism. He has neither a positive nor a viable conception of life, and his opposition to New England reformism is motivated only by a harking back to the past, by a desire for personal (and historical) revenge on the North, by a rejection of everyday reality.

Basil is a southerner yearning for the restoration of a doubtful chivalric code of male supremacy and consequently bound to a past age and a defeated cause. As such, he is pitched against the decline and the aberrations of New England reformism, which affects negatively both society and the individual, in the name of an even more negative wish for historical denial and personal retaliation. He is just as eager to assert himself at the expense of others as is Olive

a wonderfully rich, intelligent and brilliant book. I said it is an acknowledged masterpiece. . . . It could have been written only by James, and it has an overt richness of life such as is not commonly associated with him. . . . it makes the imputed classical status of all but a few of the admired works of Victorian fiction look silly" (pp. 169–70). See also Marius Bewley, *The Complex Fate: Hawthorne, Henry James, and Some Other American Writers* (London, 1968), pp. 11–30, and Henry James, *Hawthorne* (1879), ed. Tony Tanner (London, 1967), pp. 125–30.

in her wish to monopolize and dominate Verena. New England feminism has fallen away from its early idealistic motivation of transcendental origin (represented in the novel by the figure of Mrs. Birdseye).[18] It breeds "monsters" like Olive or requires victims for business and emotional speculations like Verena. Verena can only escape into Basil's arms: but this too implies her physical and psychological subjugation, the ultimate acceptance of a kind of life which, according to the final words of the author, will not be devoid of tears and distress.

Verena's psychological and emotional dilemma—indeed her drama—is that she is caught between two possible solutions, both of which are equivocal. And this is so because society itself is in a state of crisis, divided as it is between an ambiguous drive towards renewal and an equally ambiguous harking back to the past. Verena finds herself pushed, if not actually crushed, between those who want to exploit her for publicity purposes (Matthias Pardon, the newspaperman), for economic and social advancement (her parents), or for dubious private ends (Olive), on the one side; and those like Basil, on the other, who seem to want to use her for personal affirmation and historical revenge. She is tormented and torn, that is, between the restrictions, conventions, and perversions of New England reformism and the lure of a quiet life that could, however, turn out to be enslavement of an even more painful kind.

This would be sufficient to qualify the book as a kind of deterministic attempt in the direction of naturalism, both in terms of environment and, to a certain extent, of heredity. As Lionel Trilling has observed, the theme is not so much the battle of the sexes, in the manner of George Meredith or G. B. Shaw; it is the total war of the sexes (and society) in the manner of Ibsen, Strindberg, or D. H. Lawrence. It is also

[18] For James's defense of his conception of Mrs. Birdseye against his brother William's strictures, see *Letters* I, 115–17. See also David Howard, "*The Bostonians,*" in *The Air of Reality: New Essays on Henry James,* ed. John Goode (London, 1972), pp. 60–80.

the war between two cultures and two civilizations—North and South—both corroded and compromised by social ideals falsely understood and lived out ambiguously, that proves a determining factor in the characters' lives, psychological motivations, and conduct. For good reason, Trilling defines this work as a "story of the parental house divided against itself, of the keystone falling from the arch, of the sacred mothers refusing their commission and of the sacred fathers endangered."[19]

We are confronted, then, with a novel of social criticism and moral denunciation which deals with the combined aberrations of sexual, social, and political life and becomes in this way James's closest attempt to deal with contemporary society in naturalistic terms. If not the laws of heredity, the laws of social determinism and confrontation are at work here, and in no other novel of James's, perhaps, are the psychological motivations and the private lives of the characters so closely related to their social and historical milieu. Although a kind of dry humor and many amiable touches distinguish *The Bostonians* from full-scale naturalistic novels, Geoffrey Tillotson can maintain with some truth that "the result is like Gissing," and Oscar Cargill that James's *"environment of ideas* is as substantial as Zola's environment of things."[20]

[19] *The Opposing Self*, p. 117. In these years James seemed particularly interested in the "antagonism of the sexes."

[20] Tillotson, "Henry James and His Limitations," *Criticism and the Nineteenth Century* (London, 1951), p. 248; Cargill, *The Novels of Henry James* (New York, 1961), p. 137. See also F. W. Dupee, *Henry James* (New York, 1951), p. 152. James was dissatisfied, however, with his "rather reckless attempt to represent a youthful Southron. . . . Basil Ransom is made up of wandering airs & chance impressions, & I fear that as the story goes on he doesn't become as solid as he ought to be. He remains a rather vague & artificial creation, & so far as he looks at all real, he is only fait de chic, as the French say" (Letter, 13 May 1885, in *Henry James and John Hay: The Record of a Friendship*, ed. G. Monteiro [Providence, 1965], p. 97). To his brother William he wrote, "I had the sense of knowing terribly little about the kind of life I had attempted to describe" (quoted in F. O. Matthiessen, *The James Family* [New York, 1948], p. 329).

One does not want to push the point too far, but unquestionably the use of an illustrative method of presentation further qualifies the book as a realistic attempt. Here James does not avail himself of the principle of the limited point of view and the center of consciousness on which he had at least partially relied in the previous novels, and he portrays everything from the standpoint of an omniscient narrator, with scrupulous impartiality, objectivity, and completeness. Background descriptions, authorial comments, environmental analyses abound as in perhaps no other novel by James. The social world is displayed as in a great pictorial fresco; the psychological and emotional reality is fully explored and subjected to a thorough analysis, to the extent that its wide-ranging scope—one might even say its over-treatment—proves functional and justified only if referred to James's wish for pictorial and representative exhaustiveness. James himself later thought the novel redundant in descriptive psychology: "All the middle part is too diffuse and insistent—far too describing and explaining and expatiating. The whole thing is too long and dawdling." But this was so because of his attempt at documentation and comprehensiveness: "[I] felt a constant pressure to make the picture substantial by thinking it out—pencilling and 'shading.' "[21]

[21] *Notebooks*, p. 49, and Matthiessen, *The James Family*, p. 329. James did not include the book in the New York Edition mainly for questions of space, and not for any artistic dissatisfaction with it. "I have even, in addition, a dim vague view of re-introduing, with a good deal of titivation and cancellation, the too-diffuse but, I somehow feel, tolerably full and good 'Bostonians' . . . that production never having, even to my much-disciplined patience, received any sort of justice" (to W. D. Howells, 17 August 1908, *Letters*, II, 100). Cf. also letter to Edmund Gosse, 25 August 1915: "The immediate inclusion of the Bostonians was rather deprecated by the publishers . . . and there were reasons for which I also wanted to wait: we always meant that that work should eventually come in. Revision of it loomed peculiarly formidable and time-consuming (for intrinsic reasons,) and as other things were more pressing and more promptly feasible I allowed it to stand over—with the best intentions. . . . But by this time it *had* stood over, disappointment had set in. . . . All the same I *should*

In a traditional nineteenth-century manner many "big scenes" mark the development of the action, and the architecture of the novel is in fact characterized by a series of such big scenes between Olive and Verena, Verena and Basil, Basil and Olive, and so on, climaxing in the big theatrical scene of the conclusion, appropriately set in a theater. But they are sensational, melodramatic scenes—coups de theatre—rather than "dramatic scenes" in the sense which that term was to acquire in James's later experimental novels; they are the kind of scenes we find in Dickens, George Eliot, Hawthorne, or Melville, carefully prepared and fully exploited for their immediate theatrical and emotional effect. They are scenes in which the slow descriptive and analytical preparation and the web of details build up to a climax, coalesce in major highpoints of action and psychological tension which explode into crucial confrontations, fully realized in all their theatrical potentialities, and which forcibly turn the action into unexpected developments. The time has not yet come for the slow sequel and masterful counterpoint of isolated moments, each rendered intense and meaningful by a dramatic method that does away with preparation, analysis, setting, and highlights in order to concentrate on an intensity of presentation and on a gradual revelation of meaning through a carefully worked out *juxtaposition* of scenes. In the novels of the following decade, as we shall see, the narrative method will rely more and more on these flashing and *synthetic* dramatic presentations of little actions, minor events, brief episodes, psychological shades and overtones that will mark each step of the development, dictate the "march of the action," and provide its secret rhythm through the application of the

---

have liked to review it for the Edition" (ibid., p. 498); and *Discovery of a Genius: W. D. Howells and Henry James*, ed. Albert Mordell (New York, 1961), pp. 156, 157–58. Howells was all in favor of its inclusion. James's motivation was repeated in an unpublished letter of 1914 to Andrea Raffalovich, now in the University of Virginia Library, Charlottesville.

limited point of view and the "scenic form." In *The Bosto-nians* James's experimentation has to do still with his choice of subject matter and with his adherence to the illustrative and pictorial method typical of nineteenth-century realism and of naturalistic fiction.

Many of these observations apply to *The Princess Casamas-sima* as well, which was written almost simultaneously and serialized in the *Atlantic Monthly* during 1885–86 while the previous novel was still appearing in the *Century*. It repre-sents James's excursion into an almost unknown and rather uncongenial field for him, the world of political—indeed, revolutionary—activity. Here too, at least in intention, James kept an eye on the model provided by naturalistic fiction and the *roman à thèse*; in fact, in spite of its pretensions to realistic documentation and representative accuracy, the novel frequently borders on romance and melodrama.

According to James's statement in the Preface, it grew out of his habit of observation while walking the streets of London, and from the London pavement had sprung up for him the very figure of the protagonist, Hyacinth Robinson, who was to give his own personal "impression" of that public turmoil and to personify its drama. The novel, how-ever, sprang also from a number of literary reminiscences—not so much from *Tom Jones* or George Eliot, as James was later to maintain, as from Turgenev's *Virgin Soil* (*Nov'*, 1876), a book which he had reviewed and which could provide him with more than one motif for his story[22]—and from a

[22] See Daniel Lerner, "The Influence of Turgenev on Henry James," *Sla-vonic and East European Studies*, 20 (December 1941), 28–54. James did not think highly of Turgenev's novel, yet his characterization of its hero bears a strong resemblance to his later characterization of Hyacinth Robinson: "His central figure is usually a person in a false position, generally not of his own making. . . . Such eminently is the case with young Neshdanoff, who is the natural son of a nobleman, not recognized by his father's family, and who, drifting through irritation and smothered rage and vague aspiration into the stream of occult radicalism, finds himself fatally fastidious and sceptical and 'aesthetic'—more essentially an aristocrat, in a word, than any of the aristocrats he has agreed to

renewed interest in the work of Zola. *The Princess Casamas-sima* might well be called James's second book in the man-ner of Zola. James went directly not only to the streets of London but to a prison as well in order to gather firsthand realistic documentation: "I have been all the morning at Milbank prison (horrible place) collecting notes for a fiction scene. You see I'm quite the Naturalist. Look out for the same—a year hence," he wrote in a revealing letter.[23]

The novel thus displays an accurate sense of place and of the historical moment, "a brilliantly precise representation of social actuality," a "social texture . . . grainy and knotty with practicality and detail," as Lionel Trilling has re-marked;[24] and quite a few critics have detected in it a strong Dickensian flavor. But there is more to it. Besides the actual feeling of London, James reflects in his novel the atmosphere of uneasiness, tension and social upheavals that prevailed in Europe and England in the "depressed eighties." "Nothing *lives* in England to-day but politics," he wrote to T. S. Perry in 1884: "They are all devouring, & their mental uproar crowds everything out. This is more & more the case; we are evidently on the edge of an enormous political cycle. . . . The air is full of events, of changes, of movement (some

---

conspire against" (the *Nation*, 24 [26 April 1877], 252–54, now in *Literary Reviews and Essays,* pp. 190–96 [p. 192 for the quotation]). But see also Jeanne Delbaere-Garant, "Henry James's Divergences from His Russian Model in *The Princess Casamassima,*" *Revue des langues vivantes,* 37 (1971), 535–44; Ivo Vidan, "*The Princess Casamassima* between Balzac and Conrad," *Studia Romanica et Anglica Zagrabiensia,* No. 21–22 (1966), 265, for a possible influence of Turgenev's novel *On the Eve,* and his "James's Novel of 'Looming Possibilities,' " in *Renaissance and Modern Essays Presented to Vivian de Sola Pinto* (London, 1966), pp. 137–45; and Lionel Trilling's introduction to the novel (New York, 1948), now in *The Liberal Imagination* (Garden City, N.Y., 1957), pp. 55–88, for similarities between Rose Muniment and Jennie Wren in Dickens's *Our Mutual Friend.* On James's relation to Turgenev, see Dale E. Peterson, *The Clement Vision: Poetic Realism in Turgenev and James* (Port Washington, N.Y., 1975).

[23] To T. S. Perry, 12 December 1884, in Harlow, *Perry,* p. 319.

[24] *Liberal Imagination,* pp. 71, 57.

people wld. say of revolution, but I don't think that)."[25] As
W. H. Tilley has shown in a valuable contribution, 1881
had seen the assassination of Czar Alexander II in Russia,
1882 the murder of Lord Cavendish in Dublin; in March
1883 a series of "dynamite outrages" had begun; explosions
had taken place in the Local Government Board in 1883, at
Victoria Station, Scotland Yard, and Saint James's Square
in 1884, at the Metropolitan Railway and the House of
Commons in 1885; in 1886 London had seen the Trafalgar
Square riots and Chicago had been the scene of the Hay-
market tragedy. After becoming interested in Bakunin
(through Turgenev), Kropotkin, and their anarchist activities, James read extensively the publications of the French
radical circles (the *Rappel* and the *Intransigeant*), an autobiographical novel by the communist leader Jules Vallès,
and for a great deal of analysis and background information
he reverted to the London *Times* and the *Spectator,* which in
those years carried a long series of articles on the activities of
the revolutionary groups.[26]

Although, according to W. H. Tilley, in *The Princess
Casamassima* James "invented less and borrowed more than
usual," he does not carry his program of naturalistic documentation beyond a certain limit. He was himself forced to
admit in his Preface that "the more than 'shady' underworld
of militant socialism" hardly appears in the book. He found
an ingenious explanation—indeed, an excuse—for it by
maintaining that the "scheme called for the suggested near-
ness (to all our apparently ordered life) of some sinister
anarchic underworld" whose threatening presence was best
felt if suggested underneath the quiet surface, guessed at,

[25] Letter of 26 September 1884, in Harlow, *Perry,* p. 318.

[26] W. H. Tilley, *The Background of* The Princess Casamassima (Gainesville,
Fla., 1961), pp. 6–50, in particular chap. 3, "Revolution and *The Times*";
Trilling, *Liberal Imagination,* pp. 69–70. James referred to the damaging of
Westminister Hall and the Tower in a letter to Grace Norton (*Letters,*
I, 114 [24 January 1885]); see also his Preface to the novel and
his letter of 2 November 1879, in Harlow, *Perry,* p. 304.

suspected and feared rather than actually seen or met.[27] The genesis, however, and quite a few of the basic elements of the story are typical of a naturalistic intention and of an impulse toward realistic presentation. This becomes, to my mind, sufficiently clear if one accepts Erich Auerbach's pertinent definition of realism: "The serious treatment of everyday reality, the rise of more extensive and *socially* inferior human groups to the position of subject matter for problematic-existential representation, on the one hand; on the other, the embedding of random persons and events in the general course of contemporary history, the fluid historical background—these, we believe, are the foundations of modern realism."[28]

This is at least partly true if applied to Hyacinth and his social milieu, to his problematic-existential predicament, and to the presence of the historical background adumbrated in the book. Yet the overall result is another matter: as I have already suggested, it often borders on a merely pictorial—or even picturesque—background illustration, on a melodramatization of the situations and on downright romance. An unmistakable element of romance stays with Hyacinth as well as with Christina Light, taken over from *Roderick Hudson* and now become Princess Casamassima; indeed, "romance" plays an important role both in her "false seriousness," in her equivocal interest in the underworld of anarchism, and in the predicament of Hyacinth, whom James described in the Preface as "tormented but not limited," painfully kept at the most respectful of distances from "freedom and ease, knowledge and power, money, opportunity and satiety."

[27] *The Art of the Novel,* pp. 76–78; Tilley, *Background,* p. 34.

[28] *Mimesis: The Representation of Reality in Western Literature,* tr. Willard R. Trask (Pinceton, N.J., 1968), p. 491. "And it is natural," Auerbach goes on, "that the broad and elastic form of the novel should increasingly impose itself for a rendering comprising so many elements." He saw nineteenth-century France as playing the most important part in the rise and development of realism.

Here too the drama is mainly enacted in the soul of Hyacinth who, young revolutionist as he is, falls in love with "the beauty of the world, actual order and all, at the moment of his most feeling and most hating the famous 'iniquity of its social arrangements'; so that his position as an irreconcileable pledged enemy to it, thus rendered false by something more personal than his opinions and his vows, becomes the sharpest of his torments."[29] It is essentially an inner, psychological conflict taking place in the mind of the radical youth, who is led to discover the meaning of social ease and artistic beauty (first at Medley, the aristocratic country house, then in Paris and in Venice). James emphasizes more than once in the novel the role played by heredity and environment. "There was no peace for him [Hyacinth] between the two currents that flowed in his nature, the blood of his passionate, plebeian mother and that of his long-descended, super-civilized father"; the poor London setting he lives in increases that dualism and becomes a determining factor in his joining anarchism ("he was with the people and every possible vengeance of the people"). At Lomax Place he feels excluded from life—he had "to look at the good things of life only through the glass of the pastry cook's window." But when he is exposed to the grand world—"so pleasant was it to be enthroned with fine ladies in a dusky, spacious receptacle which framed the bright picture of the stage"—his dualism becomes a tragic

[29] *The Art of the Novel*, pp. 60–62, 72. Given his position, Hyacinth becomes, according to James, one of his "intelligent observers." In a review of Stepniak's *Russia under the Czars,* in *Atlantic Monthly,* 56 (August 1885), p. 270, James had significantly written of nihilism: "The great mystery of this movement for outsiders has always been its psychological side. . . . The strange enthusiasms for Nihilism . . . its power of enlisting the sympathies of women . . .—it is upon these characteristics of the movement that light would have been welcomed." See Tilley, *Background,* p. 11; John L. Kimmey, "*The Princess Casamassima* and the Quality of Bewilderment," *Nineteenth Century Fiction,* 22 (1967), 47–62; Taylor Stoker, "Words and Deeds in *The Princess Casamassima,*" *ELH,* 37 (1970), 95–135.

burden. The basic conflict, therefore, is an inner one: it takes place in the very conscience of the Young Man from the Provinces (the definition is Lionel Trilling's) who is stirred and hopelessly confused by the brilliance and the elusive snares of the big city and the great world.

A comparison of Frédéric Moreau's *éducation sentimentale* and Hyacinth's social and artistic "education" (as Edmund Wilson has originally suggested in his essay "The Ambiguity of Henry James") proves very interesting. One sees how the weary resignation and final pathos of the former hero contrast markedly with the latter's compulsion to violence and suicide. In both cases, however, the conditioning and almost deterministic background is provided by history and by a society in decline: the political dissatisfaction and unrest that led to the 1848 revolution and the coup d'etat in one case, the indifference or the even more culpable reformist complacency of a decadent English society in the other, aghast at what it cannot comprehend but eventually well in command of the revolutionary situation.[30] James, we remember, saw England "at the edge of an enormous political cycle" at the time. But the driving force was hopelessly perverted if left in the hands of irresponsible anarchists or of people like Christina and her set. Equally responsible for Hyacinth's tragedy are the ambiguities of his conscience ("He has undertaken to play a part that with the drop of his exasperation and the growth, simply expressed, of his taste, is out of all tune with his passion, at any cost, for life itself"), Christina, and the social condition of which the Princess is both expression and secular arm. Even if the central conflict is psychological, James goes to great lengths to build up the drive of environmental forces, and the social denunciation is vigorously present or implied.

---

[30] See Grover, *Henry James and the French Novel*, pp. 93–103, for a comparison of the two novels. John Roland Dove has proposed a comparison with Stendhal's *Le Rouge et le Noir*, in *Studies in Comparative Literature*, 7 (1962), 130–54; Ivo Vidan has drawn a parallel with Balzac's *Les illusions perdues* (see note 22 above).

James stays mostly with his main character, but he gives the narration such a frankly panoramic and processional movement, he works with so many characters and types, he insists so much on the sense of place, he gives such a detailed picture of London and its various milieus, its streets and pubs, its sounds and smells, its shops and palaces, moving out to Medley, Paris, and Venice, that the final result may indeed be compared to a vast chiaroscuro painting—not so much a "Titianesque effort" (as James had envisaged in *The Art of Fiction*) as an attempt in the direction of Tintoretto.

As Joseph Warren Beach has remarked, "This story is another beautiful instance of an 'idea conceived as picture.' " The events and the spectacle of the world—"the social horror" and "the glory of the world," according to Lionel Trilling—are consistently referred to and reflected in Hyacinth's conscience.[31] But it is his experience *as a social being* in a particular milieu, the social and historical context faithfully rendered in its physical details and external circumstances, that enables us to see in *The Princess Casamassima* a second example of James's commitment to realism and naturalistic themes. As Zola had written: "L'homme n'est pas seul, il vit dans une societé, dans un milieu social, et dès lors pour nous, romanciers, le milieu social modifie sans cesse les phénomènes. Même notre grande étude est là, dans le travail réciproque de la societé sur l'individu et de l'individu sur la societé."[32] This is to a great extent exemplified or implied in the novel. The "death of society," as Stephen Spender has called it, is here represented in an "inclusive" manner, "portrayed" in the completest possible

---

[31] Beach, *The Method of Henry James* (1918; enlarged edition with corrections, Philadelphia, 1954), p. 212; Trilling, *Liberal Imagination*, p. 81.

[32] Zola, "Le Roman expérimental," *Anthologie des préfaces de romans français du XIXᵉ siècle*, p. 273. Georges Markow-Totevy writes that the novel "is another Jamesian attempt to examine the social upheavals of his time. Ambitious, close to the method of Zola, James considers class-conflict and revolution" (*Henry James*, tr. John Cumming [n.p.: Minerva Press, 1969], p. 44). A slight exaggeration, in my view.

way, as had been proposed in *The Art of Fiction*.[33] It involves
each of the many characters, every level or class of society.
Here too the number of figures who surround the protagonists answer the need for an almost apocalyptic illustration
and denunciation of the abyss over which society seems to
be desperately hovering.

3

Discouraged by the poor reception of the two novels in
which he had struggled so much to renew his fiction ("They
have reduced the desire, and the demand, for my production to zero," James wrote to Howells early in 1888), the
novelist laid the blame upon his "delayed experience" and
the use of an untrustworthy vehicle.[34] This is why, perhaps,
with *The Reverberator* (serialized in *Macmillan's Magazine* in
1888) he went back not only to the short novel (following
for once his brother William's advice), but to the light comedy of manners and the international theme. His new experiences had not been wasted, however. Under the veil of
irony and cheerful satire, the lighthearted comedy of the
American girl whose marriage to an aristocratic Frenchman
is momentarily compromised by the indiscretion of a friend
who sends off "revelations" about the aristocratic family to
a paper was originally to have served the purpose of social
denunciation as well.

The germ was given by a "queer incident"—the indiscretion of an American girl who had written an "inconceivable
letter" to a New York newspaper "about the Venetian
society whose hospitality she had just been enjoying." In
perfect good faith, although "irreflective and irresponsible,"
she had caused scandal and indignation. James was impressed
by "the strange *typicality* of the whole thing" and proposed
to use that "very illustrative piece of contemporary life" to

[33] *The Destructive Element* (London, 1938), pp. 45–46.
[34] *Letters*, I, 135.

denounce "the sinking of *manners,* in so many ways, which the democratization of the world brings with it." "That mania for publicity," he wrote, "is one of the most striking signs of our times. . . . One sketches one's age but imperfectly if one doesn't touch on that particular matter: the invasion, the impudence and the shamelessness, of the newspaper and the interviewer, the devouring *publicity* of life, the extinction of all sense between the public and private."[35] In sketching the story James envisaged that the indiscretion would be committed by a friend and admirer of the girl, a journalist from New York "of the most enterprising, and consequently the most vulgar, character," whose revelations in the press cause her marriage to be called off. In the *Notebooks* "the newspaper dictates and triumphs" with the threat of *new* revelations, so that the family is compelled by blackmail to "come round" and the marriage takes place.

This rather "horrid" conclusion (which James saw as "a reflection of actual fact") was, however, abandoned in the novel. To achieve verisimilitude James moved the setting from Venice to Paris and to "an old *claquemuré* Legitimist circle, as detached as possible from *tout ce que se fait, s'écrit et se pense aujourd'hui,*" and resorted once more to "Europeanized American" characters.[36] In so doing, he shifted his attention from the vulgar journalist to the little drama of which the girl herself is both accomplice and victim. In a typically Jamesian way the international theme and the comedy of manners came thus to the forefront, while the amused, ambiguous, and lighthearted conclusion modified and minimized the polemical impulse expressed in the early notes. *The Reverberator* is today mainly interesting for the

[35] *Notebooks*, p. 82. James also remembered the "beastly and blackguardly betrayal" of James Russell Lowell at the hands of Julian Hawthorne in an unauthorized newspaper interview. For his dealings with, and aversion to, journalism, see Henry James, *Parisian Sketches: Letters to the New York Tribune, 1875–76*, intr. Leon Edel and Ilse Dusoir Lind (London, 1958), pp. ix-xxxvii; *Letters*, I, 46–47 and II, 304; and his final outburst in *The Question of Our Speech* (Boston, 1905), pp. 43–44.
[36] *Notebooks*, pp. 84–85.

delineation of the various characters and the light touch with which the international contrast—no more than a storm in a teapot—is sketched and developed. As F. O. Matthiessen remarked, "The novel is, therefore, less serious a piece of social criticism than James had at first envisaged"[37]. It is clear that while working on it James considerably altered his perspective.

If his innocent and charmingly irresponsible Americans in Europe—the Dossons, "almost incredibly *unaware of life*," "least of all conscious of deficiences and dangers"—are caught treating Europe "as a vast painted and gilded holiday toy, serving its purpose on the spot and for the time, but to be relinquished, sacrificed, broken and cast away, at the dawn of any other convenience" (as James wrote in the Preface),[38] they get indeed the best of their adventure and *they* are triumphant in the end. The opposing party—the Proberts, with their sense of Europe and conservative manners—are brought to surrender and almost total defeat by Francie's moral fiber. Her refusal to lie, her obstinate and obsessive defense of her own rights brings about Gaston Probert's conversion, *his* taking sides with her. If she has been instrumental in the breach of privacy, she does not retract; she breaks off the engagement, and it is up to Gaston to choose her rather than his family, to join the itinerant Dossons in their travels or in their weary retreat to America. In accordance with so many Jamesian heroines, Francie asserts herself and brings about Gaston's liberation from his family, his limitations, and his conditioning background; she wins in the end, and the "living doll of Europe" is joyfully left to its hollow social conventions. In any case, far from being a purely negative influence, the interference of the newspaper proves beneficent and instrumental in bringing the two young people together and in enabling both Francie and Gaston to choose freedom rather than con-

[37] Ibid., p. 86.
[38] *The Art of the Novel*, pp. 187, 188, 189.

ventions, love rather than social decorum, moral energy
rather than wordly wisdom.

The irresponsible invasion of privacy proves, after all, a
felix culpa. It is true that Francie is not fully aware of her
actions or her motivations and that Gaston is led rather
blindly and inconclusively to "have done with limits." It
is also true that James spares neither the Dossons nor the
Proberts in his good-humored criticism of their respective
ways of life and that poor George Flack, the journalist, is
subjected time and again to scathing remarks and violent
denunciations. But the girl succeeds in her peculiar sort of
way, and if the newspaper "dictates and triumphs" as far
as Gaston is concerned, this is certainly not for the worse,
but the better. In spite of its original purpose, in other
words, *The Reverberator* is made of the stuff of pleasant and
lighthearted comedy; as such, and in its adherence to the
international theme, it is to be set apart as an exception in
James's middle period. If it is documentary at all, it is documentary of a particular social situation and only indirectly,
in its original intention, of a social problem.

Writing about the book in his later Preface, James called
it an anecdote and a jeu d'esprit, and he saw it "as a small
straight *action,*" emphasizing its "blest drama-light," "the
planned rotation of aspects," and its " 'scenic' determination." [39] In fact, if he had previously aimed at illustration and
pictorial completeness, he gave here an early example of
dramatic compression, developing his story in a tight succession of episodes in which the characters mainly *act,* with
few "preparatory" parts and psychological analyses. Seeing
it, however, from the vantage point of his major phase,
James was led, I believe, to exaggerate its "scenic" quality
and his using Francie as a center of consciousness. Her
drama—and Gaston's inner conflict—become of central
importance only in the second half of the book; in the previous pages it is rather the social notation of awkward man-
ers and pompous conventions that claims our undivided

[39] Ibid., pp. 180, 182.

attention. James was right in stressing the American quality of the story and Francie's kinship with some of his other heroines. But the original social purpose of the novel, its documentary purport, and contemporary relevance were almost completely lost on the way: the comedy prevailed.

The illustrative and pictorial completeness advocated in *The Art of Fiction* had been temporarily laid aside. But it reappeared at once, and in full force, in the last of these four novels, which brought James's early middle period to a close. After Boston and London, *The Tragic Muse* (serialized in the *Atlantic Monthly* in 1889–90) was to deal with the social "picture" of Paris (and London). More than in the former novels, however, the double drama of the protagonists was here essentially an inner conflict, only partially determined by the sociohistorical conditions and depending more closely on the question of individual choice.

The germ of the novel, as recorded in the *Notebooks*, was to provide "a study of the histrionic character" and to represent a relationship between an actress and her patron based on the principle of the "transference of vitality." The "constant motto" that James set for himself was "*à la Maupassant*," and, as in *The Princess Casamassima*, he was to "depend on the collective effort." The theme, as formulated in the Preface, was that of "the conflict between art and 'the world' " and was developed into two parallel stories and contrasts: between the theater and high society (or indeed the diplomatic world), on the one hand, and between art and the political world on the other.[40] Thus the theme became typically Jamesian once again (it is hardly necessary here to mention his many excursions in this field), all the more so in that the solution of the conflicts

---

[40] *Notebooks*, pp. 63–64 (19 June 1896); *The Art of the Novel*, pp. 83–84 and passim. The conflict between art and the world is present in a number of stories of this period, from "The Lesson of the Master" and "The Aspern Papers" (1888) to "The Real Thing" (1892), "The Middle Years" (1893), "The Death of the Lion" (1894), "The Next Time" (1895), "The Figure in the Carpet" (1896). See also chapter 3, note 18, below.

depended almost exclusively on the characters' personal choice. Nick Dormer finds moral strength enough to sever the innumerable familiar and emotional links that tie him to politics so as to devote himself to painting, while the diplomat Peter Sherringham cannot bring himself to marry Miriam Rooth, to whose success as an actress he contributed so much. The "losers"—Julia Dallow, Nick's fiancée, who has set up political success as the sustaining reason of her life, and Peter, unable to overcome the social taboo of Victorian prejudice against the theater—are both headed for renunciatory marriages (Julia, it seems, will end by accepting the fledgling painter who has fallen so low in her view).

This pathetic and weary ending of the long novel sheds a twilight of disillusionment and renunciation in the mildest Jamesian vein. But the greatness of the book lies in the implacable violence of the struggle that is there enacted, in the rending tension underlying the emotional and social relations that are set off by the context of political and theatrical activities, in the "picture" of a social world that is analyzed in its laws of conduct and decorum, idols and ideals, self-imposed prejudices and limitations. Peter Sherringham's involvement with Miriam has never been a true artistic interest (as James openly states in the novel) and can therefore be linked with the "false seriousness" of the Princess Casamassima; Julia Dallow's political obsession is basically selfish and ambiguously motivated; Nick makes his choice when it is apparently too late, and will probably become a second-rate painter. They have all been conditioned and warped by their families, their backgrounds, or their careers. Miriam Rooth alone overcomes her difficulties at full stride, and shows a marked superiority to Hyacinth Robinson's uncertain and equivocal need for action. She asserts herself in a strenuous struggle for artistic success that is also a struggle for life.

Here too, as with Olive Chancellor or Christina Light, the will to dominate has taken the place of feminine wisdom. Julia Dallow's and Lady Dormer's political obsession appears cruel and demanding, almost rapacious; Mr. Carteret's cunning political game and his financial (as well as moral) blackmail turn out to be both reprehensible and degrading. Nick is linked, indeed tied, to their world by a web of relations and obligations that constrain his emotional development and very likely compromise his artistic success. That world seems to allow the challenge to its social exclusiveness represented by the amateur or the aesthete—by Gabriel Nash (perhaps a disguised portrait of Oscar Wilde), carefree and lighthearted, happy and satisfied. But it fights tooth and nail—that is, by financial might, moral blackmail, emotional oppression, and social retaliation—to prevent the escape of its members and to withstand the assault of the "tragic muse" without compromising its internal balance. In this cruel game the victims outnumber the conquerors; society imposes its own rules, commands respect for its code of behavior, sets itself up against the flowering genius, artistic "dispersion," the cultivation of intellectual or artistic pursuits. Or, more subtly, it accepts them only to keep them at bay and at a distance on the "histrionic" level, in the external world of entertainment (for Nick's mother, we are explicitly told, "art is pardonable only so long as it's bad—so long as it's done at odd hours, for a little distraction.").

The Tragic Muse, too, is therefore at least partially a *roman à thèse*, a novel of social criticism and denunciation, though it is set in a context much more congenial and familiar to James than those of the previous novels. The theme is objectively embodied and developed, set in a well-defined social context and a fully rendered milieu (the theatrical world in Paris, the London constituency, the society mansion, and so forth, each with its respective figures) which provides the background but also conditions and determines the action. Furthermore, the composition is still dominated by an explicit commitment to a "mighty pictorial fusion" that James himself compared, at least in aspiration, to Tintoretto's *Crucifixion* in Venice. This fusion is in this case of two main "pictures," and against the pictorial and illustrative background "totally objective" figures are portrayed in the round, with breadth and scope of psychological, as well as social, definition. Undoubtedly it is the "busiest" canvas painted by James, the one in which that "visualization of character and scene" of which he had written in *The Art of Fiction* is more fully pursued and achieved. It has been called by Clarence Gohdes "a series of rich prose pictures of scenes" by an "observant naturalist" and "the richest of all the James novels in pictorial suggestion."[41] It is also the last of the major "documentary" novels at least indirectly inspired by Zola's naturalism and certainly the most ambitious and substantial of the three, even if it lacks the narrative urgency of the others. As in *The Bostonians* we have here the "private story of a public woman," and as in *The Princess Casamassima* the "political case" is compromised by aesthetic sensibility, and these two themes are combined with others in a major effort at comprehensive inclusiveness that led James to real "desperations of ingenuity."

One of these arose from the fact that the double picture (the "political case" and the "theatrical case") and the objective presentation of the characters confronted the writer with a real drawback: a lack of compositional center. To overcome this difficulty, James tried to have "Miriam central to analysis, in spite of being objective." In doing this he had to adopt her as a structural center and partially as center of consciousness, and it is highly significant that his theory of foreshortening was discussed in the Preface to this

[41] Clarence Gohdes, in Arthur Hobson Quinn, ed., *The Literature of the American People* (New York, 1951), p. 694. See also Leon Edel, Introduction, *The Tragic Muse* (New York, 1960), pp. vii-ix; D. J. Gordon and John Stokes, "The Reference of *The Tragic Muse*," in *The Air of Reality*, pp. 81-167; Kenneth Graham, *Henry James: The Drama of Fulfilment, an Approach to the Novels* (Oxford, 1975), pp. 79-126; and Edward Stone, *The Battle and the Books* (Athens, Ohio, 1964), pp. 93-112, for a consideration of William Black's *Macleod of Dare*, a novel James had reviewed in the *Nation* (19 December 1878), as a possible source.

novel. By having Miriam central to the analysis as much as possible, James had in a way to restrict his proposed inclusiveness of pictorial representation, so as to avoid the danger of writing one of those much-feared, "large, loose, baggy monsters" of nineteenth-century realistic fiction. He confessed to a delight in "a deep-breathing economy and an organic form." The "economy" was indeed deep-breathing and wide-ranging. Nevertheless, James spoke of it not in pictorial but rather in dramatic terms: "the whole thing has visibly, from the first, to get itself done in dramatic, or at least in scenic conditions—though scenic conditions which are as near an approach to the dramatic as the novel may permit itself." The scenic consistency, as in the later case of *The Awkward Age,* was to be found in a "multiplication of *aspects.*"[42]

In *The Tragic Muse,* then, according to James, we would already have an application of the dramatic or scenic method (which was to be widely applied in the novels of the 1890s) within the general framework of the pictorial method. James perhaps exaggerated the scenic quality of a novel that is still closely linked in themes and methods to his previous "pictorial" works. It is doubtless, however, that both the indirect vision of the central character and the scenic form make their appearance here in some crucial episodes.[43] The "big scenes" in the nineteenth-century manner are less melodramatic and sensational than in the preceding novels. They have been reduced and refined to the measure of significant, no longer climactic, episodes. The encounters, meetings, and clashes between characters conform to a dramatic compression within the single episodes that is more controlled in its effects and therefore more conducive

---

[42] *The Art of the Novel,* pp. 84–85, 87–88, 89–90. Cf. also Alan W. Bellringer, "*The Tragic Muse*: The Objective Centre," *Journal of American Studies,* 4 (1970), 73–89.

[43] James writes of having chosen "the indirect vision" in a revealing passage of the novel itself. See Edel, *The Middle Years,* p. 263, and *The Art of the Novel,* pp. xvii–xviii, 256, and passim. See also chapter 2, note 9, below.

to a *gradual* unfolding of the narrative parable. The "multiplication of aspects," although still tentative, restrains James's theatricality and relies more and more on a meaningful juxtaposition of dramatic scenes and episodes.

The Tragic Muse was thus the swan song of the "naturalistic" period, in which the scenic form made its first appearance. In it, thematic experimentation gave way to a more properly technical experimentation. But this early period projected the shadow of its thematic concerns on the following one. The circumstantial, detailed, and systematic denunciation of society as such was reflected in a more indirect moral denunciation of spreading corruption, of the selfish and irresponsible aberrations of an upper class in decay and dissolution. In the novels of the 1890s as well, evil would work constantly on the conscience of the characters as a misdirected will to possession and power, as a misguided approach to reality. In these, however, the victims would no longer be condemned to defeat, enslavement, or renunciation by the overriding social movements and historical situations in which they were entagled (feminism, revolution, the press, politics) but rather by the predominance of particular self-centered interests or by the selfish acquiescence of a society corrupted from within—in intrinsic static dissolution, not even in movement. The refinements of technique brought about a thematic astringency: the social motive, although still present and felt, would be almost completely appropriated by and absorbed in the moral question.

"The picture, the representative design, directly and strongly appealed to me, and was to appeal all my days," James wrote in *A Small Boy and Others* (1913); "the picture was still after all in essence one's aim." In the novels of the 1890s, however, the pictorial method was broken from within. It was to reappear only in the novels of the major phase, strengthened and enlivened by the joint application of the scenic form developed in the experimental novels of the 1890s. The scenic method was a result of a search for, and an experimentation with, new techniques that led to a quite different approach to fiction and reality, and left aside or behind themes and forms of the traditional nineteenth-century novel.

II. Middle Period: (2)
Experimental Techniques

1

DISAPPOINTED by the comparative failure of his strenuous narrative efforts, for five years James devoted himself almost completely to writing for the theater. His "dramatic years" were mainly motivated by the hope of achieving popular and financial success; they brought him only disappointments and cruel humiliations.[1] James was partly to blame: he had compromised as never before, under the mistaken assumption that success in the theater depended on meeting the audience halfway and renouncing artistic rigor. He had consequently to pay a severe price for his adherence to allegedly popular demands. Yet this experience was of the utmost importance for the novels that were to follow.

First of all, it convinced James that the time had passed for sweeping pictorial frescoes in the nineteenth-century manner. As early as 1888-90 he had envisaged a ten-year period of short novels, and in 1895 he wrote to Howells: "I shall never again write a *long* novel, but I hope to write six immortal short ones—and some tales of the same quality."[2] Second, it led James to a solemn rededication to the art of fiction, now with a full awareness of the possibilities, the advantages, and the challenge of the dramatic method. "I take up my *own* old pen again—the pen of all my unforgettable and sacred struggles," he wrote in the *Notebooks* (p. 179),[3] and later on: What I feel more and more that I must arrive at, with these things, is the adequate and regular prac-

---

[1] On James's theatrical years, see Leon Edel's introductions to *The Complete Plays of Henry James* (Philadelphia, 1949), pp. 16–69, and *Guy Domville* (London, 1961), pp. 13–121; Edel, *The Middle Years*, pp. 279–345; and Elizabeth Robins, *Theatre and Friendship* (London, 1932).

[2] *Letters*, I, 232.

[3] In this chapter, page references in the text are to the *Notebooks*.

tice of some such economy of clear summarization as will
give me from point to point, each of my steps, stages, tints,
shades, every main joint and hinge, in its place, of my
subject—give me, in a word, my clear order and expressed
sequence. . . . When I ask myself what there may have been
to show for my long tribulation, my wasted years and
patiences and pangs, of theatrical experiment, the answer
[is]: . . . it will perhaps have been exactly some such mastery
of fundamental statement—of the art and secret of it, of
expression, of the sacred mystery of structure" (p. 208, 11
August 1895).

In the *Notebooks* of this period, which provide a fully
developed (although gradually discovered) theory of the
"dramatic method" on which James was to rely for his new
novels, he came to conceive of the novel no longer as picture
but as play—as narrative action based on a carefully worked-
out sequence of dramatic scenes. As Michael Egan has remarked, "Eighteen ninety-five is the pivotal year in James's
artistic evolution. His commitment to what he later called
'intense illusion' . . . resolved itself ultimately into the conviction that dramatic representation was the technical solution
for which he sought."[4] *Dramatize* is a constant invitation,
indeed a command, that appears over and over again in his
Notebooks: every germ or idea "must resolve itself into a little
action, and the little action into the *essential* drama" (p. 198).

As early as 1875 James had maintained that the dramatic
form seemed to him "of all literary forms the very noblest"
on account of its structural tightness and concentration:
"The fine thing in a real drama, generally speaking, is that,
more than any other work of literary art, it needs a masterly
structure. It needs to be shaped and fashioned and laid together, and this process makes a demand upon an artist's

---

[4] Michael Egan, *Henry James: The Ibsen Years* (London, 1972), p. 26.
Although James wrote no novels during his "dramatic years," he wrote
a number of important stories, collected in *The Real Thing and Other
Tales* (1893), *The Private Life* (1893), *Terminations* (1895), and *Embarrassments*
(1896).

rarest gifts. He must combine and arrange, interpolate and eliminate, play the joiner with the most attentive skill; and yet at the end effectually bury his tools and his sawdust, and invest his elaborate skeleton with the smoothest and most polished integument."[5] Twenty years later, after the theatrical experience, he was to find that the play offered a guidance both for the "art of preparation" and for the balanced structure of narrative blocks, often in terms of the three- or five-act structure of the "well-made" play. The "scenario" of a play proved to be an already concentrated story, and from now on James came to rely increasingly on the principle of the scenario for both dramatic and narrative purposes:

Voyons, voyons: may I not instantly sit down to a little, close, clear, full scenario of it? . . . Compensations and solutions seem to stand there with open arms for me. . . . Has a *part* of all this wasted passion and squandered time (of the last 5 years) been simply the precious lesson, taught me in that roundabout and devious way, that cruelly expensive, *of the singular value for a narrative plan too* of the (I don't know *what* adequately to call it) divine principle of the Scenario? . . . IF . . . this exquisite truth that' what I call the divine principle in question is a key that, working in the same *general* way fits the complicated chambers of *both* the dramatic and narrative lock . . . why my infinite little loss is converted into an almost infinite little gain. [P. 188]

The stage play, James was to maintain in 1913 in a letter, represented merely a case, while the dramatic situation had "connections with and into life at large."[6] But the dramatic

[5] "Tennyson's Drama," in *Views and Reviews*, ed. Le Roy Phillips (1908; rpt. Freeport, N.Y., 1968), pp. 180–81. In "Nona Vincent" (1892) he had written: "The scenic idea was magnificent . . . —the dramatic form had a purity which made some others look ingloriously rough" (*The Complete Tales of Henry James*, ed. Leon Edel, 12 vols. [Philadelphia, 1962–64], VIII, 157). Cf. Edel, *The Treacherous Years*, p. 21.

[6] *Letters*, II, 320: "The play somehow represents a Case merely, as distinguished, so to speak, from a Situation; the Case being always a thing rather void of connections with and into life at large, and the Situation, dramatically speaking, being largely of interest *just* by having these."

analogy in the novel, as we have seen above, called for "some such economy of clear summarization," such a "clear order and expressed *sequence*," "some such mastery of fundamental statement," that the result had to do away with pictorial inclusiveness and aim at synthetic compression. At this stage at least, picture and scene were not complementary but opposed principles: action, rather than illustration, was of paramount importance, and it had to rely for its development on dramatic scenes in which the characters, caught and presented in action, revealed their motivations indirectly while carrying the story forward. As James noted during the composition of *What Maisie Knew:*

Ah, this *divine* conception of one's little masses and periods in the scenic light—as rounded ACTS; this patient, pious, nobly "vindictive" ["vindicating"?] application of the scenic philosophy and method—I feel as if it still (above *all*, YET) had a great deal to give me, and might carry me as far as I dream! [P. 258, 26 October 1896]

I realize—none too soon—that the *scenic* method is my absolute, my imperative, my *only* salvation. The *march of an action* is the thing for me to, more and more, *attach* myself to: it is the only thing that really, for *me*, at least, will *produire* L'OEUVRE, and L'OEUVRE is, before God, what I'm going in for. Well, the scenic scheme is the only one that *I* can trust, with my tendencies, to stick to the march of an action. How reading Ibsen's splendid *John Gabriel* a day or two ago (in proof) brought that, FINALLY AND FOREVER, home to me! [P. 263, 21 December 1896][7]

[7] In his Preface to *The Wings of the Dove* James was to distinguish between the two opposing functions of picture and scene: "The odd inveteracy with which picture, at almost any turn, is jealous of drama, and drama (though on the whole with a greater patience, I think) suspicious of picture" (*The Art of the Novel*, p. 298). The distinction can be related to the opposing narrative principles of *telling* and *showing* as discussed by Wayne C. Booth in *The Rhetoric of Fiction* (Chicago, 1961). See also Stefania Piccinato, "*The Wings of the Dove*: dal progetto alla forma," *Studi Americani*, 15 (1969), 131–68, who refers (p. 141) to Tzvetan Todorov's distinction between the scenic style, which is "en même temps la représentation et la vision 'avec' (narrateur = personnage),"

The dramatic scene ("dialogue which is always action") is intense and compressed, not illustrative: it presents, rather than represents. It is objective, contained in itself, self-evident: it articulates a sequence, a vital, progressive, rising narrative rhythm. As James stressed in his Preface to *The Awkward Age*, "The dramatist has verily to *build*, is committed to architecture, to construction at any cost." And if his construction takes the form of "the successive Acts of a Play," then "the divine distinction of the act of a play . . . was . . . in its special, its guarded objectivity. This objectivity, in turn, when achieving its ideal, came from the imposed absence of that 'going behind,' to compass explanations and amplifications." The point was "to make the presented occasion tell all of its story itself, remain shut up in its own presence."[8]

A second, crucial point develops from this. In the theater, of course, the scene is made visible to the audience. In the novel it is made "evident" by the device of the "intelligent observer," the narrator who is involved in the action and presents it from his limited point of view. This principle, stressed by James in the *Notebooks* of this period and in the later Prefaces, becomes one of the basic "hinges" of the scenic form. It allows the novelist to achieve his highest aspiration: to reconcile objectivity of presentation with subjective vision. On the one hand, the narrator presents the relevant facts as they happen objectively, as on the stage; on the other, he invests them with a personal perspective and point of view. It

---

and the panoramic style, which is "la narration et la vision 'par derrière' (narrateur > personnage)" (Todorov, *Littérature et signification* [Paris, 1967], pp. 85–86).

[8] *The Art of the Novel*, pp. 109, 110–11. In a letter of 26 July 1899 James wrote of "the promiscuous shiftings of standpoint and centre of Tolstoi and Balzac for instance (which come, to my eye, from their being not so much big dramatists as big *painters*—as Loti is a painter)" (*Letters*, I, 327). His long letter throws light on his conception of the scenic method as opposed to the pictorial for its intensity and objectivity of presentation. See Joseph Wiesenfarth, *Henry James and the Dramatic Analogy* (New York, 1963), pp. 2–12.

is the narrator·who provides a rigorous "foreshortened" perspective, required by the dramatic form, and at the same time the angle of vision, the obliqueness, and ambiguity, of a personal, subjective view.[9] He presents and reconstructs simultaneously, in a manner that somewhat resembles Brecht's technique of the "estranged" actor.

According to Brecht's theory, his estranged, or "alienated," actor, while objectively enacting his part, makes us at the same time aware of its artificiality, of his own *interpretation* of it. He "reconstructs" scenes and events in such a way that we can tell he is *acting,* performing a role. This should lead the spectator to a full awareness of the basic issues involved and to pass a critical—rather than emotional—judgment on them. No identification of the actor with his role, or of spectator with actor, is permissible: we watch, as it were, through the actor *into* the action. In a rather similar way, though the point must not be overstressed, James's narrator is actually involved in the action but detached from it; he performs his role in the story, but, more crucially, he acts as intermediary for the reader, providing him not with a full interpretation of the scene but with hints and clues that the reader himself must interpret. In both cases much more is required of the spectator or reader than mere acquiescence in the facts presented.

In such a way, far from being in opposition, the two Jamesian principles of the limited point of view and the dramatic scene are complementary—"two ends of one stick," as R. P. Blackmur called them in his introduction to *The Art of the Novel,* "and no one can say where either end begins." In James's *Notebooks* we can see how the two devices grew and developed simultaneously, in a kind of mutual

---

[9] As James wrote in his Preface to "The Altar of the Dead": "The safest arena for the play of moving accidents . . . is the field, as I may call it, rather of their second than their first exhibition. By which, to avoid obscurity, I mean nothing more cryptic than I feel myself show them best by showing almost exclusively the way they are felt" (*The Art of the Novel*, p. 256).

dependence. The dramatic scene objectifies the indirect approach, while the narrator "colors" the scene in a subjective way. As Percy Lubbock remarked in *The Craft of Fiction,* "The story that is centered in somebody's consciousness, passed through a fashioned and constituted mind— not poured straight into the book from the mind of the author— . . . takes its place as a story dramatically pictured." If the "intelligent observer," moreover, serves the specific requirements of the dramatic scene, he is in turn subjected to the dramatic principle. The self-sufficiency of the dramatic scene is made dependent on the personal—and limited—view of the narrator; in turn, his mind and consciousness as well are dramatized. Michael Egan has recently stressed this aspect: "What is happening here is that James is passing over from the dramatization of events to the dramatization of states of mind and soul, the conditions of what is happening below the surface of the dialogue and the action."[10] This further twist must also be borne in mind in approaching James's experimental novels.

James was approaching here a form of mannerism: all the more so if we remember that for the overall structure of these novels he seemed to follow the model of the well-made play, that he took quite a few hints from Ibsen in terms of subject matter and began to use rarefied, artificial, and stereotyped forms of dialogue. It has even been suggested that the device of the limited point of view itself was adopted by James to disguise his ignorance of the signs and the shorthand of a stylized society (the English upper class) of which he had no real firsthand or full knowledge. This would be one of the reasons for his choice of children as "intelligent observers" and centers of consciousness—characters, that is, only partially aware of the facts they report or witness. Along these lines, F. W. Bateson has suggested that James's reliance on a narrator to the complete exclusion of authorial intrusions and comments was actually imposed on him by the very nature of the language he used—literary English, which Americans *had* to use in a restricted way as it belonged to another country and expressed a different civilization. Hence his disguise or retreat into the mind of a *limited* observer: a tactical device rather than a strategic victory.

Be that as it may, one must emphasize the fact that the principle of the limited point of view combined with the scenic form provided James with unexpected opportunities not only for dramatic compression but for psychological investigation as well. In using young people or children as observers, he gradually became a master of the "reign of wonder," the domain of psychological subtleties, while providing his scenes with the elusiveness and ambiguity of a limited, incomplete, and indirect knowledge. Here was the beginning of his peculiar ambiguity—a quite modern achievement that was made possible by the combination and interrelation of the two experimental principles, which were to become of the greatest importance in contemporary fiction. James's ambiguity, from now on, pertained to his situations, his characters, his centers of consciousness, and was reflected in a mannered and rarefied style. His achievement, however, was precisely in circumscribing a personal view and focusing it on foreshortened moments, episodes, and scenes, on multiplied aspects vibrant with dramatic and *objective* intensity. The rhythm of the narration was then given by the significant juxtaposition of moments, episodes, and scenes which the narrator presents and projects subjectively—either by choice, chance, or necessity—but which he also isolates in their dramatic evidence and objectifies as on a stage by his presentation. The point of view intensifies gestures, actions, and words in a subjective way; it also gives them objective evidence.

I have insisted on a preliminary definition of the implications of James's scenic method because they seem to me crucial not only for the novels that were to follow but for twentieth-century fiction at large. Among the techniques that James derived from his "dramatic years," the interrelation between the principle of the scenic method and the limited point of view seems of the greatest importance. Not merely technical, but epistemological and even philosophical in its implications, concerning as it does the novelist's way of apprehending and recreating reality, this interrelation affects the overall dramatic structure of the novel. It accounts for the aspiration to brevity and compression (implied in the *limited* point of view) as well as for the "multiplication of aspects" that leads by gradual steps to a proliferation of scenes. From the *short length* James was imperceptibly to arrive at overtreatment and stylistic diffusiveness. He was having it, as it were, both ways, combining dramatic intensity with psychological subtlety, just as he aimed at combining objectivity of presentation with subjective vision. These principles, so wide-ranging and fruitful in their implications, provided the foundation and the background for his intensely experimental novels of the 1890s and were to influence both his major phase and twentieth-century fiction.

2

When in 1893 James recorded the germ out of which *The Other House* (serialized in the *Illustrated London News* in 1896) was to grow, he wrote that he had a play in mind, but that it could be used for the other possibility, namely, fiction. He divided the story into three acts, which merged into the chapters of a novel: "the 1st chapter of my story—by which I mean the 1st act of my play!" (p. 139). He later wrote a scenario in three acts (*The Promise*), which in 1896 was reworked in narrative lines. Its definition, however, was still uncertain: "a play of 'incident'—or . . . a novel—of the same" (p. 141); "quite the subject of a story as well as of a play" (p. 146).[11] Play and / or novel, then, developed in

[11] See also James's letters on the novel to Clement Shorter, editor of

dramatic scenes, thanks to the limited number of characters and the rather melodramatic nature of the plot: the plight of a "Bad Heroine" driven to child-murder so as to pave her way to marriage with a man bound by a promise made to his first wife not to remarry so long as their child lived. For once, the original donnée was simplified in the novel, thus doing away with the possibility of a happy ending and emphasizing the melodrama of the denouement. The melodramatic quality of the novel depended also on a rather crude imitation of Ibsen in terms of subject matter and technique, carried out by James in these years through readings and attendance of plays such as *Hedda Gabler* and *The Master Builder*. As has been recently maintained, *The Other House* may be seen as James's "first full-blown Ibsen tragedy," "pure Ibsen, unalloyed, undistilled and hawked directly from the pages of *Hedda Gabler* and *Rosmersholm*." Ibsen, moreover, had shown James "not only that the theatre *should* be used as a vehicle for serious social comment, like the novel, but that modern drama *could* sustain intense investigation of character and situation, of states of mind and soul."[12]

-----

the *Illustrated London News*, in *Letters to an Editor* (London, 1916), pp. 5–8, and his letter of 2 August 1907 in *Letters to A. C. Benson and Auguste Monod*, ed. E. F. Benson (New York, 1930): "It is simply a three-act play converted into a narrative in three 'Books.' It was first written as a play . . . and then laid by. . . . Then at the end of 2 or 3 years the material was economically used *tel quel*, as it stood, for the narrative purpose: the only small scrap of arrangement (I mean departure from the scenic form) being the 3 or 4 opening pages. The rest is all 'scenic' and the thing thus perhaps a considerable curiosity: which may be its only merit!" (p. 107).

[12] Egan, *The Ibsen Years*, pp. 59–60 and 29. Egan goes on: "James discovered through Ibsen that Realism, to which he was of course committed as a novelist, was not antipathetic to the drama." See also Cargill, *The Novels of Henry James*, pp. 209 ff.; Edel, *The Treacherous Years*, pp. 27–31 and 165–67; Introduction, *The Other House* (New York, n.d.), pp. vii–xxi; Herbert Edwards, "Henry James and Ibsen," *American Literature*, 24 (1952), 208–23; Pelham Edgar, *Henry James: Man and Author* (Boston, 1927), p. 197 (the novel "reads like an Ibsen play with Jamesian amplifications").

At this stage James's adherence to Ibsen did not quite bring out the dramatic qualities of his story. *The Other House,* which he himself described as an "extended prompt-book," provides rather an interesting aperçu on his struggle to move away from the stage play in order to write "dramatic" fiction. This is not so much on account of the obvious imitation of Ibsen in terms of story and character (the bad heroine, Rose Armiger, is a case in point), as of the "scenic" development of the plot, which even included a sort of chorus, "two persons to figure as the *public,* the judging, wondering, horrified world" (p. 140). James's own contribution was his sensitive portrait of the "good heroine"; on the technical level, by introducing those two figures as horrified spectators he also foreshadowed in a way his later use of "narrators." By concentrating furthermore on Rose Armiger, he turned as much as possible the "play of incident" into a psychological drama, especially if we keep in mind that Rose's punishment was limited to her loss of moral balance and peace of mind.

In an Ibsen-like way, this time, the novel was once again a denunciation of the hypocrisy and rapaciousness of society and of the destructive violence lurking under its surface. The method of presentation, however, was no longer the illustrative fresco, as in the previous novels, but rather the quick succession of single dramatic scenes. Because of its perfect "exposition," James was later to call it, in the Notes for *The Ivory Tower,* his "blest *Other House,* which gives me thus at every step a precedent, a support, a divine little light to walk by."[13] It is in fact unique in his canon for brevity, compression, and narrative drive. But one must also note that its dependence on the theatrical experience and method is too close and mechanical. Its value lies exactly in its being a work of transition, where one can detect James wavering undecidedly between the stage drama and the

---

[13] See also Jacques Barzun, *The Energies of Art* (New York, 1956), pp. 235–36.

novel. It is not without significance that he was later (1908) to rework it into a play.

The real turning point from the play-novel to the experimental "scenic" novel is exemplified by *The Spoils of Poynton*, which was also conceived in 1893, completed before *The Other House*, and serialized in 1896 in the *Atlantic* (under the title *The Old Things*). James's *Notebooks* devote more pages to it than to any other completed novel, and they allow us to follow step by step the working-out and the application of his new poetics. The germ, in 1893, was provided by the situation, half personal and half social, of a Scottish mother who found herself deposed and dispossessed by the marriage of her son, according to "the ugly English custom." Evicted from the house she had furnished and adorned with beautiful objects, she rebeled against her son and the cruel usage, removing many of the best objects from the house and going to any length to retain their possession. Once again James envisaged the story "in three chapters, like 3 little acts" (p. 198), "splendidly foreshortened" and arranged according to the three moments of a well-made play: the exposition, leading up to the marriage of the son (Act I), the gathering storm when she cannot bring herself to return her spoils (Act II), and the denouement (Act III). At this stage, however, James began to perceive that the dramatic situation would be greatly enhanced if he used another character, Muriel Veetch (later Fleda Vetch), as a catalyst: "I have a dim sense," he wrote, "that the denouement must be *through* her" (p. 199).

He outlined here the principles of the scenic method that have been previously discussed. Later on he moved the climax of the action to the third act ("the marriage takes place . . . in Act III" [p. 209]). Meanwhile the story grew in development and sidelines, and James was confirmed in his "dim sense" that Fleda would give a "lift" to the story, thus concentrating most of his attention on her. It is precisely here, as is clear from his own detailed analysis, that Mrs. Gereth's drama fades into the background and Fleda

Vetch's inner conflict becomes the central issue and the guiding line of the story. Fleda falls in love with the young son, Owen Gereth, and with Mrs. Gereth's precious things, but she will not be instrumental herself in breaking his previous engagement to Mona; she will in fact "heroically" prevail upon Mrs. Gereth to return her spoils, so that the expected marriage takes place. In the "crowded finish," Fleda's moral stature increases with the growth of the psychological and behavioral subtleties with which James endowed the novel. Her choice becomes a moral as well as an aesthetic choice, and she sacrifices herself rather than bring herself to a breach of style and decorum. But even in the specific context of Fleda's moral and social dilemma, James insisted on the need for "SCENIC intensity, brevity, beauty—make it march as straight as a pure little dramatic action" (p. 249). "IT MUST BE AS STRAIGHT AS A PLAY—this is the only way to do" (p. 253), he noted later on, and this scenic intensity was to be achieved through a multiplication of aspects and key episodes, which by now numbered fifteen.

Fleda's growth from secondary to main character leads quite naturally to a proliferation of scenes: and it is also quite a natural development that these dramatic scenes are now not only referred to Fleda but seen and filtered by her as an "intelligent observer" involved in the action. In this way the "dramatic" novel finds its center of interest and its center of consciousness; in turn, the presence of a center of consciousness is directly responsible for the fragmentation of the narration into a sequence of scenes. These scenes are always conceived and directly presented as *action*, both on the factual and the psychological level ("it must all be an absolute and unmitigated *action*" [p. 219]); they build up a sort of rhythmic development and a *progression d'effet* (as Ford Madox Ford would call it) while being subjectively filtered in and through the personal involvement of Fleda. As Walter Isle, among others, has observed, James's shift to the dramatic novel "is intimately connected with . . . the use of a central consciousness," and the choice of a point of view itself determines a gradual involvement with the dramatic scene.[14]

James's combination of the two methods allowed him to reflect the external drama for the possession of the spoils in Fleda's inner drama of painful renunciation, both of the things themselves and of love. It allowed him, on one hand, to denounce Mrs. Gereth's "greediness" while qualifying it as aesthetic passion and attenuating it through Fleda's own appreciation of the spoils. On the other hand, it enabled him to analyze the emotional and psychological process that leads Fleda to an abdication, which is perhaps, after all, no better than the interested triumph of the others, if we see in it too much passivity of action and too close an adherence to principles of decorum. This combination, finally, determined a perfect balance between the urgency of the dramatic moments (James again: "it must be unmitigatedly objective narration—unarrested drama") and Fleda's gradual withdrawal into her own tortured and frustrated soul.

The growth of Fleda from secondary character to heroine of the book and "mirror of the subject" was analyzed by James in his later Preface to the novel in a revealing way. If "the Things, always the splendid Things," were placed in the middle light, being inarticulate, they were "barred" from claiming central position. It was then Fleda who "marked her place in [his] foreground at one ingratiating stroke. She planted herself centrally"—claiming her position as intellectual, emotional, and moral center, although "only intelligent, not distinctly able." She became the key to the drama and made "a drama of any sort possible." The march of the action, in this

---

[14] Isle, *Experiments in Form*, pp. 77–78. On the interrelation between point of view and scenic method, see Dorothea Krook, "Principles and Methods in the Later Works of Henry James," in *Interpretations of American Literature*, ed. Charles Feidelson, Jr., and Paul Brodtkorb, Jr. (New York, 1959), pp. 262–79 and p. 267 in particular: "The result is a method of presentation so organically, so necessarily and inescapably, *dramatic* that one searches in vain for anything comparable in the history of the novel."

way, "became and remained that of her understanding" (given her gift for *appreciation*), because she "sees and feels, while the others but feel without seeing."[15] Her capacity to *see* thus became her drama and her torment—made her a heroine and a victim. But it became her *technical* function as well, her structural role in the novel as intelligent observer and center of consciousness. Theme and technique are identical, inextricably interwoven. The sequence of dramatic scenes gives rhythmic structure, shape, and pattern to the novel, while providing Fleda with the material itself of her experience. Her experience lies in turn in her way of recognizing, confronting, and enacting the emotional dilemma and the moral drama with which she is faced. Hers is in short a process of coming to terms with reality, while at the time serving the purpose of a narrative reconstruction in which she acts and suffers both as heroine and as "intelligent observer."

Before her eyes, and through her eyes before us, the little acts of the drama take on concrete vividness and at the same time a profound psychological resonance.[16] The march of the action through dramatic scenes—multiplied in number at each stage but foreshortened and compressed by the very principle of the point of view—has never been so consistent, controlled, and gradual; never before had it served with such intensity the purpose of a painful, gradual recognition of reality on the part of the involved narrator. We witness here the gradual discovery and application of a complex method and a refined technique, but also the triumph of a moral vision conveyed through a well-defined and consistent *artistic* vision.

[15] *The Art of the Novel*, pp. 126–29.
[16] Wiesenfarth, *Henry James and the Dramatic Analogy*, pp. 51–56; for the presence of authorial intrusions, John Tilford, "James the Old Intruder," *Modern Fiction Studies* 4 (1956), 157–64. Other relevant studies are Nina Baym, "Fleda Vetch and the Plot of *The Spoils of Poynton*," *PMLA*, 84 (1969), 102–11; Philip Greene, "Point of View in *The Spoils of Poynton*," *Nineteenth Century Fiction*, 21 (1961), 359–69; W. B. Stein, "The Method at the Heart of Madness: *The Spoils of Poynton*," *Modern Fiction Studies*, 14 (1968), 187–202.

Ford Madox Ford saw in *The Spoils of Poynton* "the technical high-water mark of all James's work" and others regarded it as an example of "accomplished perfection . . . for structure, proportion, texture, style," "the first absolutely pure example of James's method."[17] It is a jewel in James's canon, whose richness of thematic implications and psychological subtleties would deserve a detailed analysis. Here, however, I have been mostly concerned to detect and analyze the way in which it stands out as the turning point in James's shift from the pictorial to the dramatic method. Its overall structure, as in *The Other House*, fits into the three-act division of the well-made play, and Michael Egan has shown the usefulness of such an approach.[18] But this is just one of its aspects; the step forward toward the "scenic" method is much greater. Within each act the action is carried forward through a series of compressed and tightly organized scenes. Each scene, moreover, is written as much as possible in dialogue form and with as little authorial comment as possible. The dramatic scene has called for the use of the center of consciousness, and this has in turn made possible, strengthened, and vivified the full application of the scenic method. This is further confirmed if we turn to an examination of *What Maisie Knew*. There is another side to the story as well.

[17] Ford, *Portraits from Life* (1937; rpt. Chicago, n.d.), p. 11: "and can't I remember the rapturous and shouting enthusiasm of Conrad over that story when we first read it together"; Carl Van Doren, *The American Novel* (New York, 1921), p. 210; Beach, *The Method of Henry James*, p. 233.

[18] Egan, *The Ibsen Years*, pp. 77–80. On other and related aspects, see Lawrence Holland, *The Expense of Vision: Essays on the Craft of Henry James* (Princeton, N.J., 1964), pp. 90–113; Robert C. McLean, "The Subjective Adventure of Fleda Vetch," in *Henry James: Modern Judgements*, ed. Tony Tanner (London, 1968), pp. 204–21; Alan H. Roper, "The Moral and Metaphorical Meaning of *The Spoils of Poynton*," *American Literature*, 32 (1960), 182–96; Graham, *Henry James: The Drama of Fulfilment*, pp. 127–59; the discussion carried on in *Essays in Criticism*, 16 (1966), 185–200 and 482–89, 17 (1967), 238–43, 18 (1968), 107–11 and 357–59. For a connection with Balzac, Adeleine R. Tintner, " 'The Old Things': Balzac's *Le curé de Tours* and James's *The Spoils of Poynton*," *Nineteenth Century Fiction*, 26 (1972), 436–55.

3

The process leading to the combination of dramatic scene and point of view was reversed in *What Maisie Knew* (1897, serialized in the *Chap Book*). Here the germ was not given by a dramatic situation, as in *The Spoils of Poynton*, but by the intuition of a girl "*divided* by [her] parents in consequence of their being divorced" (p. 126), who ends by determining a new, equivocal relationship between her stepparents. This new "particular relation" was to develop "through the child—over and on account of and by means of the child" (p. 127). In this case too James recorded at great length in the *Notebooks* the technical and thematic development of the story. The girl was immediately seen as "a fresh bone of contention, a fresh source of dramatic situations" (p. 127); her position of innocent go-between endowed her from the beginning with the double role of dramatic protagonist and technical center of consciousness. "The moral consciousness of a child is as much a part of life as the Islands of the Spanish Main" James had maintained in *The Art of Fiction*, when discussing *Chérie* by Edmond de Goncourt and Stevenson's *Treasure Island*. Realism claimed as its domain both the external and the psychological life. In his notes for *What Maisie Knew*, accordingly, he waved aside the temptation of trying for the *ironic* effect and he saw at once the advantages of combining "the ironic and the *other* interest (the 'touch of tenderness'—or sweetness—or sympathy or poetry)" (p. 134). And when in 1895 he sat down to write the novel, it was almost inevitable that the scenic method should be combined with the principle of the girl's limited point of view.

"Make my point of view, my *line*, the consciousness, the dim, sweet, wondering, clinging perception of the child" (p. 236), James openly prescribed in order to enhance the dramatic possibilities of the story. And immediately it divided itself into ten sections, developed through a juxtaposition of dramatic scenes dealing for the most part, after the "exposition," with a series of visits, meetings, chance encounters, and clashes between the irresponsible and corrupt grown-ups. These scenes imply Maisie's presence and hence her gradual involvement for both thematic and structural purposes. Thus we have the episodes of Maisie with Miss Overmore, the governess, at her father's house (section III); of Maisie and the Captain at her mother's (IV); an exchange of three visits (V); and then Maisie together with her stepparents, who are brought together in an equivocal way on account of the child (VI: "*Description of it in form of picture of the child's dim sense*" [p. 239]); and Maisie again who learns of her father's bolting with the "strange little lady" (VIII); Maisie and her stepparents by now "very definitively come together"; finally, Maisie with Mrs. Wix, who may save her from that vicious circle of corruption (X). "EVERYTHING TAKES PLACE BEFORE MAISIE," according to James's repeated statement: "That is a part of the essence of the thing . . . the second of the golden threads of my *form*" (p. 238).

The other golden thread was of course the scenic method. As he specified in the "detailed scenario" of the second part of the story, the problem was not to "slacken in my deep observance of this strong and beneficent method—this intensely structural, intensely hinged and jointed preliminary frame" (p. 257). The girl "serves as a sort of a dim, crooked little reflector of the conditions," James noted, and "The rest of my story—*voyons*—consists of the sharp notation, at a series of moments, of those conditions. Each little chapter *is* thereby, a moment, a stage" (p. 258). In each moment and stage James saw "the little *act* of my little drama," until he reached that joyous exaltation for the scenic method that underlies the passages already quoted earlier in this chapter ("Ah, this *divine* conception of one's little masses and periods in the scenic light. . . . I realize—none too soon—that the *scenic* method is my absolute, my imperative, my only salvation" [p. 263]). There was an absolute need not to deviate from that method: "I must now, I fully recognize, have a splendid recourse to it to see me out of the wood, at all, of this interminable little *Maisie*" (p. 263). As he later put it in the Preface to the novel: "the whole course of my design . . . would be to make and to keep her so limited consciousness the very field of my picture while at the same time guarding with care the integrity of the objects represented. . . . To that, then, I settled—to the question of giving it *all*, the whole situation surrounding her, but of giving it only through the occasions and the connexions of her proximity and her attention; only as it might pass before her and appeal to her, as it might touch her and affect her" [19]

In *The Spoils of Poynton*, as we have seen, the original dramatic conception gradually brought about the adoption of the center of consciousness. Here it is the other way round: Maisie's limited point of view and her limitations as such a center led James to rely more and more on the scenic method. The final result is the same, and it implies in either case an expansion of the initial donnée, a proliferation of scenes, and a dangerous tendency to overtreatment. This is due, as I suggested, to the need of reconciling the indirectness, the limitations and the ambiguities of the circumscribed point of view, with the required self-evidence of the dramatic scenes; the proper analysis of Maisie's mental and psychological development—her gradual acquisition of knowledge—with a sequence of objectively presented episodes whose meaning depends on their rhythmic succession and total effect.

The sequence of episodes (the completed novel is divided into thirty-one sections) gives substance and form to the story both in terms of its factual development—the external plot—and in terms of Maisie's own inner development—her personal adventure and dubious "education." James' insistence on the scenic method, far from interfering with Maisie's application of her limited point of view, provides it with the

[19] *The Art of the Novel*, pp. 144–45.

necessary field of application, and is in turn conditioned and made possible by this second golden thread of his narrative procedure. Central consciousness and dramatic technique are "so fused as to reflect almost perfectly the meaning of the novel."[20] Maisie's construing is indeed the construction of the whole book. The unrelenting "march of the action" in dramatic episodes is, moreover, combined with the proper slackening of pace, which allows James to penetrate the psychological tortuosity of the girl's mind, while the emphasized, symmetrical disposition of scenes is harmonized by an artistic vision which, although tending to diffusiveness and overtreatment, is securely "hinged" on an overall dramatic structure.

Much more than Fleda Vetch, of course, Maisie needs a few *ficelles*—those secondary characters, like Mrs. Wix, who enable her to surmise and comprehend even what she does not, and cannot, see, who help her to mature mentally, expanding her awareness and contributing to her moral development in the midst of so much corruption and irresponsibility. This fact—and the fact that Maisie, like Huck Finn some years before her, is "really keeping the torch of virtue alive in an air tending infinitely to smother it . . . drawing some stray fragrance of an ideal across the scent of selfishness, by sowing on barren strands, through the mere fact of presence, the seed of the moral life"[21]—accounts also for the multiplication

---

[20] Isle, *Experiments in Form*, pp. 122–23.

[21] *The Art of the Novel*, p. 143. I touch here only indirectly on the question of Maisie's "knowledge," for which see Marius Bewley, *The Complex Fate*, pp. 96–144; Harris W. Wilson, "What *Did* Maisie Know?" *College English*, 17 (1956), 279–82; Glauco Cambon, "What Maisie and Huck Knew", *Studi Americani*, 6 (1960), 205–20; John C. McCloskey, "What Maisie Knows: A Study of Childhood and Adolescence," *American Literature*, 36 (1965), 485–513; James W. Gargano, "What Maisie Knew: The Evolution of a 'Moral Sense,'" in *Henry James: Modern Judgements*, pp. 222–35; Muriel G. Shine, *The Fictional Children of Henry James* (Chapel Hill, N.C., 1969), pp. 109–26 (and pp. 146–70 for Nanda Brookenham); Philip M. Weinstein, *Henry James and the Requirements of the Imagination* (Cambridge, Mass., 1971), pp. 80–96. One of the best critical treatments of

of aspects and the unavoidable lengths of overtreatment. James's overtreatment is not only a cherished habit and an indulgence of his later, mannered style: it is implied in and a consequence of his experimental method itself. He wanted to confront, search, and combine too many things and too many possibilities, to pursue all possible threads, to squeeze every drop of meaning out of every technical and expressive potentiality. This was his lifelong aim and ambition; in particular, his dramatic method required by its very nature a formidable sequence and display of scenes to achieve its overall significance, while the limited point of view, again by its very nature, called for a multiplication of meaningful occasions in order to provide a comprehensive, and comprehending, perspective. In the Preface to *What Maisie Knew*, in fact, James spoke of "the growth of the 'great oak' from the little acorn," and hinted at "the vague pictorial glow" of its inception. By this time, however, he had developed a quite different method of presentation ("I was in presence of the red dramatic spark that glowed at the core of my vision"),[22] depending on the organic interrelation of the two principles of the point of view and the dramatic scene.

It is Maisie who contributes to the formation of new relationships between the characters, "weaving about, with the best faith in the world, the close web of sophistication; . . . becoming a centre and a pretext for a fresh system of misbehaviour, a system moreover of a nature to spread and ramify." At the same time, her very presence controls the proliferation of scenes with the necessary limitation of her point of view. By her imponderable presence she lends a precious element of dignity to persons and things: "she has simply to wonder, as I say, about them"—James stressed in the Preface—"and they begin to have meanings, aspects, solidities, connexions— connexions with the 'universal!'—that they could scarce have hoped for." She makes them "portentous all by the play

the novel is in Tony Tanner, *The Reign of Wonder: Naivety and Reality in American Literature* (New York, 1965), pp. 178–98.

[22] *The Art of the Novel*, pp. 140, 141, 142.

of her good faith" and allows effects of "associational magic," because by virtue of her role, and the role of her virtue, the action necessarily adheres to the scenic form.[23] In his joint Preface to *What Maisie Knew, The Pupil,* and *In the Cage,* James stressed the "subjective" adventures of his "intelligent observers" (Maisie, Morgan Moreen, the telegraphist) *and* their conforming to the "scenic law": "Going over the pages here placed together has been for me, at all events, quite to watch the scenic system at play. The treatment by 'scene,' regularly, quite rhythmically recurs." As in a musical suite, preparations and "quiet recitals" alternate: "The point, however, is that the scenic passages are *wholly* and logically scenic, having for their rule of beauty the principle of the 'conduct,' the organic development, of a scene."[24] He did most of the business of criticism for us. In the long passages of his *Notebooks* and the inspired Preface he gave us the perfect documentation of an experimental method embodied in artistic substance and artistic form, as well as the theoretical justification of the particular ways he pursued.

James, by then fully at home with his method, squeezed every drop of artistic significance from it. *What Maisie Knew* is a triumph of compositional complexity, of patterned and sustained narrative rhythm, of achieved mastery over the expressive means chosen to convey an artistic vision. It was more than a tour de force or a jeu d'artifice, for the theme explored is rooted once more in the drama of the eternal conflict between innocence and corruption and is reflected in the context of a society all the more sordid, irresponsible, and corrupt for its lack of awareness and concern. In a letter of 1886 to Charles Eliot Norton, James has seen in the frequent divorces and common affairs of the day an unmistakable sign of the increasing corruption of the English upper class—by now comparable to the decaying French aristocracy on the eve of the revolution or the depraved late Roman world.[25]

[23] Ibid., pp. 143, 147.
[24] Ibid., pp. 157–58.
[25] *Letters,* I, 124: "The condition of that body [the English upper class]

It took the eyes of a girl to reveal the carelessness of that corruption; and it took James's masterly application of his new experimental principles to give both formal rigor and tender human value to her painful and emblematic experience.

The rhythmic sequence of episodes proceeds according to a principle of functional multipication of aspects, because they must gradually acquire a value for Maisie. In order to acquire value for Maisie, who views them with (objective) detachment and (subjective) involvement, they are presented as scenic moments. As such, they provide for the successive steps and stages in the psychological and moral wonder of the girl—her gradual, bewildering discoveries. So the alternation of scenes is not only between Maisie and the grown-ups but also between Maisie *with* the grown-ups and Maisie alone *with* herself—two distinct moments or poles of one process. Around Maisie wheels the absurd and unbelievable minuet of corruption and irresponsibility—a minuet of libertines so uncontrolled that it seems the headlong rush of a society toward its moral and physical dissolution. Ida Farange, her divorced mother, pairs off with Sir Claude, while her father, Beale, pairs off with the young governess, Miss Overmore. But once they are married, the new couples dissolve and reform at random—Ida with the Captain in the Park, Beale at the mysterious lady's, while Sir Claude and the present "Mrs. Beale" are drawn together by their interest in Maisie. The wider it becomes, with the flight of Ida and Beale with their respective lovers, the tighter the circle of corruption closes around Maisie, who is left alone to provide a ground and a pretext for Sir Claude's and Mrs. Beale's guilty interest in her.

Every time the circle widens or closes around her, Maisie is more and more alone with herself (and Mrs. Wix), to face her dangers with wonder, to suggest by her very presence the need

---

seems to me to be in many ways very much the same rotten and *collapsible* one as that of the French aristocracy before the Revolution—minus cleverness and conversation; or perhaps it's more like the heavy, congested and depraved Roman world upon which the barbarians came down."

for a responsible choice, to contemplate that disgraceful spectacle, to try to account for it in both personal and moral terms. In this last case, the scenic method merges completely with the point of view reflecting on itself; it is a reflection of dramatized consciousness. The artistic vision stretches or shrinks just as the circle of corruption does, in accordance with the very movements of girl's consciousness; Maisie either reaches out to the spectacle of the world or withdraws into herself for painful reconsideration. By this kind of movement, such an artistic vision reveals its deepest nature: a unified, consistent, responsible view of the moral world. James's achievement is not only in the working-out of a new poetics, it is in the perfect application of a complex twofold method which can inimitably express that particular moral and artistic vision and which indeed *becomes* that vision.

Less than two years later, with *The Awkward Age* (serialized in 1898–99 in *Harper's Weekly*), James took up again a similar theme: the tension and the danger to which the precarious innocence of the young is exposed by the disordered life of their elders. This time the subject was to be dealt with in the spirit of "the lightest comedy" and with fewer complexities of psychological analysis, but with further emphasis on its "scenic" character. The original idea was a short tale on the subject of a *jeune fille* who is allowed too early to "sit downstairs" in her mother's drawingroom and salon and is thus exposed to the subtle corruption of the "free" speeches and "sophisticated" behavior of the adults (she "inevitably hears, overhears, guesses, follows, takes in, becomes acquainted with, horrors"), so as to be eventually "dropped" by her fiancé. In this case, too, James developed his idea into a full-fledged novel, dealing specifically with "the question of the non-marrying of girls, the desperation of mothers, the whole alteration of manners—in the sense of the *osé*" (p. 192). The girl, Nanda Brookenham (like Maisie, "conscious and aware"), kept her central position only for a short time; the character of the mother soon claimed a "focal position" in the novel as Nanda's unconcious corrupter and unwitting rival. But a further and more important experimental complication was introduced here.

On one hand, as James relied less and less on the girl's personal reflections, the principle of the dramatic scene grew predominant and was pursued as a means to the greatest possible objectivity of presentation. It will be remembered that James theorized on the objective value of the scenic method with particular reference to *The Awkward Age*. On the other hand, James emphasized as much as possible the theatrical quality of the dramatic scenes by presenting them almost exclusively as *pure dialogue*, to the exclusion of almost all narrative links and connections. The proliferation of scenes and the multiplication of aspects were in this case counterpointed by a reduction of the dramatic episodes of their purely *scenic* essence and outline. His avowed aim was "to make the presented occasion tell all its story itself, remain shut up in its own presence."[26] With this new experimental complication James set out to follow the example of such society writers as "Gyp" (pseudonym for the French author Sybille Riqueti de Mirabeau) and Henri Lavedan, who were particularly fashionable at the time for their ironic lightness of touch and who had consistently applied to their work the principle of the *roman dialogué*. " 'Dialogue,' always 'dialogue'! I had seemed from far back to hear them mostly cry: 'We can't have too much of it, we can't have enough of it, and no excess of it,' " he wrote in the Preface.[27] James went indeed so far in this direction as to cut out as narrative interferences the "stage directions" themselves, including the harmless "said he" or "said she": the dialogue, pure and simple, had to speak for itself, "present" all the facts, and indeed constitute the very substance of the book. For the conversation piece he could of course find in England the precedent of Thomas Love Peacock. But his own experiment with the *roman dialogué* seems to be well suited to the story precisely because it is through the dialogues of the grown-ups

---

[26] *The Art of the Novel*, p. 111.
[27] Ibid., p. 106.

that Nanda Brookenham is exposed to the danger of corruption.

From these premises it follows that Nanda, more than a center of consciousness like Maisie (and, significantly, she has no need for *ficelles*), became a *structural* center and pivot of the dramatic construction—a construction which for James himself, who sketched it in the Preface of the novel, took the form of concentric rings. Many distinct "lamps" revolve round Nanda, each throwing light on a particular aspect of her situation:

I drew on a sheet of paper . . . the neat figure of a circle consisting of a number of small rounds disposed at equal distance about a central object. The central object was my situation, my subject in itself, to which the thing would owe its title, and the small rounds represented so many distinct lamps, as I liked to call them, the function of each of which would be to light with all due intensity one of its aspects. . . . Each of my "lamps" would be the light of a single "social occasion" in the history and intercourse of the characters concerned, and would bring out to the full the latent colour of the scene in question and cause it to illustrate, to the last drop, its bearing on my theme.[28]

Each of these social occasions became obviously a "scene," so that the architecture of the novel came once again to correspond to "the successive Acts of a Play" and acquired a kind of total objectivity, undisturbed by subjective interpolations. (As we have seen, "the divine distinction of the act of a play . . . was . . . its guarded objectivity.") As with *The Other House*, the novel approached the condition of a play, and the analogy was here pursued and worked out to its ultimate conclusions. James himself listed the most "dramatic" scenes of the novel (the attempted "compact" between Mr. Longdon, Nanda's protector, and Mr. Vanderbank, Mrs. Brookenham's lover with whom Nanda has fallen in love; the meeting between Vanderbank and Mitchy, in love with Nanda, whom she urges to marry Aggie, and so forth). He also stressed his work of compression and coordination of

[28] Ibid., p. 110.

the episodes scenically numbered and arranged. Within his ten acts James again went to desperations of ingenuity to realize his aim.[29]

The technical process of which he spoke was pursued within the framework of the scenic method, with its complication of relationships *within* the action, with its total avoidance of that "going behind" which had characterized his earlier novels and which had been to a certain extent present in *What Maisie Knew* (where it was needed to throw light on the *subjective* adventure of the girl). "I 'go behind' right and left in *The Princess Casamassima, The Bostonians, The Tragic Muse,* just as I do the same but singly in *The American* and *Maisie,* and just as I do it consistently *never at all* . . . in *The Awkward Age,*" he wrote in 1899 in a letter.[30] As Joseph Warren Beach has remarked: "He had confined himself, for the fun of it, to the 'scene' pure and simple. He would never undertake to give us any information even as to the present scene other than what the participants shared or what might have been gathered by a 'supposititious spectator,' 'an observer disposed to interpret the scene.' "[31] In this novel the dramatic method

[29] See Robert Marks, *James's Later Novels* (New York, 1960), pp. 17–18: "The acts (or books) are ten in number, each a selected social occasion in the history and intercourse of the persons concerned, each marking a distinct phase in the development of the crisis, with an individual interest and character of its own." A detailed analysis of the "Books" follows. See also Eben Bass, "Dramatic Scene and *The Awkward Age*," *PMLA*, 79 (1964), 148–57.

[30] *Letters*, I, 324–25 (26 July 1899: the "going behind" was typical of "Dickens, Balzac, Thackeray, Tolstoi") and p. 333 (12 November 1899: "a form all dramatic and scenic . . . with no going behind, no *telling about* the figures save by their own appearance and action"). Cf. also *The Art of the Novel*, p. 111: "This objectivity, in turn, when achieving its ideal, came from the imposed absence of that 'going behind,' to compass explanations and amplifications." As for James's going behind, in spite of all claims, in chapter 10, see, however, Francis Gillen, "The Dramatist in His Drama: Theory vs. Effect in *The Awkward Age*," *Texas Studies in Literature and Language*, 12 (1971), 663–74.

[31] *The Method of Henry James*, pp. 243–44.

was applied at all levels: in the overall structure, in the sequence of scenes, and in the predominance of dialogue within the scenes. And not only, as James wrote in the Preface, was Nanda's situation presented on absolutely scenic lines, but each scene, abiding "without a moment's deflexion by the principle of the stage-play," brought the dramatic method to its fullest realization by identifying substance with form, subject and technique.[32]

The dialogue form pertains in essence to the drama as such, but it is also the best form that, given the subject of the story, can supply Nanda's experience with substance, constitute the very ground and mode of her adventure among the grown-ups. The value of the treatment becomes the value of the subject, and vice versa. Nanda's experience is dramatic and it takes place as on a stage—the drawingroom—where she acts, half spectator, half protagonist and victim, by reviewing and going through a sequence of moments that are so many "scenes" in which she takes part or to which she is exposed. She listens to dialogues, scraps of conversations, exchange of views, innuendos and allusions, half hints and half words: *they* consitute the real danger for her innocence, and they are taken up and recorded by James in their pure form. Dialogue provides the technical key to the novel, but also the thematic substance of Nanda's experience. The technical device, indeed the method itself, is part and parcel of the thematic development; it gives a particular twist to the story, but it answers the very needs of the story. Nanda is exposed to the danger represented by the free dialogues: consequently her story is developed purely and consistently in terms of dialogues.

James spoke of the novel as a scientific triumph, and I believe he had this in mind when he wrote of "dialogue organic and dramatic, speaking for itself, representing and embodying substance and form"; "it helps us ever so happily to see the grave distinction between substance and form . . . signally break down. I hold it impossible to say, before 'The Awkward

[32] *The Art of the Novel*, p. 115.

Age,' where one of these elements ends and the other begins."[33]
F. O. Matthiessen refers to the book's "strained virtuosity,"
but Frederick Dupee sees it as "technically the most brilliantly
achieved," while Elizabeth Stevenson considers it James's
most difficult book, "but taken on his terms, an absolute
success." *The Awkward Age* is experimental in the fullest sense,
and it marks the highest consummation of the dramatic
method underlying the novels of the 1890s. Percy Lubbock
was right in stressing the fact that "the whole of the book passes
scenically before the reader" and that "it might indeed be
printed as a play; whatever is not dialogue is simply a kind of
amplified stage-direction. . . . the novelist completely ties his
hands, submitting to all the restraints of the playwright in
order to secure the compactness and the direct force of true
drama."[34] Leaving the wish to engage in realistic illustration
behind, the novel no longer aims at a documentary analysis of
the corruption of society: it becomes a problematic presentation of social and moral evil seen in action and through the
action, reduced as it were to its verbal manifestation—the
corrupting levity and irresponsibility of mere dialogue. But
the corruption is there, behind and in the scenes, all the more
powerful for its devious workings in words and through
words.[35]

[33] Ibid., pp. 115, 106. F. R. Leavis, in *The Great Tradition*, speaks
of "the intense moral and tragic interest that here justifies his technique
and is justified by it" (p. 207), and calls the novel "that astonishing work
of genius" (p. 156).

[34] F. O. Matthiessen, *Henry James: The Major Phase* (New York, 1944), pp. 18–
19; Dupee, *Henry James*, p. 136; Elizabeth Stevenson, *The Crooked
Corridor: A Study of Henry James* (New York, 1949), p. 150; Lubbock, *The
Craft of Fiction*, p. 190.

[35] "By the side of *The Princess Casamassima* and *The Bostonians*, the
range of society here examined may be thought meagre. But it is as
if James, in dissecting the rotting head of the smelly fish of late Victorian
and Edwardian England, takes for granted the proverbial assumption that
the rest of the body is hardly likely to be notable for its freshness"
(S. Gorley Putt, *Henry James: A Reader's Guide* [Ithaca, N.Y., 1967], p. 243).
See also Margaret Walters, "Keeping the Place Tidy for the Young
Female Mind," in *The Air of Reality*, pp. 190–218; Ian Gregor and Brian

One might say that for the sheer artistic pleasure of it James created his own obstacles and difficulties to overcome ("it being really, at bottom, only difficulty that interests me," he wrote in 1908 to Howells).[36] In fact, he was later to attribute the "failure" of this novel to the scenic method so thoroughly pursued. If never an end in itself, however, the technical difficulty does become the most exciting aspect of the process, and it is at least partly responsible for the gradual thickening and involution of James's style, already on its way to the typical "manner" of his later phase. There was a good deal of mechanic application in all this (Van Wyck Brooks called him "an impassioned geometer"), and it is undeniable that in his experimental fiction James often bordered on mannerism.[37] Mannerism has, however, its charm and value. It is in fact equally characteristic of James, his period, and contemporary literature. Twentieth-century mannerism and experimentation in fiction—in the highest sense of the world—find in him a forerunner, a prophet, and a first example.

In his last experimental attempt before the novels of the major phase, *The Sacred Fount* (1901), James seemed to end by turning his own method on itself, or against the very form of the novel. His middle period seemed to close with an admission of possible defeat and total doubt of the possibility of writing fiction. This was, however, exemplified and resolved (as we shall see) in *narrative* terms, and in such a peculiarly modern way that James's enigmatic new novel might indeed find

---

Nicholas, "The Novel of Moral Consciousness: *The Awkward Age*," in *The Moral and the Story* (London, 1962), pp. 151–84; Elizabeth Owen, "*The Awkward Age* and the Contemporary English Scene," *Victorian Studies*, 11 (1967), 63–82; W. F. Hall, "James's Conception of Society in *The Awkward Age*," *Nineteenth Century Fiction*, 23 (1968), 28–48.

[36] *Letters*, II, 119.

[37] For James's connection with pictorial mannerism, see Viola Hopkins, "Visual Art Devices and Parallels in the Fiction of Henry James," in *Henry James: Modern Judgements*, pp. 89–115. Here I speak of mannerism, however, in its general sense—as literature that is more and more self-conscious and aware of its technical side.

a crucial position at the very center of our twentieth-century *querelle* over the possibilities, the nature, and the fate of novel writing. That this was a moment of strength rather than weakness is borne out by the flourishing of James's fiction that was to follow almost immediately. In the novels of the major phase James overcame that doubt and made use of the experimental techniques tested and developed in the 1890s—both in terms of illustrative picture and dramatic method. As he wrote in the Preface to *The Ambassadors*:

The material of *The Ambassadors*, conforming in this respect exactly to that of *The Wings of the Dove*, . . . is taken absolutely for the stuff of drama; so that . . . I had mainly to make on its behalf the point of its scenic consistency. It disguises that virtue, in the oddest way in the world, by just *looking*, as we turn its pages, as little scenic as possible; but it sharply divides itself, just as the composition before us does, into the parts that prepare, that tend in fact to over-prepare, for scenes, and the parts, or otherwise into the scenes, that justify and crown the preparation. . . . Everything in it that is not scene (not, I of course mean, complete and functional scene, treating *all* the submitted matter, as by logical start, logical turn and logical finish) is discriminated preparation, is the fusion and synthesis of picture.[38]

More precisely, as Francis Fergusson remarked, "the late novels are narrative *and* dramatic *and* plastic. The heresy would be to insist on one aspect of their form to the exclusion of the others."[39] They might indeed be described equally well as "pictorial drama" or as "dramatic picture": they are in a sense *tableaux vivants*. If in fact *The Ambassadors, The Wings of the Dove*, and *The Golden Bowl* embody both dramatic intensity and pictorial ease, the combination of these two forms was largely made possible by the work carried on by James in the two experimental moments of his middle period, by the two methods painstakingly tested and developed in the

---

[38] *The Art of the Novel*, pp. 322–23. For the act and scene structure of *The Wings of the Dove*, see Egan, *The Ibsen Years*, pp. 129–31.

[39] "James's Idea of the Dramatic Form," *Kenyon Review*, 5 (1943), 495–507 (p. 503 for the quotation).

1880s and 1890s. Most of the novels so far discussed have an artistic value of their own, claim our attention as achievements in their own right. But in them the way was paved for the novels of the major phase and for the later developments of twentieth-century fiction.

III. Rival Creation and the Antinovel

1

The Sacred Fount, written at the end of James's experimental period and on the eve of his major phase, was not properly a transition novel, a necessary stepping-stone between them. James did not include it in the New York Edition of his works, and its connection with the major phase is mainly an ideal one, in the sense that its total doubt about the possibility of fiction writing itself would be overcome by *The Wings of the Dove*, *The Ambassadors*, and *The Golden Bowl*.

The later novels exhibit the same stylistic traits as *The Sacred Fount*, but they show no signs of those embarrassments and difficulties in fiction writing that constitute its main characteristic. If *The Sacred Fount*, as I believe, was meant to test the further capacities of the traditional—and the experimental—novel, it ended on a note of undeniable hopelessness. Nevertheless, in clearing the field of any excessive complacency about his artistic role, it freed James from his own uncertainties. Life, in this case, did not imitate art. His future career did not follow the pattern set in the novel, where the doubt about fiction writing, dramatically projected and expressed, provides a subtle pretext for fictional elaboration and the very subject of the book. The novel was more closely connected to the preceding works, both in terms of thematic ideas and fictional techniques, stretched, in this case, nearly to breaking point. And one must start by emphasizing its links with the novels of the middle period as they have been examined and defined in the previous chapters.

The Sacred Fount is not an easy work to read, nor is its meaning immediately clear. So much has been written about it that one wonders (according to the refrain) whether it was actually meant to be written and written about—rather than read. Beautiful pages, exquisite descriptions, and delightful episodes emerge from a confused background noise—a ceaseless chatter of conversations, interviews suddenly interrupted, half-sentences and broken talks, inconclusive verbal duels, hints quickly denied, flimsy suggestions, sudden suspensions, false clues, tentative assumptions, hopeless surmises. The indirect method and approach are here in full dominion: despite the impressive verbal display, nothing seems to be accomplished and everything is to be reviewed, readjusted, reinterpreted, tentatively explained. One's patience is severely tried, yet one can accept the challenge of the slipping links, connect the ties, seek on the page the half-suggested meaning. And the conclusion is extraordinarily rich in interpretative possibilities, "bristling with questions," in James's cherished phrase, and some possible answers. The book opens an unexpected view on a theme—that of the artist—which is central to James's inspiration and to so much of American literature; and from such a suggestive angle that it allows us to relate it to the latest trends of fictional method and artistic ideals of the French *nouveau roman*. The concerns and the possible issues it dramatizes take on shades and overtones of unexpected modernity. Typical of James and the late nineteenth century, they reveal striking affinities with our present.

The Sacred Fount is a novel *on* the novel, or rather on the insurmountable difficulties that beset the novelist in his attempt to impose an exhaustive and conclusive order on the contrasting data and suggestions of experience: to create, in other words, through the mirror and point of view of the self, an artistic reality, objectively "true," that subjects to its ideal and artistic reasons the fleeting phenomena of human experience, behavior, relations, and contradictions. In doing so, the novel deals with a subject that had obsessed James as a critic and a writer, disturbed young Hawthorne, tormented Herman Melville's Pierre. And insofar as it foreshadows the further obsession with this subject to be found in James Joyce, André Gide, or Thomas Mann, James's book (published in 1901) may prove a first example of the novel's turning on itself, which

is typical of the twentieth century. In its disconsolate conclusion, however, in its utter negation of any vital possibility
for fiction except as a straightforward recording of events and
surfaces, *The Sacred Fount* goes farther. It finds its place,
ante litteram and before its time, on the ideal line of development that will lead to the very modern "discovery" of the antinovel.

This does not mean that the book (as has been supposed)
is a pathetic confession of personal impotence on the part of
James.[1] It represents, instead, a moment of tormenting and
total doubt concerning the actual or remaining possibilities of
the novel in its nineteenth-century sense, built in a unified
way according to a plot—a doubt which James was soon to overcome brilliantly but which he nonetheless felt deeply at this
time and transposed artistically in purely narrative terms. In
The Sacred Fount, life seems really to oppose the demands of
art; it does not submit to ordering and interpretation. It
baffles the attempts and mocks the pretensions of the pathetic
Narrator who finds, or rather puts, himself at the center of
a situation that he can neither dominate nor clarify.
The book is the chronicle of his attempts and his
failures—a subtle exposure of the Jamesian method and of
novel writing as such which is, however, transposed and
resolved in *narrative* terms. This is the crucial point for any
further interpretation. The story, of course, involves an awkward
artist, far too eager and personally interested in his dealings, an
easy victim of his own excesses and doomed therefore to failure,
who may fully deserve his fate. But this does not detract from
the fact that the story deals ultimately, and from the inside,
with the very problem of the possibilities and the limits of
fiction writing.

[1] Wilson Follett, "The Simplicity of Henry James," *American Review*, 1
(1923), 315–25, and "Henry James's Portrait of Henry James," *New York
Times Book Review*, August 22, 1936, pp. 2, 16; Raymond Mortimer,
"Henry James," *Horizon*, 7 (1943), 318; R. A. Perlongo, "*The Sacred Fount*:
Labyrinth or Parable?" *Kenyon Review*, 22 (1960), 635–47. See below, note 10.

The Sacred Fount is experimental in subject and form, for its manner of presentation as well as the nature of its theme and for its clear linkage to the series of avowed experiments in James's fiction that preceded it. The stages of his experimental period, as we have seen, brought him from the psychological and sociological realism of *The Bostonians* to the melodramatic and often "romantic" realism of *The Princess Casamassima*; from the lighthearted, half-serious comedy of *The Reverberator* to the "double picture" of *The Tragic Muse*; from an interest in documentary and pictorial fiction and an unsuccessful theatrical experience to the play-novel (*The Other House*) and then gradually to a meaningful combination of limited point of view and scenic method in *The Spoils of Poynton* and *What Maisie Knew*, up to a final attempt at *roman dialogué* in *The Awkward Age*.

We noticed that mannerism and mechanical solutions played a part in these novels. From a different standpoint, retrospectively provided by *The Sacred Fount*, we might say that we were often confronted with the utmost formal exploitation of minimal thematic suggestions and narrative substance. Far too great formal "oaks" grew out of elusive, insubstantial "acorns": James himself admitted more than once to being exposed to the danger of overtreatment.[2] Most of those novels betray a disproportion between the slightness of the germ and the formal scaffolding imposed upon it. It is not only a question of excessive length: the overtreatment lies in the fact that the exploration of the possibilities of technique tends to expand in a disproportionate way, almost for its own sake, quite independently of the action itself. This is obviously connected with the gradual thickening and complication of the language, already verging on James's late manner. His final resorting, as much as possible, to the dialogue form may be even construed as a means of avoiding this danger. It is undeniable that such complicated language, organically or mechanically growing in sheer stylistic exhilaration, is often applied

[2] *The Art of the Novel*, pp. 57, 117. See Carlo Izzo, "Henry James, scrittore sintattico," in *Studi Americani*, 2 (1956), 127–42, and following note.

to a material still insufficiently articulated to bear its weight. The material itself, therefore, tends to appear all the more rarefied and flimsy, even as the language betrays the effort to cover and make up for the underlying emptiness. A full integration will be achieved in the novels of the major phase: in the experimental novels James is still exposed to dangers that might be related to fin-de-siècle aestheticism. The very fact that after *The Bostonians* he abandoned the "American scene" and laid his novels in an English setting may explain, to a certain extent, his gradual loss of the once cherished "solidity of specification."

If these observations apply only partially to the previous novels, they have a direct bearing on *The Sacred Fount*. James himself considered the book an overgrown tale (*"given the tenuity of the idea,"* he wrote to Howells, "the larger quantity of treatment hadn't been aimed at"), and the multiplication of scenes, episodes, and dialogues, the endless sequence of hypotheses, theses, and antitheses reach here the limit of pure abstraction.[3] But the formal and thematic justification of the gigantic verbal scaffolding lies in its very excess: *it* becomes

[3] *Letters*, I, 408–9 (11 December 1902). But the whole passage is worth quoting: "I am melted at your reading *en famille The Sacred Fount*, which you will, I fear, have found chaff in the mouth and which is one of several things of mine, in these last years, that have paid the penalty of having been conceived only as the 'short story' that (alone, apparently) I could hope to work off somewhere (which I mainly failed of), and then *grew* by a rank force of its own into something of which the idea had, modestly, never been to be a book. That is essentially the case with the S. F., planned, like *The Spoils of Poynton, What Maisie Knew, The Turn of the Screw*, and various others, as a story of the '8 to 10 thousand words'!! and then having accepted its bookish necessity or destiny in consequence of becoming already, at the start, 20,000, accepted it ruefully and blushingly, moreover, since, *given the tenuity of the idea*, the larger quantity of treatment hadn't been aimed at. I remember how I would have 'chucked' *The Sacred Fount* at the 15th thousand word, if in the first place I could have afforded to 'waste' 15,000, and if in the second I were not always ridden by a superstitious terror of not finishing, for finishing's and for the precedent's sake, what I have begun. I am a fair coward about *dropping*, and the book in question, I fear, is, more than anything else, a monument to that superstition."

the narrative center and the theme itself of the book, which shows in fictional terms the failure of the Narrator who is responsible for the verbal proliferation and who flounders in his own verbal maze.

This verbal obsession of the Narrator originates, moreover, in his own ambiguous wish for knowledge and spiritual mastery. A similar motivation, with the necessary qualifications for each separate case, is present in most of the protagonists of the preceding novels. The antagonists in *The Spoils of Poynton* are defined by their capacity for appreciating, and their struggle to possess, the "spoils"; Maisie is the heroine and the victim of a gradual acquisition of knowledge, is qualified and characterized by "what she knows," and is in turn fought over in a pitiless and selfish struggle for possession; the young girls of the "awkward age" move among the gleams of a process of awareness stimulated by the "social lamps." One may recall the telegraphist of "In the Cage" (1898), with her hopeless reconstruction of events, and the governess in "The Turn of the Screw" (1898), both grappling with the problem of knowing.[4] Strether, of course, in *The Ambassadors*, will embody such an experience in its fullest sense. They are all characters eager to know, indeed, qualified and defined as characters by their degree of knowledge. And it must be added that the limit between knowing and possessing, knowledge and spiritual mastery, is often blurred and hardly defined, as is, parenthetically, that between the innocence due to ignorance and the awareness of evil given by knowledge.

In the Narrator of *The Sacred Fount*, more than elsewhere, knowledge and spiritual mastery tend almost to identify and to appear as complementary modes of the same activity; and the milieu itself of these tantalizing adventures is significant. For all these characters, as for the Narrator, it is a question of knowing, possessing, and dominating a world that thrives on ambiguity and equivocation. They move in an

---

[4] Tanner, *The Reign of Wonder*, pp. 311–19, seeing in "In the Cage" the exploration of the theme of the wondering imagination *receiving* and *deciphering*, relates it to *The Sacred Fount* in a very convincing way.

English upper class without moral order, which is wasting away in its own contradictions, leaning for support on the shaky gewgaws of threadbare conventions. It is a society in dissolution, torn by inner contradictions, watching unawares over its own destruction, and almost complacent about it. It stimulates an unhealthy curiosity, and for this very reason exercises a tyranny over its adepts and initiates: the knowledge of evil is a form of mastery and possession, but it soon proves a kind of enslavement.

The Sacred Fount is set in this society, and it is unnecessary to stress the obvious parallels with the preceding novels. Here we are in a country house during a weekend: the perfect setting and occasion for equivocal dealings, false situations, the barely disguised play of irregular relationships, the thriving of corruption under the glittering surface. The suspicion remains—here, as in "The Turn of the Screw"[5]—that it may be all a projection of the guilty conscience of the Narrator, carried by his own sense of guilt and inadequacy to see evil and ambiguities everywhere. Be that as it may, for the Narrator of *The Sacred Fount* the problem is to unravel, clarify, unmask, perhaps even vicariously experience, an equivocal and dubious reality of evil. His problem—as with Fleda Vetch, Maisie, Nanda, the telegraphist, or the governess—is to know, to understand the relationships, to achieve a perception of the basic elements of the picture in order to project them in a more comprehensive and articulate vision of reality. In this case, however, the heuristic obsession of the Narrator becomes more than ever a means of spiritual mastery; it verges on cognitive hubris. In putting himself by a sheer act of will (and willfulness) at the center of the relationships and the presumed intrigues, the Narrator ends by wanting to determine them. And so much self-will goes into this mania for knowing, for imposing an order—if only fantastic or *fictional*, in every sense of the word— on his vague perceptions that one can detect in his behavior

[5] See Edmund Wilson, "The Ambiguity of Henry James," in *The Triple Thinkers* (New York, 1948), pp. 88–132; *A Casebook on "The Turn of the Screw,"* ed. Gerald Willen (New York, 1965).

the typical attitude of an artist. He is of course an artist
sui generis, but his adventure can be seen as a parable on
the pathetic failure of the ordering and expressive skills on
which the artist's greatness depends.

He reconstructs in order to narrate, and James, recording
step by step his uncertain and faulty process, ended by making
it the very subject of his story and by subjecting formal
and stylistic redundancy to a thematic function. He was later
to call the book a "profitless labyrinth," "fantastic and
insubstantial," "the merest of *jeux d'esprit*," "a small fantasti-
cality" which was not "worth discussing" as he had tried "only
to make it—the one thing it *could* be—a *consistent* joke." But he
also added: "Let me say for it, however, that it has, I assure you,
and applied quite rigorously and constructively, I believe, its
own little law of composition."[6] In another letter to Howells he
called it "a fine flight into the high fantastic." To his literary
agent, however, he wrote that "it is fanciful, fantastic—but very
close and sustained, and calculated to minister to curiosity."[7]
Wavering in his own conception of the novel, James did
minister to curiosity: if the "little law" about which he was so
vague cannot be pinned down with complete assurance, it is
nevertheless worthwhile trying to examine its possible implications.

2

James's first idea of the story, as recorded in the *Notebooks*,
was that of the transference of vitality in a married couple,

[6] These statements are in letters to the Duchess of Sutherland and to
Mrs. Humphrey Ward (15 March 1901) quoted in Leon Edel, Introduction,
The Sacred Fount (New York, 1954), pp. xxx-xxxi; longer quotations
from them are to be found in the English edition (London, 1959),
pp. 14 and 9 (see below, note 11). In an unpublished letter (to William
Morton Fullerton, 9 August 1901, now in Princeton University Firestone
Library) James calls the book a jeu d'esprit and a pure and single accident
of technique, not worth writing about.

[7] Quoted in Edel, *The Treacherous Years*, p. 339.

which suggested a similar and concomitant "transfusion" of *intellectual* vitality in another couple. The interest shifted immediately to the *analogy* between the couples, and to the idea of "the *liaison* that betrays itself by the *transfer* of qualities"—to the process of discovery, that is, set in motion by the envisaged transference of vitality.[8] One "process" (that of the old-young pair) was to lead to "the spectacle of the other (covert, obscure, unavowed)"; the idea of the *secret* to be revealed by the concomitant processes came therefore to the forefront, and the Narrator of the book—the only one in James's canon to speak in the first person—sets out on a typically heuristic quest, which takes on gradually the characteristics of an artistic endeavor.

On his way to Newmarch, the country house where his "intellectual adventure" will take place, the unnamed Narrator has already chosen his "elements" and devoted himself to his task. Mrs. Briss appears to him to have grown incredibly younger; their mutual friend Long seems suddenly brighter. Mrs. Briss suggests that his improvement may be the result of a love affair; and when the Narrator detects in Mr. Briss's early aging the source of his wife's rejuvenation, by a principle of analogy he sets out to look for Long's source of inspiration— the "Egeria" who may have drained herself in transferring her intellectual qualities to him. We are in the midst of riddles and mathematical equations: if Long's "sacred fount" is discovered, the plight of Mr. Briss will be confirmed;

[8]*Notebooks*, pp. 150–51 (17 February 1894): "The notion of the young man who married an older woman and who has the effect on her of making her younger and still younger, while he himself becomes her age. . . .— Mightn't this be altered (perhaps) to the idea of cleverness and stupidity? . . . Or the idea of a *liaison*, suspected, but of which there is no proof but this transfusion. . . .—this exchange or conversion? The fact, the secret, of the *liaison* might be revealed in that way." Cf. also p. 275 (15 February 1899). A third entry (p. 292) records the idea under the heading "Anecdotes"; this is noteworthy, as James gave a particular meaning to the word: "The anecdote consists, ever, of something that has *oddly* happened to some one, and the first of its duties is to point directly to the person whom it so distinguishes. . . . The anecdote has always a question to answer—*of whom necessarily is it told?* (Art of the Novel, p. 181, my italics).

if Briss's situation is proved true, it will strengthen the supposition concerning Long.[9]

In his search the Narrator has at first the support of Mrs. Briss and Ford Obert, a painter "who could see as much as most" (p. 28). He evaluates and examines one possible candidate after another, troubles friends and acquaintances, asks everyone for their opinions, advances and abandons suppositions incessantly. Inevitably he has moments of doubt and reasons for distress. There is nothing sure on which to build, and yet his search must rest "on psychologic signs alone," without any concession to the ignoble means of "the detective and the keyhole" (p. 66). It must be pure in aim and means. Nothing much, therefore, comes out of it—all the more so because, if his assumptions are right, he is bound to touch open wounds, to reveal jealously guarded secrets, to jeopardize delicately balanced relationships and private affairs. He meddles with explosive situations and alarms almost everyone with his endless prying and probing. Furthermore, he claims— but it is obviously a delusion—that he is protecting the victims, while carefully avoiding to make the guilty suspicious. He is thus compelled to reticence and half statements, to operate chiefly by hints and guesses, to conceal his real or supposed knowledge. He thinks he is covering his tracks but he muddles up instead the ones he is following.

He is, therefore, gradually deprived of collaborators. Mrs. Briss realizes that the possible or eventual discovery of Long's mistress might compromise her own position; Obert withdraws his support. On the other hand, as the threads of the investigation get more and more tangled, there is no end to the possible developments and solutions. If it is true that the sacred fount depends on a link of affection or intimacy in order to work, suppositions and surmises too become endless. Couldn't Mrs. Briss herself be Long's mistress? And couldn't

[9] Beach, *The Method of Henry James*, pp. 252–53, gives us indeed the proper equations (X : D :: A : B; C : D :: A : B; A : C :: B : D, etc.); see also Follett, "The Simplicity of Henry James." In this chapter, page references in the text are to *The Sacred Fount* (New York, 1954).

a relationship be established between the two victims if there is one between the exploiters? And wouldn't it be in their best interest, in any case, to divert and mislead the investigation?

The Narrator flounders in a maze of possibilities.[10] The heart of man is fathomless and the sacred fount is by its very nature mysterious. Mrs. Briss eventually defies the Narrator openly and on his ground: their last confrontation provides the ambiguous conclusion, and perhaps the key, to the whole story. Put on her guard, Mrs. Briss pushes the Narrator to complete uncertainty and confusion, close to physical and psychic depression. One might even be led to believe that the Narrator himself has become *her* sacred fount—a source of awareness and youth for his antagonist. But the important point is not here, just as the motif of the transference of physical and spiritual vitality is only a pretext for the Narrator's intellectual adventure. What matters is that Mrs. Briss throws dust in the face of the presumptuous investigator and, in doing so—whether she betrays her own guilty game or a total opposition to his approach to reality—she defines the nature of his interest, his adventure, and his failure.

It is possible that she reacts in desperate and ruthless self-defense, when she sees her position in danger ("Mrs. Briss's last interview with the narrator being all an ironic *exposure*

---

[10] And quite a few critics with him. Criticism of the novel has reached such proportions that I can only refer here for details to the bibliographies in my Italian translation of *The Sacred Fount* (Venice, 1963, pp. xxi-xxii and xxxviii-xli), in Wiesenfarth, *Henry James and the Dramatic Analogy*, pp. 131–39, and in Jean Frantz Blackall's book-length study *Jamesian Ambiguity and* The Sacred Fount (Ithaca, N.Y., 1965), pp. 176–88. Among the latest contributions, see Naomi Lebowitz, *The Imagination of Loving: Henry James's Legacy to the Novel* (Detroit, 1965), chap. 7; Isle, *Experiments in Form*, 210–31; Philip M. Weinstein, in *The Interpretation of Narrative: Theory and Practice,* ed. Morton W. Bloomfield (Cambridge, Mass.; 1970), pp. 189–209 and in his *Henry James and the Requirements of the Imagination*, chap. 4; Charles Thomas Samuels, *The Ambiguity of Henry James* (Urbana, Ill., 1971), chap. 1; Barbara and Giorgio Melchiori, *Il gusto di Henry James* (Turin, 1974), chap. 8; William B. Stein, "*The Sacred Fount:* The Poetics of Nothing," *Criticism*, 14 (1972), 373–89.

of her own false plausibility, of course," James was to state in a letter).[11] It is also possible that she opposes the method of intuitive perception with which the Narrator looks at reality. If that is so, we might describe her position as a blank denial of the possibility of enriching life imaginatively: she seems content with a positivistic acceptance of the simple data of experience, which allow for no interpretation or artistic elaboration. In this sense her strongest opposition is directed against the Narrator's attempts to reach an integrated vision of the data of experience, to achieve a unified and coherent, even if fanciful, view of life. She charges him with *seeing* (let alone talking) too much. His beautiful "palace of thought" is to her a crumbling "house of cards" (p. 262). She will eventually call him crazy and demented.

Neither of them, it must be noted, denies the existence and the nature of their opposing views and of their radical divergence: their interpretation of its value is widely different. And this might already qualify the attitude of the Narrator in an "artistic" sense. Their opposition is not simply epistemological: besides *seeing* too much, he *connects* too much. This way of reacting to the data of experience and the suggestions of reality is the "constructive" one typical of the artist, who connects, links, interprets, who must find, create, or impose an order. This is how one of James's characters, in the tale "The Story in It" (1903) significantly defines the activity of the artist:

The adventure's a relation; the relation's an adventure. The romance, the novel, the drama are the picture of one. The subject the novelist treats is the rise, the formation, the development, the climax, and for the most part the decline, of one.

. . . .

What's a situation undeveloped but a subject lost? If a relation stops, where's the story? If it doesn't stop, where's the innocence?

[11] Quoted in Edel's introduction to the novel (London, 1959), p. 9. As for the possibility of the Narrator's becoming the "sacred fount" of Mrs. Briss, cf. Norma Phillips, "*The Sacred Fount:* The Narrator and the Vampires," *PMLA*, 76 (1961), 407–12.

It seems to me you must choose. It would be very pretty if it were otherwise, but that's how we flounder. Art is our flounderings shown. [12]

The definition fits our Narrator, his activity as well as his "flounderings." His pursuit must be "a high application of intelligence," resting as we have seen "on psychologic signs alone." He looks for "the evidence of relations," for "combinations," for a theory that will make things "hang together." In a "blaze of suggestion" he is the only one "aware"; in his "plunges of insight" and "flights of fancy" he himself determines the situations he anticipates in his mind. He talks about appropriating the characters, of "the impossibility of my indifference to the mere immense suggestiveness of our circumstances" (p. 240); of the "impunity of my creation" (p. 74). In a revealing passage he tells of Mrs. Server: "It was exactly as if she had been there by the operation of my intelligence, or even by that—in a still happier way—of my feeling" (p. 129). He is disturbed by the suggestions that do not fit his "book," and he asks Mrs. Briss what she would do with it, *artistically*. His effort is devoted to "the art of putting things" (p. 262); he talks, almost in a Shakespearean way, of "the whole airy structure I had erected" (p. 144)—of "the interpretation of my tropes and figures" (p. 284). He speaks of "the joy of intellectual mastery of things unamenable, the joy of determining, almost of *creating* results" (p. 214, my italics).

These hints could not be more explicit: both R. P. Blackmur and Leon Edel have noticed that the Narrator follows an artistic urge, the impulse to meet the challenge of reality and organize the data of experience according to the laws of a system. More recently, among others, Tony Tanner has maintained that "there is little doubt that the narrator epitomizes the artistic instinct." [13] In this impulse Blackmur saw the greatness of the

[12] *Complete Tales*, XI, 319–20.

[13] See R. P. Blackmur, *"The Sacred Fount,"* *Kenyon Review*, 4 (1942), 328–42; idem, "In the Country of the Blue," *Kenyon Review*, 5 (1943), 595–617 (rpt. in *The Question of Henry James*, pp. 191–211); Edel, introductions to *The Sacred Fount* and *The Treacherous Years*, p. 343; Tanner, *The Reign of Wonder*,

Narrator, who seemed to him to succeed in his avowed attempt to become the consciousness of the other characters. I would say rather that his is a pathetic failure, in which life overcomes art. If "he is in the position of the alienated artist, cherishing his product, and nervously guarding it against what Yeats called 'the brutality, the ill-breeding, the barbarism of truth,' " he suffers from a "morbid imagination": his efforts are misdirected and baffled.[14]

If his artistic impulse is legitimate, he builds up his interpretations on flimsy grounds and without "collateral support" (p. 248): he yields, by his own admission, to the "idle habit of reading into mere human things an interest so much deeper than mere human things were in general prepared to supply" (p. 156). He "groups" his elements "into a larger mystery (and thereby a larger 'law') than the facts, as observed, yet warranted" (p. 23). His "vision of life is an obsession" (p. 23), and his experience relies on fancy rather than facts. He lacks, of all things, "a sense of proportion" (p. 301): he draws "extravagant inferences" from what he sees. He is "abused by a fine fancy" (p. 261), led astray by a "failure of detachment" (p. 210). His palace of thought crumbles too easily, like a mere house of cards. Here lies its beauty, and its danger.

---

p. 325 ("he also wants to add something to the world, in particular those symmetries and harmonies which are alien to its gratuitous configurations") and the whole section, pp. 319–31. Also Wiesenfarth, *Henry James and the Dramatic Analogy*, p. 102 ("basically a novel which represents the process of imaginative fabrication of a 'structure' from a 'germ' that has been conceived as a 'subject' ").

[14] Tanner, *The Reign of Wonder*, pp. 326 and 328: "James has subjected the activities of the 'morbid imagination' to their most damaging criticisms." See also Ralph Ranald, "*The Sacred Fount*: James's Portrait of the Artist *Manqué*," *Nineteenth Century Fiction*, 15 (1960), 239–48; D. W. Jefferson, *Henry James and the Modern Reader* (New York, 1964), p. 177 ("The narrator reflects aspects of the novelist himself, but with lurid and comic distortions. . . . He has obsessions akin to an artist's, but apparently no artist's medium."); Bernard Richards, "*The Ambassadors* and *The Sacred Fount*: The Artist *Manqué*," in *The Air of Reality*, pp. 219–43.

It is possible that the Narrator, as Leon Edel suggested, is hopelessly caught in the gap between appearance and reality, but his failure is also traceable to personal, intrinsic reasons. As an artist, he is far too "intelligent," too intellectually eager, devoid of any intimate and direct knowledge of reality. He involves too many people—his very "characters"—in his game: a game of chess, eventually, where the pieces no longer have any reciprocal value. James was to warn about the danger "of imputing to too many others, right and left, the critical impulse and the acuter vision": "the truth for 'a young man in a book' by no means entirely resides in his being either exquisitely sensitive or shiningly clever. It resides in some such measure of these things as may consort with the fine measure of other things too." And he was also to warn against "the undue simplicity of pretending to read meanings into things absolutely sealed and beyond test or proof."[15] The Narrator is in a sense a victim of this "undue simplicity," lacking in discretion, rash in imputing "the critical impulse and the acuter vision" "to too many others." He lacks, moreover, that "amount of felt experience" that James himself deemed essential not only for the success but for the morality of the artist. The quality of his mind—again in James's terms—is not a sufficient guarantee for the quality of his work: hence, his failure.

But there is perhaps something more, since otherwise his case would be simply pathetic, a mere illustration of the

[15] *The Art of the Novel*, pp. 155, 69, 162, and 64: "The wary reader for the most part warns the novelist against making his characters too *interpretative* of the muddle of fate, or in other words too divinely, too priggishly clever. 'Give us plenty of bewilderment,' this monitor seems to say, 'so long as there is plenty of slashing out in the bewilderment too. But don't, we beseech you, give us too much intelligence; for intelligence— well, *endangers*; endangers not perhaps the slasher himself, but the very slashing, the subject-matter of any self-respecting story. It opens up too many considerations, possibilities, issues; it *may* lead the slasher into dreary realms where slashing somehow fails and falls to the ground.' " See also Yvor Winters, *In Defence of Reason* (Denver, 1947), p. 331, on James's and his characters' "marked tendency . . . to read into situations more than can be justified by the facts as given" (in *The Spoils of Poynton, The Turn of the Screw*, and even in *The American*).

Jamesian principle (stated in the Preface to *The Tragic Muse*) that only the *failed* artist can be a proper subject for artistic treatment. The failure of the application of a given method casts doubts on the method itself. And one need hardly stress the fact that the Narrator applies here, with all the risks involved, the principles of the Jamesian method. He willfully acts as central intelligence in a given situation and filters it through his limited point of view; he resorts to a great number of *ficelles*; he avoids descriptions for the most part (but not always), and relies on scenes, dialogues, and interviews that he himself reconstructs for the reader. He is detached and at the same time involved in the story; his approach is—and must be—as indirect as possible. He lacks foreshortening, but he knows very well where and how to pick his straws, how to arrange his mosaic and give us the overall picture.

Shall we hastily conclude that we are then faced with a self-parody? That seems too simple. If, in a novel so intentionally abstract and impersonal,[16] a doubt is expressed about the validity of a method so characteristically Jamesian, is it not more correct to see in it an *artistically objectified* expression of that doubt? In *The Sacred Fount* the organizing principle of art, the predominance of art over

---

[16] See Ezra Pound, *ABC of Reading* (London, 1951), p. 90: "There [in *The Sacred Fount*] for perhaps the first time since about 1300 a writer has been able to deal with a sort of content wherewith Cavalcanti had been 'concerned' "; and idem, *Literary Essays*, p. 327: "In *The Sacred Fount* he attains form, perfect form, his form. . . . it seems to me one work that he could afford to sit back, look at, and find completed. I don't in the least imply that he did so." A word must be spent on the style of the book, so complex and involuted, worked out to the limit of preciosity: ambiguities of meaning, intentional obscurities, double entendres, and half sentences abound. The dialogues or half dialogues are such that we do not always exactly know who is speaking, who is being talked about, and so on. The Narrator is in the dark, and we grope in the dark with him. Obscurities and difficulties, however, have a thematic function; they are essential to the illustration and embodiment of the subject—the difficulties of the artist himself, which gradually become the very theme of the novel.

life, thanks to the operation of technique, fails miserably. We are at the opposite pole, as it were, from an exemplary story such as "The Real Thing" (1892), where James had explicitly maintained and dramatized the artist's innate preference "for the represented subject over the real one," "the perverse and cruel law in virtue of which the real thing could be so much less precious than the unreal"—"that odd law which somehow always makes the minimum of valid suggestion serve the man of imagination better than the maximum," as he was later to repeat.[17] Just a year later Strether, in *The Ambassadors*, would be allowed in the end to see clearly in a situation (the affair between Chad and Mme. de Vionnet) in which a transference of physical and spiritual vitality also takes place. Our Narrator is denied any real knowledge or discovery.

James's doubt is, therefore, not about his own artistic possibilities, but rather about the validity of a method of discovery and presentation, and this doubt is transposed and projected in an autonomous and impersonal story—not theoretically expressed but artistically embodied. The answer he gives is the same one received by Melville's Pierre, by Hawthorne's artists and scientists: life baffles and eludes art; fiction cannot really cope with reality. But Melville and Hawthorne dealt with the difficulties of the artist in a specific historical and social situation—either in Puritan America or in a country insensitive to art, which clipped the wings of the fragile butterfly of fancy and decreed the failure of the artist for his hubris in being and remaining an outsider, a rebel, an individualist. James had left America behind, and although using the theme of the artist to test and define the relationship between society and the individual, he projected and dramatized it in an abstract way, with greater subtlety and complexity and less dependence on the historical and social situation.[18] The

---

[17] *Complete Tales*, VIII, 258; *The Art of the Novel*, p. 161.

[18] In *Roderick Hudson* (1876) there are still Hawthornesque overtones; in "The Story of a Masterpiece" (1868) art did reveal life, while in "The Madonna of the Future" (1873) it required a technical application

Narrator is placed in the midst of English society—a milieu James considered most fruitful for the novelist—where social conventions and idolized manners have been raised to principles of behavior and rules of life. It is not only, or not so much, society that in *The Sacred Fount* defeats the narrator and his artistic impulse: the greatest fault lies in himself and his method—in the claims and pretensions of his organizing effort. James's doubt about fiction writing involves the novelist who aims at dominating reality, who wants to impose order and symmetry on life, to incorporate and embody it into a higher artistic vision. In expressing this doubt, James seems to shake the very foundations of the nineteenth-century novel; and it is precisely here that his link with the twentieth-century novel, and with the antinovel, becomes apparent.

3

The nineteenth-century novel was based on a conception of art as "rival creation." This conception was diametrically opposed

---

more than a tumultuous experience of life. The contrast between life and art is central to "The Author of 'Beltraffio' " (1884), "The Lesson of the Master" (1888), and *The Tragic Muse*. Subtler relationships are explored in "The Real Thing" (1892), "The Middle Years" (1893: the artist's hopeless longing for a "second chance"), "The Death of the Lion" (1894: sudden fame bringing the writer to a lonely death), "The Next Time" (1895: the irreversible fate of the popular and the "refined" writer), and "The Figure in the Carpet" (1896: the frustrated need for perceptive critical appreciation). Pathetic figures of self-willed and inhibited artists are sketched in "Broken Wings" (1900), "The Story in It" (1902), and the lesser tales "The Tree of Knowledge" (1900) and "The Coxon Fund" (1894). The frequency of the artist motif is particularly notable in the "experimental period" leading up to *The Sacred Fount*, and it is hardly necessary to recall that an artistic impulse is detectable in many of the leading characters of the novels. See F. O. Matthiessen, "Henry James's Portrait of the Artist," *Partisan Review,* 11 (1944), 71–87, rpt. as introduction to Henry James, *Stories of Artists and Writers* (New York, n.d.), pp. 1–17; R. P. Blackmur, "Henry James," *LHUS* (New York, 1959), 1-vol. ed., pp. 1039–64.

to the medieval idea of art as "incremental creation"—to
use Dostoevski's and Saint Augustine's contrasting definitions.[19] Down to the end of the Renaissance, art was seen
as an *incrementum* to God's creation: and it is useful to
keep in mind that the rhetorical term *incrementum*, as used
for instance by Quintilian, indicates tension and elevation
toward a climax. In Christian art, God was the climax, and
the *incrementum* was ultimately to God. Artistic creation accepted
the order of things and the great chain of being; the
artist contributed in his work to a definition and an em-
bellishment of that order: he never sought to change it. He
created copies and "duplicates" of—not alternatives to—God's
creation. He may have added something, but within the established framework of a harmonious correspondence of beings
and forms. He increased the value of substance by enriching
the accident; he aimed at a representation of beauty that
tended to "increment" the objective validity of the whole. The
act of denial, the no-saying—the first act by which the individ-
uality of man, not only of the artist, was asserted—came later.

Although the rigorously theocentric emphasis was lessened in
the Renaissance, the climax of incremental creation was still
nature and the world of God. The artist held the mirror up
to nature and, in spite of all doubts and quivers, still found
his order there. In the mirror of art, an essentially divine
nature was reflected and refracted in harmonious compositions:
and if man sometimes looked for his own image there, there
was yet no real disturbing of the balance. Artists still created
in the image of God, and of the universe, and if they did
create in their own image, they still saw and felt themselves
as an integral part of creation. Almost to the very end of
the Renaissance the proper term for their activity was *fiction
making* rather than *creating: effingere*, not *creare*. Both terms are

---

[19] The background for what follows is provided, among others, by
Ernest Robert Curtius, *European Literature and the Latin Middle Ages*, tr.
Willard R. Trask (New York, 1963), and Arthur O. Lovejoy, *The Great
Chain of Being: A Study of the History of an Idea* (Cambridge,
Mass., 1936).

used for instance in Sidney's *Apology for Poetry*; and here for the first time, in a much debated passage influenced by the Italian theorists of the late Renaissance, Scaliger and Fracastoro, one reads of the poet who, "lifted up with the vigour of his own invention, doth grow in effect into another nature, in making things either better than Nature bringeth forth, or, quite new, forms such as never were in Nature."[20] If not yet the metaphor of "rival creation," something approaching it is present here; a trace of it can be detected in Shakespeare's passage in *The Winter's Tale* where Polixenes, though speaking of grafting, and with the qualification at the end, ventures to maintain:

> over that art,
> Which you say adds to nature, is an art
> That nature makes.
> . . . . . .
> This is an art
> Which does mend nature—change it rather; but
> The art itself is nature.
> [IV.4.90–97]

The shift in conception, from *effingere* to *creare*, appears to have taken place in the poetics of mannerism and early baroque art, where the artist was no longer seen as imitating nature, but rather, in neoplatonic terms, his own mental idea of it. "Imitating" an idea that the artist himself could form and control, rather than external reality, would soon lead to a full-fledged conception of art as independent creation. It is only in recent times, however, from romanticism onwards, that the

---

[20] Sir Philip Sidney, *An Apology for Poetry*, ed. Geoffrey Shepherd (London, 1965), p. 100 (the crucial "into" appears in Ponsonby's, not Olney's, text [1595]; and see the introduction, pp. 61–66, and notes, pp. 155–56, where the sources and the implications are discussed. Scaliger (*Poetices Libri Septem*, 1561) had spoken of "naturam alteram" and "Deus Alter"; Fracastorius (*Naugerius*, 1555) of something "more perfect, dearer and more agreeable than anything in nature" provided by the poet. Cf. also Anthony Blunt, *Artistic Theory in Italy, 1450–1600* (Oxford, 1956), Erwin Panofsky, *Idea* (Leipzig, 1924), and Meyer H. Abrams, *The Mirror and the Lamp: Romantic Theory and the Critical Tradition* (New York, 1953), among others.

attitude of the modern artist, in keeping with theological, historical, social, and psychological changes, altered in a radical way. He now aims at a rival creation that will surpass and outdo the created world, God's creation, and have a self-contained, independent, autonomous existence. The artist, in the extreme case, rivals God. His creation has its own aim and purpose. It no longer imitates or represents, nor does it add to the existing world: it *creates* its own world, its subject matter and its form.

This is particularly true of later European romanticism. It is clear that if incremental creation flourished in a theo-centric, unified culture, rival creation is closely connected with the origin and the development of individualistic subjectivism. In the history of ideas, this second attitude may be traced back to the typically romantic concept of organic form, to the idea that a work of art grows according to its inner, intrinsic, shaping form, like a flower, a tree, a living being. It is obviously significant that in Coleridge the eighteenth-century concept of fancy is subordinate to the new concept of creative imagination. Imagination is such a creative force that it creates its own reality over and above the existing one. If we keep the idea of rival creation in mind, we may find a deeper truth in Matthew Arnold's statement that literature is essentially anti-Christian or in Stanislas Fumet's dictum that "art, whatever its aims, is always in sinful competition with God." Nietzsche was to discover that no artist can "tolerate reality"; Van Gogh reproved God for creating a botched sketch of the world, which the artist is called upon to recreate and endow with style. Artistic hubris knows no limits, and one could fill many pages with relevant quotations.[21] For our purposes, it is suffi-cient to note that the postromantic artist, while in no position to escape reality, does everything in his power to create an *artistic reality* more in keeping with his expectations. And it is needless to point out that the question, as we try to see it,

---

[21] The emergence of the artist as hero—both in life and art—is obviously closely connected with all this. See R. P. Blackmur, "The Artist as Hero," *Art News,* September 1951, pp. 18–19.

has nothing to do with the problems of realism or aestheticism. It is a basic, fundamental change in the artist's attitude toward the world and in his approach to both external reality and artistic creation.

This is no less true of the nineteenth-century novel than it is of postromantic poetry. By becoming gradually aware of its formal possibilities, the nineteenth-century novel was soon to seek or discover its own rival creation. Without taking them at face value, at the end of this brief excursus it may be worthwhile to consider some of Albert Camus's observations on the novel in his *L'homme révolté:*

> Il est possible de séparer la littérature de consentement qui coincide, en gros, avec les siècles anciens et les siècles classiques, et la littérature de dissidence qui commence avec les temps modernes. On remarquera alors la rareté du roman dans la première. . . . Avec la seconde, au contraire, se développe vraiment le genre romanesque. . . . Le roman naît en même temps que l'esprit de révolte et il traduit, sur le plan esthétique, la même ambition.
>
> . . . . . .
>
> Qu'est-ce que le roman, en effet, sinon cet univers où l'action trouve sa forme, où les mots de la fin son prononcés, les êtres livrés aux êtres, où toute vie prend le visage du destin. . . .
>
> . . . . . .
>
> Voici donc un monde imaginaire, mais créé par la correction de celui-ci. . . . Le roman fabrique du destin sur mesure. C'est ainsi qu'il concurrence la création et qu'il triomphe, provisoirement, de la mort. Une analyse détaillée des romans les plus célèbres montrerait, dans des perspectives chaque fois différentes, que l'essence du roman est dans cette correction perpétuelle, toujours dirigée dans le même sens, que l'artiste effectue sur son expérience. Loin d'être morale ou purement formelle, cette correction vise d'abord à l'unité et traduit par là un besoin métaphysique.[22]

Camus's generalizations are breathtaking and ought therefore to be carefully and tactfully applied. The important thing for our purpose is to note that James's conception of the novel and of fiction writing, taken as a whole, comes very close

[22] Camus, *L'homme révolté* (Paris, 1951), pp. 319–20, 324, 326–27. All of chap. 4 ("Révolte et art") and in particular the section "Roman et révolte," pp. 319–31, are relevant here.

to this description, and can be seen as a consistent effort toward a fictional kind of rival creation. The central intelligence of his novels controls, and indeed creates, the very substance and form of the narrative; the limited point of view, by circumscribing the angle of vision, intensifies its subjectivity and makes it the only standard of judgment. The novel itself is a creation of the narrator, rather than a reflection of life. The self-contained world and the form of the novel challenge and defy outward reality: it is not a duplicate or an imitation of life but an alternative to it.

→ We may recall here the significant position expressed and exemplified in "The Real Thing." Elsewhere, in a well-known letter to H. G. Wells, James was to maintain with passionate intensity that "it is art that *makes* life, makes interest, makes importance." Art *makes* life: in this statement James, a child of his time, brings to mind similar fin-de-siècle aesthetic declarations. But to understand how he identified himself with the idea—and the need—to make art a powerful substitute for life one should recall the proud claim that underlies all his fiction. Not only did he admit significantly that "reading tends to take for me the place of experience—or rather to *become* itself (pour qui sait lire) experience concentrated": the novelist of *The Art of Fiction* was to "compete with life." And in a passage of his "London Notes" (1897) perhaps his closest approach to the idea of "rival creation" is poignantly expressed: "The great thing to say for them [novelists] is surely that at any given moment they offer us another world, another consciousness, an experience that, as effective as the dentist's ether, muffles the ache of the actual and, by helping us to an interval, tides us over and makes us face, in the return to the inevitable, a combination that may at least have changed. What we get of course, in proportion as the picture lives, is simply another actual—the actual of other people; and I no more than any one else pretend to say why that should be a relief as great, I mean, as it practically proves."[23]

[23] *Henry James and H. G. Wells: A Record of their Friendship, Their*

In spite of some concession to the concept of art as "relief," his definitions could not be clearer: "another world," "another actual." In his novels he strove incessantly to create and project imaginary worlds that were to be truer than life, more actual than actuality, more real than reality. By organizing the fleeting moments and data of experience in a unified vision and a consistent whole, the novelist transcended reality, was in full pursuit of his own kind of rival creation.[24] In this sense James can be linked with Joyce or Proust—a novelist who, according to Camus, "a démontré que l'art romanesque refait la création elle-même, telle qu'elle nous est imposée et telle qu'elle est refusée."[25]

If followed to its logical consequences and extreme limits (as for instance in the case of the later Joyce), this position would ultimately become untenable, verging on absurdity or impotence. At an earlier stage writers such as André Gide and Thomas Mann had become aware of the fact, and in some of their works had openly faced the problem of the limitless claims of the novelist in his attempts to reproduce, recreate, organize reality in fictional terms. And quite naturally, as we shall soon see, novels about the very possibility of writing novels began to be written, where the claims of rival creation began to be scrutinized and exposed in narrative terms. These claims were later to appear quite untenable to the practitioners of the *nouveau roman* and the "open form" of the novel. Without stressing too much the importance of the *nouveau roman* and its epistemological and philosophical premises, one can say that the antinovel (whether latent as in Gide and Mann, or deliberate as in Nathalie Sarraute, Alain Robbe-Grillet, or Michel

Debate on the Art of Fiction, and Their Quarrel, ed. Leon Edel and Gordon N. Ray (London, 1958), p. 267 (10 July 1915); *Letters*, II, 11 (19 January 1904); "London Notes", in *Notes on Novelists*, p. 436.

[24] Cf. also Tony Tanner in an earlier version of his study of the novel (*Essays and Studies*, English Association, 1963), quoted in S. Gorley Putt, *Henry James: A Reader's Guide*, p. 261.

[25] *L'homme révolté*, p. 330.

Butor) represents the avowed dialetical negation of the nine-teenth-century (and Jamesian) claim to rival creation.

The antinovel is basically opposed to the traditional novel and to the claim that it can recreate reality in its terms and its own image. As theorized by Sartre and Robbe-Grillet, for instance, and envisaged by Gide in *Les Faux-Monnayeurs*, the antinovel radically denies the creative or organizing powers of the artist and brings him down to the role of mere recorder of events, surfaces, and things. It is a presumptuous mistake to explore reality for its significance and to describe it—let alone recreate it—in anthropomorphic terms: the novelist can only avail himself of his eyes, of his physical, not inner, vision. Fiction must limit itself to an accurate recording of the outlines of things, of the physical data of experience, the partial and hazy images offered to our unbiased perception by actuality. The novelist is denied psychological analysis, the full rounding-out of characters, the significant display of setting and milieu, the working of the story according to a plot. Fiction is reduced to a photographic role, indeed to the simple taking of snapshots: it must not cross the border of visual notation; it piles up hints and guesses, images and measurements without explaining or interpreting them. It mirrors the static form and superficial nature of objects, not the flow of life or the stream of consciousness. The artist does not add a single stroke, a personal touch: he *records,* gives back what he sees or dimly perceives—does not in any case create.[26]

[26] Alain Robbe-Grillet, *Pour un nouveau roman* (Paris, 1963); Nathalie Sarraute, *L'ère du soupçon: Essais sur le roman* (Paris, 1956); Alberto Arbasino, *Certi romanzi* (Milan, 1964), p. 56 in particular: "the density of any author 'may be that of missing his destiny; to reverse it, he has only to represent it' (Piero Citati). The next step will be that the temptation arises to write a novel no longer *of* or *on* the novel, but on the impossibility or the refusal to write a *given* novel. 'When he has nothing left to say, the realist can still tell us how and why he has nothing left to say' (Moravia on Fellini). Hence a quite different novel is born" (my translation); R.M. Albérès, *Metamorphoses du roman* (Paris, 1966); Laurent Le Sage, *The French New Novel: An Introduction and a Sampler* (University Park, Pa., 1962).

This is a new kind of incremental creation, where the *incrementum* is to the object, no longer to cherished order but to accepted chaos. Its "form" is by its very nature *inorganic*: no organic form is conceivable in art just as it is not possible, to begin with, in life or in the viewing self. One accepts and describes the "labyrinth" of appearances for what it is worth. No mirror is held up to nature: the eye or, better still, impersonal camera lenses are directed on a petrified forest, devoid of all echoes or correspondences. We have reached the opposite pole from the Jamesian ideal. To get there, one had to pass through Sartre's *nausée* and through a fully experienced and expressed doubt about the possibility of keeping up the nineteenth-century ideals.

This doubt runs through Gide's *Les Faux-Monnayeurs* (and, at least partially, Mann's *Doktor Faustus*). We find it consciously experienced and expressed in a novel, Nathalie Sarraute's *Portrait d'un inconnu* (1949), which is considered one of the first *nouveaux romans* and, according to Sartre's later preface, a prototype of the antinovel. This is how Sartre theorized on antinovels in the opening pages of his preface: "Les anti-romans conservent l'apparence et les contours du roman; ces sont des ouvrages d'imagination qui nous présentent des personnages fictifs et nous racontent leur histoire. Mais c'est pour mieux décevoir: il s'agit de contester le roman par lui-même, de le détruire sous nos yeux dans le temps qu'on semble l'édifier, d'écrire le roman d'un roman qui ne se fait pas, qui ne peut pas se faire, de créer une fiction qui soit aux grandes oeuvres composées de Dostoïevsky et de Meredith ce qu'était aux tableaux de Rembrandt et de Rubens cette toile de Miro, *Assassinat de la Peinture*."[27]

Among the forerunners, Sartre mentioned Nabokov and Evelyn Waugh and, of course, Gide's *Les Faux-Monnayeurs*, which deals, among other things, with the writing of a novel. He insisted on the fact that *Portrait d'un inconnu* could be read as a detective story, but he went on to qualify his statement: "C'est

[27] Jean-Paul Sartre, Preface to *Portrait d'un inconnu* by Nathalie Sarraute (Paris, 1956), p. 7.

d'ailleurs une parodie des romans de "quête" et elle y introduit une sorte de détective amateur et passioné qui se fascine sur un couple banal—un vieux père, une fille plus très jeune—et les épie et les suit à la trace et les devine parfois, à distance, par une sorte du transmission de pensée, mais sans jamais très bien savoir ni ce qu'il cherche ni ce qui'ils sont. Il ne trouvera rien, d'ailleurs, ou *presque* rien. Il abandonera son enquête pour cause d'une métamorphose."[28]

One may stop here and notice the extraordinary resemblance between this situation and that of *The Sacred Fount*—a similarity which, in James's cherished phrase, can make us startle.[29] The Narrator knows what he is looking for and what his "elements" or characters are supposed to be: but does he really know—seeing that his search ends in a miserable failure, that he finds nothing or next to nothing, that all relations and connections escape him, and he himself undergoes a metamorphosis? And isn't possibly the very aim of James's novel to question the possibility of a fictional organization of experience by means of the novel itself? *The Sacred Fount* has the appearance and *"les contours"* of a novel: it is my contention that, as in the case of *Portrait d'un inconnu*, the novel form is used to question and "contest" the novel itself, to write "the novel of a novel that is not written, that cannot be written"—"to destroy it under our eyes while seeming to build it." The aims and the method adopted in the two novels seem to be the same, if the unknown and unnamed protagonist of *Portrait d'un inconnu* too spies on the lives of others and tries to find their possible "law," if he too is puzzled and baffled by their actions and relations, by the role he can play in them, if he resorts as well to half sentences and *sous-conversation*, endlessly connecting and achieving nothing. It does not really matter much if Nathalie Sarraute's

[28] Ibid., p. 8.

[29] And indeed Philip Toynbee did startle in a review of Nathalie Sarraute's novel (*Sunday Observer*, 22 November 1959). He only referred, however, to James's book; his intuition confirmed, rather than suggested, the possibility of linking the two novels. See also H. A. Bouraoui, "H. James's *The Sacred Fount*: Nouveau roman avant la lettre?" *International Fiction Review*, 1 (1974), 96–105.

"detective" seems superficially devoid of a specific artistic impulse. He too is obsessed by the need to discover meanings, envisage dramas, clarify situations: his failure, which according to Sartre foreshadows the failure of the possibility of writing fiction itself, is close in nature to the failure of the Narrator in *The Sacred Fount.*

We can read, then, in James's novel a daring and unsuspected prefiguration of an artistic problem that took many years to be fully expressed. We can see in it the germ or the premise of a fictional impasse and a narrative dialectic that came to be openly faced a few decades later. If the way leading to the *nouveau roman* and its surface realism must needs go through the experience of the antinovel as embodied in *Portrait d'un inconnu,* in an ideal sense it must also go through *The Sacred Fount.* The return to a kind of fiction that accepts and records the outward aspect of reality, its disordered and disconnected surface, without trying to impose any artistic unity, formal organization, and aesthetic order on it, presupposes that the fallacy of that principle be postulated and openly expressed in fictional terms. If this is the historical function of Nathalie Sarraute's novel—a link in the process, a stepping-stone, and a turning point—then this is also, in a theoretical sense, the role of James's puzzling novel.

If this contention is correct, such an exasperating tour de force acquires a contemporary relevance. And it is an exciting intellectual adventure to find links and connections that enable us to remove *The Sacred Fount* from its place and period and to set it in a network of ideal relationships with contemporary works and narrative problems, so far ahead in space and time. James is more than an American or an English writer, he is the novelist *tout court,* even when he dramatizes the painful experience of the total failure of fiction. When he most seems to approach silence, he finds echoes and interlocutors everywhere. He reaches out in all directions—toward the French *esprit de finesse* and British composure, our dilemmas and artistic anxieties. He looks to the future—our future—and envisages and foreshadows our doubts. In this sense *The Sacred Fount* is a monument, and an admonition, to *our* artistic superstitions.

Part Two

For real excitement
there are no such adventures
as intellectual ones.
The Sacred Fount

IV. *The Whole Family* and the Lonely Author

1

It is not easy to think of James as coauthor of books and collaborator with other writers. He was by long practice and inner conviction a lonely author. Yet in the aftermath of his major phase, before the two unfinished novels that were to seal his experimental search, he contributed to a joint venture—a "novel by twelve authors" serialized in 1906–7 and published in book form the following year. *The Whole Family* is seldom considered in critical analyses of his fiction, and one might contend that we have enough masterpieces to look after and should not waste time on an occasional deviation from his path.

James is, however, a special writer, and his deviations are sometimes more rewarding in the insights they offer into his workshop and his craftsmanship than the finished products. This may be only partially the case of *The Whole Family*, which is characterized by a light attitude of mere amusement. But it provided James with a rather striking fictional experience and it deserves a brief analysis. The long chapter he contributed to the novel is not only very Jamesian from a technical, thematic, and stylistic point of view. It shows him in the throes of composition and in the masterful application of his technique to a garbled narrative situation and to the needs of joint composition; in his growing attempt to monopolize the story and direct it to his ends; and in his idiosyncrasies and dangerous effects. While his contribution was yet to appear, we see him more and more dissatisfied with the turn taken by the events. James is of course at least partly to blame. As was to be expected, he steps in to break the pace and bring the story almost to a standstill. He adds lights and perspectives, but winds the situation into a kind of maze. He plays with it to the utmost, only to leave it open and suspended in the air at the end of his chapter. Resumption after him is bound to prove hazardous, almost impossible. He has envisaged and at the same time checked all possibilities. His narrative skill and his exploration of motives, applied to the central chapter, seem to have the effect of keeping all the other contributors at bay. He does his stunt, and leaves the others to pick up his impossible threads as well they may.

James had collaborated with George Gissing, Rider Haggard, Joseph Conrad, H. G. Wells, Stephen Crane, and others in a play presented at a Christmas-week party by the Stephen Cranes at Brede Place in 1899.[1] There he was in very good company, and the play (called *The Ghost*) was more a social than a literary occasion. In *The Whole Family* he was involved for the most part with second-rate writers, except for Howells, who had started the project. Moreover, joining the group had been his choice. The idea had originated with Howells, who suggested to Elizabeth Jordan, then editor of *Harper's Bazar*, the possibility of publishing a novel of twelve chapters written by twelve authors. In a letter to Miss Jordan (presumably in 1906) Howells had sketched the general plan to be submitted to the other contributors, specifying that they were not expected to conform rigidly or at all to his conceptions of the various characters. He declared himself ready to conform to *their* ideas, while stressing his view of the outline of the story: "What I wish to imply is that an engagement or a marriage is much more a family affair, and much less a personal affair than Americans usually suppose." Proceeding from his typical awareness that family ties are the strongest in life and that "a marriage cannot possibly concern the married pair alone" (though in that notion many were made and most of them unmade), Howells indicated his thematic and social aim: "I wish to indicate in my advocacy of coeducation that young people ought to know at least the workings of the male and female minds as fully as they can." Their differences were exaggerated by separate training; Howells's idea, in keeping with the reformist tendency of his fiction, was to show the

[1] The printed program is extant; see Harry T. Moore, *Henry James* (New York, 1975), p. 86.

danger of, and the need to abolish, that separation. But, he added, nothing was to be *seriously* insisted upon: "there ought to be full space for the light and humorous play of anybody's preference in the treatment of the characters."[2]

In another letter (21 May 1906) Howells suggested the various members of the family, from the Grandmother to the Young Girl, who were to be at the center of the various chapters. He would do the Father, and "believed" that Mark Twain "would like to do the Small Boy." The story would be summed up by a Friend of the Family. As for the contributors, they were not to know who else would do the other characters; they would be given the whole group of characters and left to "imagine the family for him or herself." Howells suggested a good share of women writers as collaborators (eight out of twelve) and proposed to portray the family in a moment "of vital agitation as that attending the Young Girl's engagement, or pending engagement, and each witness could treat of it in character." He also insisted that "each should try seriously to put himself or herself really into the personage's place" and that seriousness of purpose and treatment was perhaps to be preferred.[3]

Howells did not consider Henry James as a possible contributor. It was Elizabeth Jordan who evidently invited him to participate. While Mark Twain and others refused, James gladly accepted. He may have felt some kind of obligation toward Miss Jordan, who had been helpful to him on the occasion of his 1904 trip and lecture tour in America and for whom, out of his American experiences, he was then writing the long essays "The Speech of American Women."[4] But that

---

[2] *Life in Letters of W. D. Howells*, ed. Mildred Howells (New York, 1928), II, 223, and "Henry James and the *Bazar* Letters," ed. Leon Edel and Lyall H. Powers in *Howells and James: A Double Billing* (New York, 1958), p. 31.

[3] *Life in Letters of W. D. Howells*, II, 224–5. Quite consistently with his fictional credo, Howells added that the family "could be in middling circumstances of average culture and experiences. . . . The note of the whole might be confidential, but kindly criticism, reciprocal, among all the characters."

[4] Published in *Harper's Bazar*, November 1906 to February 1907

was a period of great literary success and commitment on his part, and some other, deeper reason must have motivated his acceptance. The novels of the major phase had just been published, and *The American Scene* was on the press; back at Rye, James was revising and preparing his novels and tales for the New York edition, and in particular was heavily revising the early ones; in 1907 he would write a crucial story such as "The Jolly Corner."[5] If he found time and energy to comply with the request to participate in what must, after all, be described as a literary stunt, he must have been attracted, first, by the novelty and the risks of the enterprise; second, by the secrecy as to the names of the contributors, which would allow him to sneak in on the others' efforts and bend them to *his* fictional aims; third, by that most enticing of Howells's envisaged possibilities, and most cherished of his own personal leanings—"putting himself really into a personage's place." This must have appealed to his ever-awake search for new fictional and experimental experiences. Challenged by the idea, James was to find satisfaction as well as exasperation in the process. He seems to have jumped at the possibility of intervening in the development of the story to steer it his own way and, in the network of relations among characters, to give it his imprint. Yet, as a master craftsman, he also resented the fumbles of his coauthors, their failure to follow his leads, their blindness as to his suggestions and aims. Ultimately disappointed in the venture, James still managed to give us an interesting example of his fictional technique and style—enhancing if applied by him to his peculiar material in his typical way, yet crippling and unrewarding when applied to a preestablished situation by other hands, or with a different awareness of their implications.

By 16 October 1906, on receiving the plan and the three first instalments of the novel from Miss Jordan, James already

and April to July 1907; rpt. as *The Speech and Manners of American Women*, ed. E. S. Riggs (Lancaster, Pa., 1973).

[5] See Leon Edel, *Henry James: The Master* (Philadelphia, 1972), p. 340, and *A Double Billing*, pp. 30–31.

inclined to accept. Howells's suggestion to focus on the theme of how an engagement affected, and was affected by, the whole family had been adopted, and he had himself opened the story and set the stage with a circumstantial (though indirect) statement of the situation. James considered stepping in with a portrayal of the Married Son (chapter 4 in Howells's early plan) but wanted first to see *"all* of what leads up to him." In a subsequent letter James declared his readiness to "go it at him blind, trusting to my pure genius and letting devil take the hindmost" should he fail to receive the preceding parts.[6] By the end of November he had stipulated (by cable) to come in as the Married Son and to follow Miss Edith Franklin Wyatt's and Miss Jordan's own instalments. He was, that is, to come in at the very center of the book, at chapter 8. His dissatisfaction with Miss Wyatt's "misguided effort—discretion forbids me otherwise to quality it"—led him to make his contribution chapter 7. By this time he would have liked to do chapter 8 as well, and his letter of 11 January 1907 provides one of his typical statements about the challenge, the insufferable limitations, the exclusiveness, and the joy of the writer's task: "I am deep in the Whole Family— quite up to my neck—and buffetting the flood as best I can. I shall not sink, I shall swim, and scramble out on some coral strand. Also I shall not keep you waiting long. . . . Yet now that I am at it tooth and nail my hopes are high. My difficulty is only, alas, that I verily tend to burst my bonds or my frame; to blow, that is, the roof off the house. But to prevent this uneasy consciousness I should have had to do them *all* myself! I shall have strictly and loyally played the game, however, and prepared, or left, their due job to my (as I understand it) two or three successors."[7]

Even in such a jeu d'esprit he tended to burst his bonds and his frame, and his contribution proved the longest of all, almost twice as long as any other. Yet even in a joint effort of

[6] Cf. letters no. 12 (16 October 1906) and no. 13 (31 October 1906) to Elizabeth Jordan, in *A Double Billing*, pp. 41–42.

[7] Ibid., no 18 (2 January 1907) and no. 19 (11 January 1907), pp. 43–44.

such kind his loyalty and his mastery of technique would be at work to further the story and prepare for the contributors to follow. To Miss Wyatt James thought that he would leave a proper canvas. But he felt "*too* launched" and in need of more space. As he significantly wrote in another letter (which confirms James's tendency to overtreatment): "I shall have spread myself so much on the picture and presentation, the atmosphere and circumstances, of my Couple at Eastridge, that my fond hope of doing *as much* with the situation in the second half of my Chapter, which takes C. E. on to New York after the fugitives, that I shall have, I find, to compress this latter feature and thereby sacrifice the most precious golden matter. I can't sacrifice what precedes—feeling that also auriferous." Here he also expressed his fear about the inadequacy of the other writers (including Mark Twain) to crown his edifice. And no sooner had he sent his chapter than he doubled his warnings as to what was to follow: "Obviously, a firm hand is required to take up the rest of the business of the 'fugitives'; it was impossible to me to adequately *prepare* my interest in C. E. and his wife (for I may murmur ever so softly in your ear that the others hadn't, to my battered imagination, so very overwhelmingly prepared it) and then carry on the 'action' all the rest of the way: I should have had to do thus much more than any of the others have done. So I have, of course, but left my conduct of it—of the 'action' where whoever follows me must take it up. I rather hope, confidentially, that some one more potent than Miss Edith W., if she *is* to 'rewrite' and tread on my heels, may be the appointed narrator." He wanted to give the Engaged Youth a showing, and thought that he himself "should have taken *him*— reporting *on* C. E. from his view, on all the rest of it, and above all on the frolic Aunt." Carried away by his enthusiasm, James then confessed a broken heart "at not having been able to work in (as C. E.) a direct chance at her," and was moved to a surprising avowal of his aims: "She [aunt Eliza] is the person, in the whole thing, to have been, *objectively*, done; Miss Wilkins making her, to my sense, too subjectively sentimental. My own restricted effort, with C. E., was frankly, to objectify them all as much as possible."[8]

An analysis of the chapter will show the way in which James went about "objectifying" the whole family in a typical mixture of subjective statements, characterizing touches, and as little action as possible. Objectifying was clearly for him a way of showing characters in action according to the guideline provided by a limited, subjective point of view. For James outward reality could be represented only in terms of a personal vision; but the subjective vision itself, the limited point of view, was not so much an aim in itself as a means to present reality in its objective features. Objectivity was to be reached through the view of the self; his chapter was not only narrated from the point of view of the Married Son, but in the first person. We could stop here, and proceed with the analysis of the book, if James's correspondence with Miss Jordan did not offer further hints of his intentions, difficulties, and attempted solutions. Miss Jordan apparently objected to "the Chataway part"—a short episode toward the end of the chapter on New York's East Side—and James specified that it had seemed indispensable "for giving *movement* to my Instalment, otherwise so stationary &, as it were, merely preparatory." He had to defend his conception of the chapter with Miss Jordan, and in so doing he gave one further lesson in fiction writing and technique. That short episode, he wrote,

had for me an intention & seemed to me an indispensable *Accent*— "Accents," in what had been given me by my predecessors, mostly, seeming to me rather alarmingly (for the effect of the Whole) absent; & moreover it represented what I myself was conceiving possible for C. E. to do about "Eliza" [the Aunt]. One of course can't do such a piece at all without one's imagination's projecting a coherent sequel & consequence (to one's own Part—as if one were to do it all one's self,) & my basis for Eliza—i.e. for the rest of that business—was, in C. E.'s intention & line taken, something as to which that bit about Mrs. C.

[8] Ibid., no. 20 (22 January 1907), p. 45, and no. 21 (25 January 1907), pp. 45–46. "C. E." stands for Charles Edward, the name of the Married Son: he calls his aunt "Eliza," while for the others she is Elizabeth.

was *preparatory*—though I didn't mean she should in person appear again. She represents, in short, something *to go on with & to turn round on*—which the data as up to that time given don't seem to me to supply at all, & in the absence of which I fear not a little debility for the future developments; that is not seeing, *myself*, what they have (of at all *"accented,"*) to develop on. That is all I want, a trifle pleadingly, to say—& how the morsel in question was meant to *help* my successors, & to avert flatness from the mere *drop* of my own Section.[9]

This is the master craftsman and fictional theorist at work—preoccupied with the need for "accents," coherent sequels and consequences, preparations and relations, perfectly aware of the *functional* value of the characters in terms of action and structure ("something *to go on with & to turn round on"*). If the Chataway part had to go, he was willing himself to do the little doctoring and patching required, and "yearned" for the proofs. Once he had corrected them, James was still willing to omit the Chataway part, if necessary, but new characters had captured his imagination: the Mother, whom he would like to "do" even "under a false, an extemporized name!" and aunt Eliza. He was "duly inconsolate at not having been able to get straight at her" himself and added that "the touch of C. E.'s observation in N.Y. was a *step toward that.*" Unhappy about the other characterizations and afraid that his "leads" would not be followed or developed, James proceeded to an imaginative appropriation of the whole novel and its characters. No wonder that his disappointment soon increased. When he began to receive the following in-stalments all hope was apparently lost. Chapter 8 ("The Married Daughter"), by Elizabeth Stuart Phelps, he felt had been "subjected to so pitiless an ordeal in the searching artistic light & amid the 'intellectual & literary' associations of Paris" (from where he was writing) that he "tenderly for-

[9] Ibid., no. 22 (18 February 1907), pp. 46–47. "Mrs. C." stands for Mrs. Chataway. A "P.P.S." specifies that he meant "to keep the bit about her for an illustrative bit in relation to E. [Eliza] Talbert & to dealing with her (to C. E.'s dealing with her) in N.Y."

bore, & laid it away."[10] Chapters 9 to 11 left him with
nothing to say—except that he thought it "not bad" that aunt
Eliza should be "referred back" to Mrs. Chataway and that
her sentimental predicament had not been patched up.
James's letter on the subject reveals his painful delusion, not
so much for the bad turn taken by the novel as for the
cheapening and the betrayal of its possibilities. Though
weak and not very promising, the "little Flurry" had stirred
James to give it a *direction*, but nothing seemed to have come
about:

I think there was a little to be done, from the end of VIII (if that was
my number?) on, with the Situation, with the effected presence of
3 of the Persons, in New York, & with the picture of Charles
Edward's action & passion (so to speak) there, his dealings with
Eliza & the young man, his "line taken" on behalf & in the
interest of his Mother &c—with more other things &c than I can
say. I tried to suggest some *values* for this & to *leave*
them suggested: his confrontation with the kidnapped & "compromised" youth in the Park as a Value, his then meeting[,] his
"having it out," with Eliza &, as it were, *disposal* of her, as a
Value; & I left them these Values, fairly dangling there, to my
best ability, as it were, for my successors to catch at. But alas
they haven't, by my vision, caught much—& my vision, such
as it was, of the elements, such as *they* were, has fallen to the
ground. (Of 9 & 10, as they stand, I can't—in a manner—"trust myself
to speak"!)[11]

He was again talking in terms of *values*, situations, relations,
"effective *Interest*, a really economic use of chances,"
while repeating his regret at not having done the Mother.
He had grown more and more aware of the possibilities of
presenting each picture and scene from single but at the same
time *related* points of view: "I see a thing of the highest value—
for the Whole—to have been done, in fine, with the Mother—
the Mother on what C. E. has *done*, the Mother in respect now

[10] Ibid., nos. 23, 24, and 25 (5 and 14 March and 3 May 1907), pp. 48,
49, and 50.
[11] Ibid., no. 26 (13 August 1907), p. 51.

to Eliza, to Maria, to the Father &c, the Mother above all in respect to C. E. himself (which his part was all a *preparation* for, 'leading' up to the effect of.)." He wished he had hypnotized his successors, but both the Small Boy chapter and the Mother chapter struck him as dismal failures of perception, awareness, and vitality: "the Mother treated as she actually stands seems to me . . . a positive small convulsion of debility!" This led him to question the wish of the public for "that so completely lack-lustre domestic sentimentality" and to reiterate his lonely and almost painful plea for a sustained, ordered, and organized form of fiction: "I saw, as a sequel to that, the ensuing steps of the little action so fully, vividly & logically, that I must have been thinking of them since very much as if I had really 'written them out,' & that turning to them in fact, as to find them so written, I feel them, all ruefully, anything *but* Yours most truly HENRY JAMES."[12]

Two months later he was sorry he had not taken the remaining chapters upon himself ("which I would have done ingeniously &—well, *cheap*!"). "I had engaged to play the game," James wrote, "& take over the elements as they were & hated to see them so helplessly muddled away when, oh, one could one's self (according to one's fatuous thought!) have made them *mean* something, given them sense, direction and form. It was, & still is, I confess, for me, the feeling of a competent cook who sees good vittles messed".[13] He failed to see that he was applying strict narrative principles to a semiserious fictional endeavor and that he was asking too much of his coauthors. He also failed to recognize that nothing could have come up to his rigorous conception of narrative relevance and coherence, and that by his all-devouring wish to monopolize the developments of the story he betrayed the main rule of the enterprise. Above all, he failed to see that the very application of his consummate technique and fictional awareness was at least partly to blame for the stalemate he had imposed on

[12] Ibid., p. 52.
[13] Ibid., no. 27 (2 October 1907), pp. 52–53.

the story while trying to "launch" it. James thought he had given it a turn and beautifully prepared for what was to follow. But this was true only in *his own* terms. No one but him could have carried the story forward once he had put his skillful hand to it. If James's chapter in *The Whole Family* is a perfect example of his latter style and technique, seen from another angle it did prove a stumbling block for anyone else having to start from there. James's contribution froze the action, stopped all movement, and brought the novel to a standstill.

2

In chapter 1 Howells had spoken as a newspaper editor in the village of Eastridge, who got permission to announce in his paper the engagement of Peggy Talbert to Harry Goward, a former fellow student of hers at a coeducational college. Through an amiable chat of the editor with her father, Howells managed to indicate the characters involved and to suggest their basic relations within the family. In the following chapters each writer added complications to the original situation.[14] The old-maid aunt Eliza (chapter 2) is presented as

[14] The novel ran serially in *Harper's Bazar* from December 1906 through November 1907. While the names of the twelve writers were listed, they were not identified as authors of the single chapters, and the readers were invited in an editorial note to determine which wrote each chapter. It became almost a guessing contest: James was indicated as the author of chapter 1 (correctly attributed to Howells by another reader). The authors were identified in the December 1907 issue, and in the book-form edition of the novel, published in 1908. Here is their list: chapter 1, "The Father," by William Dean Howells; 2, "The Old-Maid Aunt," by Mary E. Wilkins Freeman; 3, "The Grandmother," by Mary Heaton Vorse; 4, "The Daughter-in-law," by Mary Stuart Cutting; 5, "The School-Girl," by Elizabeth Jordan; 6, "The Son-in-law," by John Kendrick Bangs; 7, "The Married Son," by Henry James; 8, "The Married Daughter," by Elizabeth Stuart Phelps; 9, "The Mother," by Edith Wyatt; 10, "The School-Boy," by Mary Raymond Shipman Andrews; 11, "Peggy," by Alice Brown; 12, "The Friend of the Family," by Henry van Dyke.

obstinately trying to assert her youth and femininity by
wearing pink dresses and seeing all men (young or old) as
suitors. Harry Goward, the fiancé, had been one of her "loves,"
and when he suddenly leaves for New York and does not write,
all surmises and complications are possible. For the Grandmother (chapter 3), who considers the aunt "a case of arrested
development" and was strongly against sending Peggy to a
coeducational college (and who reads William James's *Varieties
of Religious Experience*), the engagement "has been like a stone
thrown into a pond, and it takes only a very little pebble to
ruffle the water farther than one would believe it possible"
(p. 78).[15] When it is discovered that aunt Eliza has telegraphed
Harry in New York, Grandmother is proved to be right.
Lorraine, the daughter-in-law (chapter 4), who never identified herself with the family, can throw an amusing light on
its staleness and limitations and see the situation with irony
and detachment. Neither she nor her husband is going to help
much. It is left to the younger daughter, the School-Girl
(chapter 5), to mix up things completely by means of a mislaid
letter from the fiancé (which has no trace of address left once it
is found) and by spreading her mistaken "discovery" that
Lorraine is in love with another man. Tom, the son-in-law
(chapter 6), bungles things as well in a long conversation he
has with Harry Goward; he obtains an explanation and
becomes his "friend," but forgets to ask about the address of
the letter. By the time he remembers, the fiancé has again
left for New York, on the same train as aunt Eliza. Everybody
fears an elopement. And Henry James makes his entrance in the
very thick of these complications.

Howells, in his opening chapter, has already characterized
Charles Edward, the married son, as some kind of artist, of
easy temper, who leaves all the push to his father and "still does
some sketching outside." He "putters over the aesthetic details
in the business, the new designs for the plated ware, and the
illustrated catalogues." His wife, Lorraine, whom he met at

---

[15] In this chapter, page references in the text are to *The Whole Family: A
Novel by Twelve Authors* (New York, 1908).

the Art Students' League, is "popularly held just such another as her husband" (p. 13). Mary E. Wilkins Freeman added that he is "a round peg in a square hole" (p. 32), and in drawing her sketch of Lorraine as the daughter-in-law in chapter 4, Mary Stuart Cutting capitalized on their being different from the other members of the family. Perfectly loathing "that long-winded Walter-Scotty name" (Charles Edward), Lorraine calls her husband Peter and refuses to make him conform to the family rules; he "perfectly detests the business, and will *never* be interested in it and never make anything out of it" (p. 84). Much to the horror of the family, Lorraine dreams of their going to Paris in six months, when a small inheritance is coming to him. She calls her mother-in-law Madonna ("even if she does think it a little Romish or sacrilegious or something queer" [p. 94]); her portrait is clearly meant to indicate her "artistic" and bohemian leanings. Her bed is not made at four o'clock in the afternoon and "Peter" is often late for work. In chapter 5 Elizabeth Jordan has the School-Girl face an incredible mess in her house, "books and teacups and magazines on the floor" (p. 107), and it is not surprising that Lorraine is briefly suspected of an adulterous attachment. Throughout the first six chapters, Charles Edward and his wife are seen in strong opposition to the other married couple—Charles Edward's sister Maria and her husband Tom Price—who represent conformity to the family rules and ideals and possess a developed business sense.

In his chapter, as was to be expected, James capitalized on Charles Edward's difference and partial detachment from the family, but from the subtler point of view of his psychological attitude rather than of his bohemian life. In so doing, he did not upset the preestablished network of relationships; he touched, in fact, on some of his cherished thematic oppositions. But so much of James's style, technique, and thematic awareness are injected into the chapter that the action is almost forgotten. Relationships are redefined and frozen in perfect balance: taking up the story again would have been difficult for anyone except James himself. He was justified in

his insistence that he alone could have carried the story forward. We, in turn, are no less interested in the Jamesian
quality of the chapter than in its shattering consequences
for the rest of the story.

James's very first sentences are almost a parody of his later
involuted style and are sufficient to stop any action and to
turn the narrative to the highest level of abstraction:

It's evidently a great thing in life to have got hold of a convenient
expression, and a sign of our inordinate habit of living by words.
I have sometimes flattered myself that I live less exclusively by them
than the people about me; paying with them, paying with them
only, as the phrase is (there I am at it, exactly, again!) rather less
than my companions, who, with the exception, perhaps, a little—
sometimes!—of poor Mother, succeed by their aid in keeping away
from every truth, in ignoring every reality, as comfortably as possible.
Poor Mother, who is worth all the rest of us put together, and is
really worth two or three of poor Father, deadly decent as I admit
poor Father mainly to be, sometimes meets me with a look, in some
connection, suggesting that, deep within, she dimly understands,
and would really understand a little better if she weren't afraid to:
for, like all of us, she lives surrounded by the black forest of the
"facts of life" very much as the people in the heart of Africa live
in their dense wilderness of nocturnal terrors, the mysteries and
monstrosities that make them seal themselves up in the huts as soon
as it gets dark. She, quite exquisite little Mother, would often understand, I believe, if she dared, if she knew *how* to dare; and the vague,
dumb interchange then taking place between us, and from the
silence of which we have never for an instant deviated, represents
perhaps her wonder as to whether I mayn't on some great occasion
show her how. [Pp. 144–45]

This is one of the few cases in which James writes in the
first person, but the beginning is far from inspiring. One is
brought down to the business of gradual unraveling. Charles
Edward is first defined in relation to his mother and in a mild
opposition to his father. Soon after, he begins to put on the
Jamesian garb of the nondoer, the sensitive soul, the detached
spectator of life: "save in this private precinct of my overflow . . . I have never either said or done a bold thing in my

life" (p. 145). James catches him, physically and symbolically, in the nonaction of waiting: as for so many predecessors of his, "what I seem always to feel . . . has been that it isn't yet the occasion, the really good and right one, for breaking out" (p. 145). Kept in check by the superior courage of his family ("this habit of their so constantly casting up my poverty at me—poverty of character, of course I mean") he can still "designate *them* as Poor" (p. 146). He keeps a diary to work off his nerves and as a resource that helps him to "hold out." He and Lorraine[16] are then presented as members of a kind of secret resistance movement, in a conspiracy of opposition to the family and their values: "It's in fact in this beautiful desperation that we spend our days, that we face the pretty grim prospect of new ones, that we go and come and talk and pretend, that we consort, so far as in our deep-dyed hypocrisy we do consort, with the rest of the Family" (p. 148). In this way they also subtly oppose the characterization they have been so far subjected to. If their "holding out" has become for them "the very basis of life" so that they hug each other "over the general intensity of it," it must have a deeper motivation and justification.

In fact, James presents Charles Edward as another incarnation of the antibusiness spirit, a man who is caught in the business world but must eventually escape from it. The son is "fully aware" of the "deep amusement" he excites at the Works; there is no doubt as to the couple's "proved business incompetence." The family takes them to task for their "lack of first-rate artistic power as well": no single type of ice-pitcher they have designed has ever yet "taken" with the awful public. As with so many other Jamesian artists, they are doing "the worst they can do": "We've tried again and again to strike off something hideous enough, but it has always in these cases appeared to us quite beautiful compared to the object finally turned out, on their improved lines, for the

[16] James has him comment on her name as she had done on his (p. 84): "My wife's inimitable name, which I feel every time I write it I must apologize even to myself for!" (p. 147).

unspeakable market" (p. 149). The couple's basic opposition is to the business world; yet within that basic opposition James manages to develop a quite interesting series of subtler, binary oppositions.

Their seeming "giving in" to the family is a better way of "holding out"; they appear as "meek" while being "ferocious" inside. Their opposition to the Works equals their opposition to the family, but there is room for articulation. Opposition from the Mother is on account of their supposed living in shame, and could be easily removed, as it later will be; opposition to the Father has an archetypal overtone and is not devoid of a "tender" touch: "poor Father, the fine damp plaster of whose composition, renewed from week to week, can't be touched anywhere letting your finger in, without peril of its coming to pieces" (p. 151). But their opposition to the other married couple, the Prices (a perfect name), is a good example of James's perception. If over-powering Maria and blunt Tom Price go about their father's business, they do so with callousness, blatancy, and avidity, without any social or moral sense worthy of note. Tom cannot be met "on that ground, the furious football-field to which he reduces conversation, making it echo as with the roar of the arena—one little bit" (p. 154); "He just hums, Tom Price, with business ideas, whereas I just gape with the impossibility of them; he moves in the densest buzzing cloud of them—after the fashion in which we carry our heads here on August evenings, each with its own thick nimbus of mosquitoes" (p. 155). Although done in a funny and semiserious way, James's characterization of Tom strikes a note of malaise and moral suspicion. He can be dangerous, he does make people pay: "He's sprightly in proportion as he's in earnest, and innocent in proportion as he's going to be dangerous; dangerous, I mean, to the competitor and the victim. Indeed when I reflect that his jokes are probably each going to cost certain people, wretched helpless people like myself, hundreds and thousands of dollars, their abundant flow affects me as one of the most lurid of exhibitions" (pp. 155–56).

James seems very careful in distinguishing this crude and cruel business attitude from the Father's attitude ("business genial and cheerful and even obstreperous, without detriment to its *being* business, has been poor Father's ideal" [p. 156]). And James seems quite aware of the dark secrets that, as in *The Ivory Tower*, are behind the great possessions. He speaks of "how exceeding small some of the material is consciously ground in the great grim, thrifty mill of industrial success; and indeed we grow about as many cheap illusions and easy comforts in the faintly fenced garden of our little life as could very well be crammed into the space" (pp. 156–57). As so often in James, Charles Edward's poverty of character, presumed or real, his negative approach to life, his lack of business ability and real artistic talent, his "void" and emptiness, become positive qualities in an opposition that is of moral no less than social (and family)[17] values. Thus James is perfectly consistent in stressing the fond relation that binds him to the Mother, who is also characterized by James through negative terms: her not mentioning the disagreement about her son's house, which "falls in so richly with all the other things, all the 'real' things, we never mention" (p. 150), her not asking anything or being anywhere, her son's helping her rather "not to see than to see." A detached brother, Charles Edward is presented as "a clinging son," and in the beautiful pages that James devotes to portraying his relation to the Mother one is tempted to see a deeply felt autobiographical projection.[18] Another link is established with the Grandmother, who is characterized as the living embodiment of premodern times dating back to the Civil War and the burning

[17] "I'm but too conscious of how, on the other hand, I'm desolately outlined to all eyes, in an air as pure and empty as that of a fine Polar sunset" (p. 155), he significantly adds to his view of Tom's "humming" with business ideas.

[18] "I'm in respect to *her* as achingly filial and as feelingly dependent, all the time, as when I used, in the far-off years, to wake up, a small blubbering idiot, from frightening dreams, and refuse to go to sleep again, in the dark, till I clutched her hands or her dress and felt her bend over me" (p. 152). One is reminded of Proust.

of witches. A character from the past, far as she is from modernity and the business world, she appeals to Charles Edward. And, contrary to the intention of Howells, who had wanted to show the advantages of coeducation, Charles Edward sides with her in "her deprecation of the idea that Peggy should be sent, to crown her culture, to that horrid co-educative college from which the poor child returned the other day so preposterously engaged to be married" (p. 159).

This allows James not only to draw a fine relation, but to vent his dislike and distrust of the "co-educative college," half-humorously and half-seriously referred to as a "bear garden" and a "general menagerie-case," where poor Peggy would only learn "to roar and snarl with the other animals." "Think of the vocal sounds with which she may come back to us!" Charles Edward had warned, and one can see here more than an echo of James's essays on the speech and manners of American women that he had just contributed to *Harper's Bazar*. In the same vein James is later in the chapter to launch on one of his familiar attacks against journalists.[19]

His own personal concerns and ideas are thus redefining, if not modifying, the given situation. Once the basic relations have been rearranged, James's interest seems to shift to an almost direct consideration of their fictional potentialities and of his own role in them. Through a fine break in the narrative tempo, he subjects the novel itself to scrutiny and analysis. For James the gist of the situation is that "every one wants to get someone else away." "Father would like to shunt Granny"; Mother to "shoo" off Eliza; the Tom Prices to extirpate Charles Edward and Lorraine, and these in turn to clear the sky of the Tom Prices; all want to get rid of Eliza. We are on the level of mild amusement, but either consciously or unconsciously James's sentences touch on some of his most typical themes. It is a question of "converting our aunt's lively presence into a lively absence"; "the strange stultification of the passions" in the characters "prevents anything ever

---

[19] "A journalist, a rolling stone, a man who has seen other life, how can one not suspect him of some deeper game than he avows" (p. 172).

from coming to an admitted and avowed head" (pp. 165–66). Converting presence into absence; nothing ever really coming to a head—these are two of James's familiar and deepest fictional motives.[20] And his correlating, or indeed contrasting, this fact with the proliferation of the narrative threads appears just as typical. In the following quotation James is speaking in his own voice:

As I read over what I have written the aspects of our situation multiply so in fact that I note again how one has only to look at any human thing very straight (that is with the minimum of intelligence) to see it shine out in as many aspects as the hues of the prism; or place itself, in other words, in relations that positively stop nowhere. I've often thought I should like some day to write a novel; but what would become of me in that case—delivered over, I mean, before my subject, to my extravagant sense that everything is a part of something else? When you paint a picture with a brush and pigments, that is on a single plane, it can stop at your gilt frame; but when you paint one with a pen and words, that is in *all* the dimensions, how are you to stop? [P. 167]

No matter how static the situation, James clearly implies that to look at it straight in a fictional way is to make it reflect endless aspects and relations. Fiction thrives in pursuing the never-ending connections that are thus revealed. Yet the reverse seems also true. Fiction freezes the flow of life, and by its very nature brings action to a stop. When Lorraine answers, "Stopping, that's art," I cannot refrain from taking it in two senses: art is knowing how and when to stop, but it also stops action and situations, as James does in his chapter. While the writer proceeds, life as it were stands still. Only the novelist, in James's image, not his character or his subject, is prepared to go any distance and may head for a probable smash: "as Lorriane says, 'Stopping, that's art; and what are we artists like, my dear, but those drivers of trolley-cars, in

---

[20] For the crucial role of "absence" in James, see Tzvetan Todorov, "Le secret du récit" (1969) and "Les fantômes de Henry James" (1969) in his *Poétique de la prose* (Paris, 1971), pp. 151–96, and chapter on *The Ivory Tower* below.

New York, who, by some divine instinct, recognize in the forest of pillars and posts the white-striped columns at which they pull up? Yes, we're drivers of trolley-cars charged with electric force and prepared to go any distance from which the consideration of a probable smash ahead doesn't deter us' " (pp. 167–68).

James goes here all the distance he can, and almost twice the length he is given. Yet while his definitions proceed and his relations multiply, nothing really happens, and the situation, far from springing into life, is more and more entangled. Again one can see a trace of his deeper concerns and most cherished ways in Charles Edward's avowal that he and Lorraine have not defined their position—they have "*re*fined it, to the last intensity" (p. 169). They have refined it by being artists (and walking rather "uncannily" to the Works together every morning). It is to their sense of independence that, toward the end of the chapter, when something must at last be made to happen, James wanted to attribute a decisive role for the "solution" of the story.

The couple's "holding out" and "saving up" have been "for an exercise of strength and a show of character," and they are now given the chance. In keeping with the trend of James's development, Charles Edward will step in to *dis*engage Peggy from her fiancé, to free her from the clutches of the family and the limitations of American life. Once he is moved to action, the Married Son will make up for lost time and missed opportunities. He is to take command, to show his strength of character, and to prove that he is the genius of the family. He will go to New York, and, by freeing Peggy, he will also free himself and Lorraine. His scheme—and here we fall back on a Jamesian cliché—is to take Peggy with them for a year's true culture in Europe. James wants to prepare for such a step, and at this point he inserts the much discussed "Chataway part."

Looking for Eliza at her friends the Chataways, in East Seventy-third Street, Charles Edward is exposed to the pretentious sordidness of the East Side setting. In a few paragraphs James spared no pains to sketch the heavy and greasy atmosphere of the parlor, the frowzy appearance of the overpowdered "massive lady" in her wrapper, the debased quality of her dialogue. This sharp note of social criticism of the American setting was clearly to serve as a justification for Charles Edward's proposed flight to Europe. Similarly, his subsequent stroll in the park was to serve as a transition. Just as the New York East Side represents the "side" of America one had to leave, in Central Park he feels almost in Paris: "so that when I at last fidgeted into the Park, where you get so beautifully away from the town, it was surely the next thing to Europe, and in fact *had* to be, since it's the very antithesis of Eastridge" (p. 180).[21] He already feels free from the burden of the Works and his family, almost grateful to Eliza for the chance. It is, again, a typical Jamesian stroke, a characteristic "turn of the screw" of his, that in the park he is suddenly made to meet Harry Goward, the fiancé, on whom he pounces as on his prey. Yet in an almost perverse Jamesian way, far from being a turning point or a conclusion, the episode is left open, suspended in mid air. When James writes that Harry Goward, surprised at being found there, "wanted everything told him—but every single thing; as if, after a tremendous fall, or some wild parabola through the air, the effect of a violent explosion under his feet, he had landed at a vast distance from his starting-point" (p. 183), we recognize the touch of the master but also his maddening predilection for the unsaid and the unstated, for absence as a better form of presence.[22] All have been landed at a vast

[21] In accordance with James's ambivalence toward America, the interior of the East Side house, with its boarding house smell of "wash" and inferior food (p. 181), is significantly contrasted with the (then) idyllic and almost poetic atmosphere of the park, the only place in all New York "where the stricken deer may weep" (p. 182).

[22] The final sentence of the chapter relates beautifully to the first in its involuted vagueness: "Well, the charming thing was that this affected me as giving the very sharpest point to the idea that, in asking myself how I should deal with him, I had already so vividly entertained" (p. 184).

distance from the starting point, including the poor writers
that were to follow.

In spite of James's repeated claim that he had "launched"
the story or "given a good blow of wind" into the sail of this or
that character, the early anonymous reviewer in the *Nation*
was right in maintaining that James, "as he would say, gets
beautifully nowhere."[23] He was getting ahead with *his own*
kind of novel, so poignantly concerned with states of absence,
of refined consciousness, relations and suspended situations.
His coauthors had no way to go, except painfully extricating
themselves from his mazes. The following chapters reveal
not only the obvious inferiority of the other contributors
but also the ravages wrought by James's personal interven-
tion. While he found it hard to stop himself, there is no
question that his chapter did manage to stop the others. His
main lead for the denouement—having Peggy break her
engagement and go off to Europe—was followed, but the
action limps clumsily along through repetition, mere mechanical complications, and a sense of fatigue. One feels the effort
of taking it up again *after* James.

Chapter 8 simply repeats the previous plot in the suggestion of a second false elopement by having Maria follow
to New York with the village doctor in order to throw *him* in
the path of Eliza and in the complications ensuing from
Charles Edward's loss of the address where he is to meet Harry
Goward. As a next step *everybody* goes to New York while poor
Harry is injured in a train crash and sent to hospital; the
Young Girl then concocts an incredible story of her own to
account for Peggy's behavior (she is supposed to be in love
with the Doctor, and innumerable new complications follow).
Poor aunt Eliza is caught in another love story of her own
making (another repetition of the early plot), and even
Mrs. Chataway, in spite of James's fears, reappears on the
scene in chapter 11. At last Stillman Dane, Charles Edward's

<hr />

[23] Cf., among others, letter of 14 March 1907 to Miss Jordan, in *A
Double Billing*, p. 49, and "Current Fiction," in the *Nation*, 87 (3 Dec.
1908), 553, quoted in Cargill, *The Novels of Henry James*, p. 459.

old college friend and Peggy's psychology professor, is providentially brought on the scene as a typical deus ex machina. Peggy discovers she loves *him,* elopes with him, and arrives just in time at the dock, happily married, to leave for Europe with Charles Edward and Lorraine. James receives his due, as far as the solution goes, but at the price of long suffering over the fumbles and bungles of his "followers." When the Friend of the Family is introduced by Henry Van Dyke in chapter 12 to arrange the happy ending, and is made to comment on the family, he seems paradoxically to comment at once on their behavior as characters and on the pointless "interferences" of their authors. Each is "at heart lovable and fairly good; but, taken in combination, bewildering and perplexing to the last degree" "Independence was a sacred tradition . . . but interference was a fixed nervous habit, and complication was a chronic social state" (pp. 296 and 297).

"It was all extremely complicated and unnecessary (from my point of view)" seems to sum up the Friend of the Family's as well as James's attitude to the story, at least in its final stages. We have seen James's growing dissatisfaction with the turn taken by the novel and his regret at not being able to "save" it in his own way. In spite of its comparative *succès d'estime,* he was perhaps asking too much of a "literary stunt".[24] Above all, he was asking too much of his coauthors, especially in the light of his particular contribution. It may be, as B. R. McElderry suggests, that James appears here in a light mood and that his collaboration to *The Whole Family* does to a certain extent qualify our stereotype of him as an austere artist.[25]

---

[24] The contemporary reviewer of the *North American Review* praised "the reasonableness and balanced power of the story as a whole," its character drawing and feeling: "In its play of psychological moonlight over the troubled surface of a spiritual sea which remains in its depth undisturbed, *The Whole Family* seems typical of the 'new literature' of the country"! One of the collaborators, however, Elizabeth Stuart Phelps, thought James's chapter "long and heavy." See Bruce R. McElderry, Jr., "Henry James and *The Whole Family,*" *Pacific Spectator,* 4 (1950), 355–56 and 359.

[25] McElderry, Jr., "Henry James and *The Whole Family,*" pp. 359–60.

Yet in his chapter he was thoroughly faithful to his typical inspiration, his thematic concerns, technical devices, and stylistic idiosyncrasies. He may be seen at play, but in a serious mood. It was this that caused endless trouble for the others. Once he had stepped in, there was no hope for them. On the other hand, just because he is caught red-handed in such a typical piece of fiction writing, the chapter has much to reveal about James's fictional habits and ideals. As the Friend of the Family says in the concluding line, "we don't want the whole family"—we want the lonely author.

Cargill (*The Novels of Henry James,* p. 457) suggests that at least the opening section of James's chapter is "deliberate spoofing." None of James's letters on the novel supports the suggestion.

V. The Sense and Nightmare of the Past

1

The Sense of the Past, one of the two unfinished novels post-humously edited by Percy Lubbock in 1917, deals in an original way with the international theme that runs through all the phases of James's fiction. It is also characterized by a further complication—stretched to its breaking point—of those technical procedures that he had experimented with in his middle phase and applied with perfect mastery in his major phase.

That two novels were left unfinished seems at least partially due to the novelty of their thematic assumptions and developments. In the case of *The Sense of the Past* this seems also due to the predictable impasse reached by a too complex elaboration of the technical principle of the intelligent observer. This elaboration seems here indeed to undergo that defeat which James had avoided, in the similar case of *The Sacred Fount,* by turning it into the very subject of the book. The international theme is here assumed as a problematic contrast between Europe and America, *and* between past and present. It is, moreover, dealt with in a surprising, paradigmatic way, while the technical elaboration—just because it is stretched to its breaking point—can be followed *in fieri,* in its making, as it is found and tested, rejected and resumed, twisted and developed to serve (or to discover) its purpose.

In *The Sense of the Past,* given its incomplete state, the combination of dramatic scene and limited point of view is perceivable in its actual forming and tentative approach. Two thematic moments are also recognizable. While in the first part the archetypal contrast between Europe and America is defined, discussed, and debated in a paradigmatic, exemplary way, in the central part this theme is defined and dealt with in the purely Jamesian terms of a problematic and anguished dialectic between past and present, which will almost compel the protagonist, as we shall see, to live a kind of nerve-racking, continual discovery of the future. Here the particular elaboration of the principle of the intelligent observer becomes of paramount importance. By a stroke almost of genius it is given a twist that affects the development and the meaning of the story itself. On account of those aspects the novel is clearly related to James's experimental period; it seems to originate directly from it, over and above the fruitful interval of the major phase, with which it also betrays revealing links. If the play of words were not too much, its purport could be expressed in a formula: *The Sense of the Past*; or, the Present as Future.

One has to proceed slowly and cautiously to unravel the enigma of its story and its making. According to a typically Jamesian procedure, complexities and complications developed while the story and the book were being conceived and figured out, discussed in the *Notebooks* and laid out in the Scenario, tentatively drafted and written. "*Solvitur ambulando*," James himself wrote here. Quite often, as he went along, instead of being solved complications were found, cheerfully pursued, followed to their farthest ends. As always in James, they develop according to an irresistible principle of inner growth from quite a scanty germ. But in their proliferation is their richness; and in their richness is their fascination and value. James had conceived and "figured out" the novel (already called *The Sense of the Past*) in the autumn of 1899, in answer to a request from Doubleday that he write a pair of tales of terror to make another volume like *The Two Magics* (published in 1898 and containing "Covering End" and "The Turn of the Screw"). The original suggestion seems to have come from Rudyard Kipling, whom James was later to blame for the publisher's subsequent lack of interest in the project. In the spring of 1900, however, Howells asked him to write a novelette on an "international ghost" and James readily agreed. He had been working on exactly that type of story.[1]

[1] *Letters*, I, 354–56; *Notebooks*, pp. 298–301. "I brood with mingled

In the *Notebooks* he wrote of aiming at something as simple as "The Turn of the Screw," in fact "less grossly and merely apparitional." Looking for a "possible alternative," he thought that "there dwelt a possibility in something expressive of the peculiarly acute Modern, the current polyglot, the American-experience-abroad line." "Hasn't one got hold of," he went on, "doesn't one make out, rather, something in the general glimmer of the notion of what the quasi-grotesque Europeo-American situation, in the way of the gruesome, may, *pushed to the full and right expression of its grotesqueness*, has [*sic*] to give?" He toyed with the picture of three or four "scared" and slightly modern American figures moving against the background of three or four European milieus and different situations, in the hope that one of these American situations abroad might "lend itself to some sort of little fantastication."[2]

He specified that the basis of the idea of *The Sense of the Past* was not simply that of a young American lost in the European past, but rather the fact that he—and not the ghostly figures from the past—was to become a source of terror for the others. The young American was soon identified as the center of consciousness of the story, whose central idea was to be "the *revealed* effect of 'terror,' . . . the fact of the consciousness of it as given, not *received*, on the part of the central, sentient, person of the story."[3] Ingenuity and *expertise* might save the story, if the author succeeded in telling it from the point of view of the protagonist and in compressing his prologue and his exposition:

---

elation and depression on your ingenious, your really inspired, suggestion that I shall give you a ghost, and that my ghost shall be 'international.' I say inspired because, singularly enough, I set to work some months ago at an international ghost, and on just this scale . . . entertaining for a little the highest hopes of him" (*Letters*, I, 351–52).

[2] *Notebooks* pp. 299–300. The reference to "The Turn of the Screw" ("grossly and merely apparitional") ought to profide a check to the Freudian and "hallucinatory" interpretations.

[3] Ibid., p. 300.

When I think of the expedient of making the narrator's point of view that of the persons outside—that of one of them—I immediately see how I *don't* get that way, the presentation by the person who is the source of the "terror" of his sense of being so. On the other hand I don't, if I tell the thing from his point of view *in* the "1st person" get, easily, that I can see, the intense simplification. At the same time, I seem clearly to see, I don't get the hope, and the chance, of real simplification save *by* the first person. . . . My «"prologue" . . . is my overwhelming space-devourer; my exposition encroaches awfully on the time, on the field, of the poor little drama itself.[4]

Given these uncertainties, when only a week later Howells lost interest in the project, James seemed almost relieved and laid it aside. "My tale of terror," he wrote, "did . . . give way beneath me. It *has*, in short, broken down for the present. I am laying it away on the shelf for the sake of something that *is* in it."[5] He had written two-and-a-half sections (110 pages, according to his statement to Howells), stopping at a crucial moment in what was to become Book 3, in the very middle of the protagonist's talk with the ambassador. Nothing is heard of the project until 1903 when, as it appears from an unpublished letter of 1 September to Scribner's,[6] James had arranged with Harpers to bring out the book toward the end of the next year. He was then busily working on *The Golden Bowl*, which was finished by the end of 1903. The effort involved must have first delayed and then postponed indefinitely his plan of bringing out *The Sense of the Past* together with the three novels of his major phase.

That he had probably given up his project completely is borne out by the fact that he used some of its elements

[4] Ibid., p. 301.

[5] *Letters*, I, 359 (14 August 1900, to Howells). And earlier on: "Preoccupied with half a dozen things of the altogether human order now fermenting in my brain, I don't care for 'terror' (terror, that is, without 'pity') so much as I otherwise might. . ." (Ibid., p. 357, and F. O. Matthiessen, *The James Family*, p. 510).

[6] The letter is now in the Scribner's Archives, Manuscript Room, Firestone Library, Princeton University.

in quite a few of his tales of this period. Although in a dream, the protagonist of "The Great Good Place" (1900) flees from the harassing world of the present into the cherished cloister of tranquility and youth, while his place is taken by a young admirer who is almost his alter ego. In "The Third Person" (1900), in a house haunted by the past like the one in *The Sense of the Past*, two spinsters are visited by the apparitions of a man from another epoch (the "third person" of the title), whom they succeed in laying to rest by doing "a bold deed" for him—an act of smuggling. "The Tone of Time" (1900) deals with the theme of the mysterious portrait—the portrait of a man unknown to the painter, which causes a strange relationship of tension and rivalry between her and the woman who commissioned it. James seems here to be playing with the supernatural in a worldly manner. In "Flickerbridge" (1902), however, which is so charged with the sense of Europe and the past as it reveals itself to a "passionate pilgrim," we find a number of motives that are of paramount importance in *The Sense of the Past*. Its protagonist is drawn to the past by a deep feeling of identification, while his fiancée (as in the first part of the novel) is all for America and the present, and he spends an intense and ecstatic vigil in an old European house. Though in this tale James probably remembered *The Reverberator*, he also drew on some aspects of his abandoned novel.

As James himself noted in a guarded way, "The Jolly Corner" (1908) draws largely and exhaustively on the motives and themes he had envisaged in 1899-1900.[7] Here we find not

---

[7] He wrote in the *First Statement: (Preliminary)* to the novel of "having made use of a scrap of that fantasy in *The Jolly Corner*—distinctly do I remember saying to myself in writing that thing that I was filching in a small way this present put-away one and might conceivably afterwards regret it. But I don't mean to regret it if I prove not to want to, or to consider my idea at all compromised by the *J.C.*: the whole thing is so different and so much more ample, and precautions in short can be taken" (*Notebooks*, p. 364). And see L. C. Knights's idea of the "trapped spec-

only the haunted house and the long vigil but the protagonist's homecoming in search of his "possible" past, and his encounter with a ghostly double, a nightmarish alter ego—what Spencer Brydon might have been had he stayed in America. The atmosphere, the suspense, the quiver and the shudder of this story have much in common with *The Sense of the Past*. Allowing for the obvious reversal of roles (here it is an expatriate who goes back to America to discover his lost self and his "possible" past), the central motive, the nightmarish experience and the anguish of the tale, are openly reminiscent of, if not indeed modeled on, the pages of the novel.

James waited until 1914, however, to resume his project, having found it impossible to go on with *The Ivory Tower*. While waiting for the original manuscript to be sent from Rye (where it had been stored) to London, he wrote a "First Statement: (Preliminary)" in which he took up the story where he had left it, in order to test its possible developments. "Under pressure of our present disconcerting conditions"—the beginning of World War I—he felt that the old manuscript offered "matter for possible experiment." "The beauty of it was just that it was complicated"; it was "too difficult to try on a mere chance." James considered the first section (the protagonist's interview with "the young woman") an introduction to the Introduction, and the young man's call at the legation—where the original draft had broken off—as the climax of the "Introduction or Prologue." This scene seemed to James a good way of dodging the difficulty of bridging the gap between the present and the past.[8]

In the past where he found himself, his protagonist was to remain conscious of the present. While acquiring the consciousness of his predecessor in the past, he was to keep his own, to enjoy—or to suffer from—a double consciousness, "the consciousness of being the other and yet himself also, of

tator" in his "Henry James and the Trapped Spectator" (1938), now in *Explorations* (Harmondsworth, 1964), pp. 162–75.

[8] *Notebooks,* pp. 361–62.

being himself and yet the other also."[9] Hence his obvious role as intelligent observer and at the same time his terrible predicament: the "romantic" had to be allowed for, as the whole thing was "the pure essence of the romantic and to be bravely faced and exploited as such." Even if the young man, however, could be characterized as "of Tory or Loyalist blood, and therefore never really effectively dissevered,"[10] his predicament and his tragedy would have developed out of his growing sense of alienation:

What his miraculous excursion into the past, his escapade into the world of that Sense of it that he has so yearned for, what it does to him most of all, he speedily becomes aware with sick dismay, is to make him feel far more off and lost, far more scared, as it were, and terrified, far more *horribly*, that is, painfully and nostalgically misplaced and disconnected. . . . His whole preconception has been that it would, that it should, be an excursion and nothing more, from which as by the pressure of a spring or a stop . . . he might get out and away from, get back to his own proper consciousness, his own time and place and relation to things. What is terrible, he perceives after a bit, is that he feels immersed and shut in, lost and damned, as it were, beyond all rescue.[11]

The longed-for past, as in "The Jolly Corner," was to prove a nightmare. Yet James insisted on the further twist of the story, whereby the young man himself would become a source of terror and uneasiness for the other people. The most intimate idea, James avowed, was that of a hero "turning the tables" on a "ghost," "winning a sort of victory by the appearance, and the evidence, that this personage or presence was more

[9] Ibid., p. 364. The representation of this "double consciousness," James added, "makes the thrill and the curiosity of the affair." *The* difficulty, at this point, however, was "the production of the 'old world' atmosphere, the constitution of the precise milieu and tone." This had sent James "beating about" for an alternative—writing of an "ancient young man in the actual" (p. 365), which would have been easier to do, but which he soon dropped.

[10] Ibid., p. 366.

[11] Ibid., p. 367.

overwhelmingly affected by him than he by *it*." One aspect of
the story was indeed to depend on the other. Either the young
man betrayed his anguish (thus appearing like a madman to
the others), or he accepted it (thus becoming a madman to
himself). In any case his uneasiness and his homesickness
were to make him appear strange, and then sinister, to the
others, to widen the gap between him and his predecessors
and to increase his alienation from them.[12] This is what
happens in the book, in which one further possibility,
glimpsed at, at the end of the Preliminary Statement, is explored and developed.[13]

The young American of 1910 was to find himself in 1820 and
to repeat the experiences of his alter ego and predecessor in
the past. He was, moreover, to find himself betrothed to an
English girl. On the one hand, he does not fully know his
situation, and he has gradually to discover it. On the other
hand, though finding himself in a preordained situation that
has already happened and must therefore be followed consistently in each of its fixed steps, the protagonist discovers
that he cares most for the sister of his fiancée. As we
shall see, his "wrong" feeling—wrong in terms of a necessary
adherence to the past—is motivated by the fact that the sister of
his fiancée is more "modern," more open to the future (which
for her is represented by the young man from 1910) and better
equipped, therefore, to sense his uneasiness and his anguish;
better suited, that is, to understand and share his feelings.

This is the most interesting twist of this long preparation.
One sees immediately that if the protagonist has to discover
step by step his role in the past, and if, moreover,
he is given the chance of *not* following step by step the
experiences preordained for him in the past; if, in a word, he

[12] Ibid., pp. 367–68.

[13] Ibid., pp. 368–69. This First Statement ends on the words "Above all
I see—"; the book itself is interrupted on the words "he could see. . . ."
A further proof of James's obsession and preoccupation with "seeing."
See Holland, *The Expense of Vision* and Tanner, *The Reign of Wonder,* among
others.

can follow his own independent steps, this means not only that he can *modify* the past but that he has to reenact it as if it were for him at each step a kind of impending *future*. Not only *is* he the future for the others, ¹and in particular for the girl he chooses to love, but he himself has to discover and reenact at each step an experience that is not merely a past experience but a new experience, a new story—an experience that is not restricted in the grooves of the past but is projected and enacted, rather, as an open possibility in a *virtual future*.

This is what happens—with the obvious doubts and limitations of such a case—in the completed chapters of the book. There, and in the Scenario of the whole story, it is clear that James meant to emphasize the complexities of the central section, and this can at least partially account for the enormous difficulties he encountered and for the unfinished state of the book. As matters stand, as soon as he received the original (1900) manuscript from Rye, James revised it rapidly and proceeded to draft a Scenario of the story to its conclusion (67 pages in Percy Lubbock's edition). He worked on the novel on the basis of this Scenario until the autumn of 1915, completing Book 3 and a sizable portion (171 pages, unrevised) of Book 4, which deals with the central and crucial experience of Ralph Pendrel's "jump" into the past.[14] He interrupted his work only to write his important introduction to Rupert Brooke's *Letters from America*. On the eve of his fatal stroke in 1916 he had apparently been looking over some pages of his novel: but there was no time and no energy left to complete it. It proves, all the same, a small master-

---

[14] Cf. Percy Lubbock, Preface and note to *The Sense of the Past* (New York, 1945, a reprint of the 1917 edition), pp. i and 291. On 1 December 1914 James had written to Edith Wharton: "I have got back to trying to work—on one of the three books begun and abandoned—at the end of some '30,000 words'—15 years ago, and fished out of the depths of an old drawer at Lamb House (I sent Miss Bosanquet down to hunt it up) as perhaps offering a certain defiance of subject to the law by which most things now perish in the public blight. This does seem to kind of intrinsically resist—and I have hopes. But I must rally now before getting back to it" (*Letters*, II, 426).

piece, both for its exemplary treatment of some crucial Jamesian themes and for its experimental development of a typically Jamesian principle—that of the intelligent observer and the limited point of view—which determines and is closely connected to the particular twist of the story.

2

Faithful to his peculiar method, James chose his protagonist, Ralph Pendrel, as the central consciousness, but resisted the temptation of the first-person narrative. "I of course, under penalty of the last infamy," he wrote in the Scenario, "stick here still, as everywhere, to our knowing these things but through Ralph's knowing them" (p. 350); [15] and similar statements are often repeated in the discussion of most of his episodes.

Structurally, the novel is built according to the principle of Chinese boxes: Books 1 and 2 constitute the introduction, followed by a kind of Prologue (Book 3) which leads to the core of the novel (Book 4, unfinished). Books 1 and 3 are essentially built on the principle of the dramatic scene—facts, feelings, and contrasts are basically conveyed through dialogues—while in Book 2 (Ralph's vigil in the London house, with the climax of the apparition of his alter ego) the inner experience of the "intelligent observer" predominates. This becomes of paramount importance in Book 4, where it alternates with a sequel of dramatic scenes. "I see my procedure ruled by the drama, the quasi-scenic movement," James wrote. "There must be . . . enormous foreshortenings, great compression and presentation of picture" (p. 306), though he realized that for Ralph's experiences in the past he had to resort to the purely narrative method, as he had done in "The Turn of the Screw." "The very essence of all this," he wrote, "is to stick as fast as possible to the precedent of the 'Screw,' in which

[15] In this chapter, page references in the text are to *The Sense of the Past* (New York, 1945).

foreshortening abounded and I didn't, and couldn't, at all hand my subject over to the scenic. . . . the crescendo of the malaise, really demands and depends upon the non-scenic for its full triumph. . . . I see how 'narrative representation' most permits, most effectively prepares and accompanies, my turning of the present screw, and what a part picture and image and evoked aspect and sense can play for me in that connection" (p. 307).

This combination of fictional methods had been beautifully applied to the novels of the major phase. Here we shall note that the sense of place, expressed in the dialectical contrast between Europe and America, dominates in Books 1 and 2. From this physical and geographical sense of place, which causes the "magic spell" of Book 2, we move on imperceptibly to a subtle consciousness and awareness of time. This operates at first as a contrast between the present and the past, and then, in Book 4, as an anguished sense of imprisonment in the past, yearning for the present, and effort of unnatural enactment in a virtual future. In Book 4 as well the sense of time (as defined here) has its obvious, but not numerous links and objective correlatives in the sense of place—the milieu, the habits, and customs of 1820. But the experience is here internalized and essentially temporal, after the great opening of the initial debate on the international theme.[16]

[16] According to Cargill, *The Novels of Henry James*, p. 489, James "excluded most of the externals of dress and décor" and tried to suggest the difference between past and present mainly "in terms of manners and sensibility." T. S. Eliot noted that James had taken Hawthorne's "ghost sense" in *The House of the Seven Gables* and given it substance, "at the same time making the tragedy much more ethereal" ("The Hawthorne Aspect," in the *Little Review,* 5 [August 1918] 52–53, rpt. in *The Question of Henry James,* ed. F. W. Dupee [New York, 1945], pp. 118–19). According to Eliot, it is in *The Sense of the Past* that Hawthorne's influence is particularly felt. F. O. Matthiessen, too, in *Henry James: The Major Phase* (London, 1946), p. 135, spoke of a "mood of eeriness" in the book. This might distinguish it from such possible "sources" as H. G. Wells's *The Time Machine* (1895), which James had just read in 1900, Mark Twain's *A Connecticut Yankee in King Arthur's Court* (1889: a possible comparison is sug-

Book 1 establishes the premises of the story in a wager and a challenge at the end of what might be termed a "flyting," and it presents a debate on the international theme in which the terms of the contrast between Europe and America acquire a startling new definition and foreshadow the value that the actual experience of the contrast will have for the protagonist. The theme is superficially that of James's early short story "A Passionate Pilgrim" (1871). It is true, as Elizabeth Stevenson suggests, that to compare the two works "is to compare his entire development. One is all innocent expression, the other, all considerate composition."[17] Yet this "considerate composition" seems also to reverse the symbolic value that James had usually attributed to Europe and America.

Ralph Pendrel and Aurora Coyne are at first glance two archetypal Jamesian characters. He is a "negative" character, a "library beetle," "a mere thinker" who has encountered life "mainly in the form of loss and of sacrifice" (p. 1). He has been kept from a full knowledge of life by "hindrances, infelicities of circumstance, imperfections of opportunity" (p. 2). He is obviously related, in this sense, to Lambert Strether in *The Ambassadors*, George Stransom in "The Altar of the Dead" (1895), and Herbert Dodd in "The Bench of Desolation" (1909). He is at the beginning in the same position as John Marcher in "The Beast in the Jungle" (1903): "*the* man, to whom nothing on earth was to have happened," who has, however, "the sense of being kept for something rare and strange, possibly prodigious and terrible, that was sooner or later to happen to you, that you had in your bones the foreboding and the conviction of, and that would perhaps overwhelm you."[18] Ralph will meet his "beast in the jungle," and will be almost overwhelmed. He has reacted to the empti-

---

gested by Edmund Wilson in his "The Ambiguity of Henry James"), and Henry Newbolt's *The Old Country* (see *The Legend of the Master*, ed. S. Nowell-Smith [London, 1947], p. 129).

[17] *The Crooked Corridor*, pp. 117–18. See also Maxwell Geismar, *Henry James and the Jacobites* (Boston, 1963), p. 425.

[18] *Complete Tales*, XI, 401 and 359.

ness of his life with a keen intellectual sense, with a deep feeling for the past—feeling for the European past and European values revealed in a historical booklet he has written.

This typical Jamesian character shares with many characters of the later tales collected in *The Finer Grain* (1910), in James's own words, a "finer grain of accessibility to suspense or curiosity, to mystification or attraction."[19] He is confronted by Aurora Coyne, a woman of grand and calm beauty, characterized by a "congruity with things" and a full experience of life. She is a sort of "Italian princess of the *cinque-cento,* and Titian or the grand Veronese might . . . have signed her image" (p. 7). She might do with a Malatesta or a Sforza, a filibuster or a buccaneer, a great soldier or a pirate. She has known marriage and, of course, Europe. Ralph sits at her feet though he has "nothing in common with her apprehension—so particular, so private as that would be—of the kind of personal force, of action on her nerves and senses, that might win from her a second surrender" (p. 8).

From *Roderick Hudson* (1876) onwards, these are the terms of a well-known and well-exploited contrast. The novelty lies in the fact that in this case Aurora has come back from Europe to *stay* in America. Europe has been poisoned for her and she is never to go back there: she has been prescribed "as a balm or vengeance, the abjuration of the general world that had made it possible" (p. 15). She is attracted by Ralph, but her condition is that he should never go to Europe—in his "starved state" he would find himself staying indefinitely; his intellectual knowledge would be spoiled. She has chosen America and her hero is now "the cowboy" or "the ranchman": "If I could have known how I was now to feel I would never have gone," Aurora maintains. "One must choose at last . . . and I take up definitely with my own country. It's high time; here, *en fin de compte,* one can at least do or be something, show something, make something. . . . I want in short to be an American as other people are—well, whatever they are" (pp. 26–27).

[19] *Complete Tales,* XII, 9.

Ralph retorts ironically: "You want a fellow only who shall have had adventures. . . . You want the adventure to have been, or necessarily to be, of the species most marked and determined by our climate, our geographical position, our political institutions, our social circumstances and our national character" (p. 29). The usual terms of the contrast are reversed. It is not simply that the European experience is a source of corruption for American innocence (and ignorance) of the world. America is accepted by Aurora as a positive value *in itself.* She appreciates Ralph's deep and intuitive knowledge of the past as long as it is not spoiled by the actual experience of Europe. She appreciates his having learned it all "over here." In some obscure way the European experience, unless it is purely intellectual, is evil. Now that Ralph, having inherited a house in London from a distant cousin, can go there, he and Aurora part on a wager and a challenge.[20] He is convinced that she will follow him to Europe, where he shall have the great adventure that will make him "worthy." She wants him to go and promises that she will follow him if *moved* to go, or that she will have him if he comes home loyally with a desire to stay.

The challenge is charged with dark forebodings. In Book 2, on a spring day, Ralph is a "passionate pilgrim" in London, ecstatically experiencing all the stages of an emotional recognition of old Europe. He plunges into the atmosphere of London and the past: "He lived, so far as a wit sharpened by friction with the real permitted him, in his imagination; but if life was for this faculty but a chain of open doors though which endless connections danced there was yet no knowledge in the world on which one should wish a door closed" (p. 46). He gives himself up in a kind of watchful ecstasy to the sense of the past. He is supported by an artistic faith (and an

[20] The donnée is the same as in "The Passionate Pilgrim" (1876); among later tales it is found in "The Third Person" (1900). The setting of the old family home, with all its usual symbolic connotations, is found in "Flickerbridge" (1902) and in "The Birthplace" (1903), where it is cheapened by advertising and commercial exploitation.

artistic fever), by a "desire to remount the stream of time," to look behind and still behind:

his interest was all in the spent and the displaced, in what . . . had been presented as a subject and a picture, by ceasing—so far as things ever cease—to bustle or even to be. It was when life was framed in death that the picture was really hung up. If his idea in fine was to recover the lost moment, to feel the stopped pulse, it was to do so as experience, in order to be again consciously the creature that *had* been, to breathe as he had breathed and feel the pressure that he had felt. The truth most involved for him, so intent, in the insistent ardour of the artist, was that art was capable of an energy to this end never yet to all appearance fully required of it. [Pp. 48–49]

His faith (and his fever) is such that everything in the house seems alive to him, or indeed haunted. It was "a museum of held reverberations still more than of kept specimens" (pp. 67–68). A new Columbus ("He had sniffed the elder world from afar much as Columbus had caught on *his* immortal approach the spices of the Western Isles" [p. 59]), "he liked to think, as he took possession, that his kinsman was watching, and therewith waiting, beyond the grave" (p. 45). His solitary visit in the late afternoon turns into a vigil—a typically Jamesian vigil. "As the house was his house, so the time, as it sank into him, was his time" (p. 66); yet Ralph is troubled by a kind of "divination . . . that from such a plunge . . . he might possibly not emerge undamaged—or even . . . not emerge at all" (p. 70). The suspense deepens, moments of vision and of troubled perception increase. Having reached the sanctum sanctorum of the house, facing the mysterious portrait of a young man with averted face, Ralph has the impression that the portrait lives.[21] In the darkness of the night, holding a candle in his

[21] According to Cargill, *The Novels of Henry James*, p. 488, the idea of the living portrait derives from *The Castle of Otranto* (1764) by Horace Walpole. In the Scenario Sir Cantopher is characterized as a "little Horace Walpole man," though no such character seems to be in that novel. It would simply take too long to list here the numerous tales and novels in which James used the motive of the portrait: among the latest, "The Tone of Time" (1900). James expatiates on the function and the

hand, Ralph confronts the climax of his initiation—the reward of his long vigil. He is met by someone with another candle, the figure in the picture had turned, and: "The young man above the mantel, the young man brown-haired, pale, erect, with the high-collared dark blue coat, the young man revealed, responsible, conscious, quite shining out of the darkness, presented him the face he had prayed to reward his vigil; but the face—miracle of miracles, yes—confounded him as his own" (pp. 87–88).

The possibility cherished by Ralph has become reality, a kind of ghostly and supernatural experience. He exchanges role and personality with his 1820 kinsman; he is going to take his place in the past. But according to James's principle expressed in the *Notebooks*, nothing is said of the way in which the exchange takes place. Nothing is said of the fantastic substitution, of the pact that must have sealed it, of the plunge itself into the past. This is according to another habit of the later James, who would often state in the Scenario the outlines and the details of the action and deal in the book only with the "sense" and the outcome of the "mere" facts recorded in the Scenario or the notebook entry. The reader who does not know the Scenario is thus very often compelled to wander in a maze of possible interpretations and ambiguities; he is involved in a process of gradual discovery of meaning. It is a peculiar process of "abstraction" on the part of the writer, which deserves a closer scrutiny. It operates in the case of *The Ambassadors* (a full Scenario of which is also extant), and it is clearly stretched to its utmost limit in *The Sense of the Past.* [22]

---

thematic meaning he would attribute to the portrait in the central part of *The Sense of the Past* in pp. 344–48 of the Scenario. The motive of the mysterious and almost ghostly "Holy of Holies" of the house is found, among others, in "The Aspern Papers" (1888) and "The Birthplace" (1903).

[22] Enrique Gomez, in a most perceptive early review of James's "Two Unfinished Novels," *Egoist*, 5 (1918), 3–4, writes of "the progressive devouring of the novel by the rapacious 'scenario'" as "the malady to which his writing had succumbed." In our novel one sees how James

After Ralph's shock of recognition, we see him, in fact, in the house of the ambassador, engaged in a sort of lay confession that reminds James himself of Hilda's confession in Hawthorne's *The Marble Faun*. Ralph's confession is developed as a dramatic scene but it is seen from the point of view of the protagonist: "the very law of my procedure here is to show what is passing in his excellency's mind only through Ralph's detection and interpretation, Ralph's own expression of it" (pp. 292–93). It is for Ralph a way of communicating his secret to the world, of leaving a trace behind before plunging into the past. For James it is instead the means of giving as little necessary information as possible, while at the same time subjecting it to the scrutiny of the ambassador's wary skepticism.

Ralph is, then, no longer himself. He has exchanged epoch and personality with his predecessor, who was as much interested in the future as he is in the past. But he is scared by the enormity of the fact and fears the possible outcome of the experience on which he is setting out. It is at this point that such an experience betrays all the complexity of its temporal levels, of its dislocation in time. "I've brought him, I've given him, I've introduced him to, the Future," Ralph announces, and this has been possible because he himself is, for his kinsman, the future: "Why, I am the Future. The Future, that is, for *him*; which means the Present, don't you see—?" "The Present, I see, for *me*!" the ambassador rejoins (p. 104).

But it is not that simple. As is immediately clear from what happens in Book 4, the past in which Ralph finds himself on going back into the mysterious house and in which he lives as if it were the present, conceals at least part of its secrets. Ralph finds that he has to *divine* at each step the *course* of his action. He must live, that is, not in a past he is acquainted with, not in an easy-going present, but in an abstract and unreal time that he must at every moment discover. He lives in what he believes is the past while

---

"touch after touch would have gone on obliterating the outline which had in conception such sharpness and distinction."

ignoring its facts; he is compelled to reenact and to recon-
struct the past while living it. He is *free* to choose his movement
in a situation which—being past—is *preordained*, has already
happened.

It is a complication of no little moment—as James himself
noted in the Scenario—which may partially account for his
decision not to follow the parallel adventures of the other man
(the 1820 man) in 1910. But it is also a stroke of genius:
this is the real motive of Ralph's anguish in the past, a past
which he does not fully know and which threatens to betray
him at every moment. And it is the real motive of his
anguish just because Ralph Pendrel is the center of consciousness. Ralph, according to the very nature of this fictional
principle, is a *limited* center of consciousness and point of view;
and this very limitation is the source of his anguish, of
his particular predicament, of his shame. Once more, as in
The Sacred Fount, the technical device is responsible for the
complexity of the story, which is all the more complex in
The Sense of the Past in that Ralph's consciousness is divided
between his consciousness of the past and his consciousness of
the present.[23] He reflects and registers his own anomalous form
of experience in an abstract time that, among other things,
compels him to divination.

Ralph intuits that in the past he must have been a suitor
for Miss Molly Midmore's hand. This is the moment when he
feels that "things came to him . . . in the very nick
of being wanted" (p. 121)[24]. It is a recognition, however, of

---

[23] As James wrote in the Scenario: "The very beauty of the subject is
in the fact of his at the same time watching himself, watching his success, criticising his failure, being both the other man and not the other
man, being just sufficiently the other, his prior, his own, self, not to be
able to help living in that a bit too. Isn't it a part of what I call the beauty
that this concomitant, this watchful and critical, living in his 'own' self
inevitably grows and grows from a certain moment on?—" (p. 300).

[24] It is worth noting that in the typescript of Book 4 (now in the Houghton Library of Harvard University) the words "in the very nick of being
wanted" are added over three cancelled lines. (Parenthetically, Aurora
was originally called Charlotte.)

what he himself terms a "foretaste";[25] a recognition of small facts (the death of his father, an estrangement between the two families, and so on) which gives him at first a sense of harmony and assurance, of exhilarating consciousness ("he knew the flood of consciousness within him to raise its level" [p. 125]). One is reminded of the Narrator in *The Sacred Fount*. "Knowing myself and yet being someone other—", in T. S. Eliot's words in *The Four Quartets*; and sometimes, as in the case of Eliot, "the words sufficed / To compel the recognition they preceded."

Ralph "was in the actual free use of the whole succession of events, and only wanted these pages, page after page, turned for him" (pp. 125–26). Even when he feels he is "lagging a bit behind," "he had for the next thing even the sense of being, and in the gallantest way, *beforehand* with her" (p. 126: my italics). He himself must at times "inform" the ignorance of the others, who may take "inspiration" from him. A heuristic exaltation ("Every question became answerable, in its turn, the moment it was touched"; "each improvisation, as he might fairly have called them all, gave way without fear to the brightening of further lights" [pp. 129 and 134]) turns Ralph into a "most prodigious professor of legerdemain" (p. 135). But if he hopes to find and to bring peace, soon his gift of divination puts him in a false relationship with the characters in the past and—in the long run—with himself.

At every moment Ralph is shaken by some need he has to fulfill, by a risky decision he has to make. But, for the first time, and significantly about the identity of Nan, Miss Midmore's young sister, the flash of consciousness and of divination fails him. Now it is time for Ralph to get "as in the glimmer of a flash the measure of the wonders he had

---

[25] "That he was to make love, by every propriety, to Molly Midmore, and that he had in fact reached his goal on the very wings of that intention, this foretaste as of something rare had for days past hung about him like the scent of a flower persisting in life" (p. 121). Further on we shall read of "those fruitions of the Future which have constituted his state" (p. 337).

achieved, and getting it through this chill of the facility stayed" (p. 175). He must realize the misery of his abnormal state. As James wrote in the Scenario: "Ralph has 'taken over' from the other party to his extraordinary arrangement certain indications that have been needed for starting the thing . . . very considerably, very enormously, assimilated. Enormous, however, as the assimilation may be, it is not absolutely perfect, and I don't exactly get out of this wavering margin, this occurrence of spots and moments, so to speak, where it falls short, just one of those effects of underlying distress, of sense of danger, as I comprehensively call it, which are of the finest essence of one's general intention?" (p. 300).

Here is the beginning of Ralph's predicament, in the failure of awareness, in the impossibility of guessing at every step the path he has to take. Here is the source of his anguish, of his fear of having forfeited the present in an avowed incapacity to be equal to his task, to act in the projection of a virtual future that he has to discover at every step. James speaks in the Scenario of a "quake in the dread of muchness" (p. 295), of a dismay in the face of the number of possibilities. Ralph, like the Narrator of *The Sacred Fount*, may flounder in the sea of possibilities. Maxwell Geismar, in spite of his many misreadings, is right in speaking of a "psychological nightmare very close to *The Sacred Fount*," in which the protagonist assumes that he can get over hurdles through his "intellect" and must, therefore, suffer an alteration of mood between false omnipotence and true panic.[26] Ralph, too, is an "observer-manipulator," ruling the scene from a tightrope and finding himself at a disadvantage *because* of his need to know. As in the case of the Narrator of *The Sacred Fount*, the other characters "affected him as really hanging on his choice." "It was as if he did precipitate wonders, at a

---

[26] *Henry James and the Jacobites*, pp. 426–30. It is a pity that in his brilliant essay "Henry James and the Trapped Spectator" L. C. Knights did not deal with *The Sense of the Past*, which would have perfectly suited his argument.

given juncture, just by some shade of a tone, a mere semi-quaver . . . . to surmount and surmount being exactly his affair, and success in it his inspiration" (p. 240). His drama is once more that of the baffled need—and will—to know, of the gap between reality and the imagination.

But if there are links, there is no mere repetition. F. O. Matthiessen is, to my knowledge, the only critic who grasped the deepest meaning of Ralph's predicament. He perceived the drama of Ralph's double consciousness and the "abstract" quality of his terrors, but he also grasped the burden of his forced projection into an unnatural future ("he can know his situation only as he enacts it"). In this tour de force, Matthiessen warns us, we are led to share "Ralph's excited consciousness of discovering, in the very nick of time, the reactions appropriate to the unforeseeable situations." But the key to this attitude is to be found for Matthiessen in an appropriate statement that A. R. Orage made shortly after James's death: "James was in love with the next world, or the next state of consciousness; he was always exploring the borderland between the conscious and the superconscious."[27] Ralph is in this sense a victim of his "superconsciousness," which has driven him into the past and supported him in his process of gradual discovery but which then leaves him in a state of painful frustration and leads him—or compels him—to the ambitious attempt of *modifying* the past.

Courting "the next state of consciousness," as Ralph does, is to be projected into the future. To modify the past is to violate its innermost nature, betray its reasons, deny its validity. Ralph is led to this by the fact that the sense of his real self, his 1910 self, begins to predominate in him:

His divination and perception of *that* [the others' malaise] so affect and act upon him that little by little he begins to live more, to live

---

[27] Matthiessen, *Henry James: The Major Phase*, pp. 135–36, and *The James Family*, p. 592. The statement by A. R. Orage quoted by Matthiessen is in *Readers and Writers* (1922), p. 10.

most, and most uneasily in . . . his own, his prior self, and less, uneasily less, in his borrowed, his adventurous, that of his tremendous speculation, so to speak—rather than the other way round as has been the case at first. When his own, his original, conquers so much of the ground of that, then it is that . . . his anguish gets fuller possession of it. [P. 301]

It comes back to him, it comes over him, that he has freedom, and that his acting in independence, or at least acting with inevitability, has laid this trap for him—that he has deviated, and of necessity, from what would have happened in the other fellow's place and time. [P. 322]

By going back to his real self not only does Ralph jeopardize his divination (even if the visit of Sir Cantopher restores much of his power); he also takes on the role of savior to Nan, his fiancée's younger sister, who has been kept in the country and may face a marriage of convenience. "He didn't *want* to back away—he but wanted again . . . to have a perch held out to him across the fall-away of familiar ground, long enough to be grasped without his moving" (p. 253), James warns us. Nan's appearance on the scene arouses a "sudden earnestness" in Ralph, who feels immediately like a knight-errant and a rescuer of maidens because he finds in her not the charm of the past but, significantly, a trace of modernity. " 'Why she's modern, *modern*!' he felt he was thinking—and it seemed to launch him with one push on an extraordinary sea" (p. 280). The extraordinary sea is still the sea of possibilities, and of the future.

The man who has gone back into the past almost by sheer force of imagination finds a true link with the girl who has a sense of modernity and of the future. The inexperienced young man who had ministered to Aurora Coyne (the majestic lady who had known the world, the cinquecento princess out of a picture by Titian or Veronese) has now had his adventurous experience; and he now leans toward the girl who reminds him of some Virgin by Van Eyck or Memling, the girl who has suffered. Ralph, it is true, is attracted by Nan's imaginative nature ("There were things

in her world of imagination . . . which might verily have
matched with some of those, the shyer, the stranger, the
as yet least embodied, that confusedly peopled his own"
[p. 282]) and by their mutual understanding ("she sees—
that is *he* sees *that* she sees" [p. 310]). But the purport of this
development, unfortunately present in the Scenario only, as
the draft of the book breaks off here, is sufficiently clear.
Ralph unconsciously looks for and finds in the past the link
with the present. The past, sought after and experienced as
such, has given him only anguish and unease. Being compelled to project himself at each step onto a virtual future,
he chooses the way of modifying the past. Yet modifying
the ordered development of the past amounts to a refusal of
the past as such, to a disowning of his early enthusiasm.
Furthermore, he modifies the past in order to escape from it.

   This was to be the reproach leveled at Ralph by his alter
ego, who has reappeared in the past to make him aware that
"he, Ralph, has done the other fellow a violence, has
wronged the personality of the other fellow *in him,* in himself, Ralph, by depriving him of the indicated, the con-
sonant union with the fine handsome desirable girl whom
the 1820 man would perfectly and successfully have been in
love with, and whom he would have kept all unalarmedly
and unsuspiciously in love with him. Deviation, violation,
practical treachery, in fact . . . aggravated moreover by the
interest taken in, the community of feeling enjoyed with,
the younger girl—for whom . . . the other fellow wouldn't
have cared a jot." (p. 322).

   It is clear that in this sense Ralph has not lived in the past
at all, or has lived in it only to deny and to refuse it. This is
so true that James himself had doubts in this respect.
Further on he was to write that if Ralph does not repeat the
past, "where is definitely that Past, that made and achieved,
that once living and enacted Past which is the field of his
business?" (p. 341). But this is exactly the point. Despite
James's attempts to reestablish a correspondence between
the actions of the two characters in the past, he himself states

that Ralph "deflects in the midst of it, yes, by the uncontrollability of his modernism" (p. 341). In whatever way one sees it, Ralph does something that is completely foreign to the very concept of the past. And this is not all. As a proper knight-errant Ralph was at first to offer to stay in the past in order to save Nan. But he was eventually to ask for her help and to accept *her* sacrifice in order to be able to come back to the present. The dramatic choice is between his giving up the present to stay with Nan, and her giving up love and safety to free him from the past and allow him to go back to the present. It is significant that Ralph's need for the present would have prevailed. This means, of course, a total failure of his longed-for experience in the past. It also means that in the end he would have reverted, both structurally and thematically, to Aurora Coyne.

A last book would have given the novel a harmonious and symmetrical conclusion by bringing Aurora Coyne back on the scene to provide "the solution of the solution" (p. 350). Aurora has gone through a "psychic evolution" in America and has "understood" the prodigy of his adventure. She comes, therefore, to London to rescue him this side of time, just as Nan had rescued him on the other side. James thought at first of a "climax" between Ralph and Aurora—Ralph face to face with Aurora—which would correspond to the big opening scene of Book 1. But here as elsewhere, according to the abstracting procedure typical of his later years, a second thought led James to imagine a "triumph of indirection" for his conclusion: an interview between Ralph and the ambassador, who has found him coming out of the haunted house, during which he learns of Aurora's arrival and sends her a message that he will be glad to see her. As this seems to me the perfect example and the clearest statement of James's abstracting and indirect method, I shall quote his final, exultant chuckle over his discovery: "A far more ingenious stroke, surely, and to be made more ministrant to effect and to the kind of note of the strange that I want than the comparatively platitudinous direct *duo* between the parties! He has only to give us in advance all that the duo must and will consist of in order to leave us just where, or at least just *as*, we want!" (p. 358).

3

Ralph would have won the initial wager and the challenge. After his experience he is no longer "the 'mere' person, the mere leader, of the intellectual life, the mere liver in a cultivated corner" (p. 351). He has become like Aurora, both for the quality of his experience and for the final choice he makes. Thematically they are bound to correspond, just as structurally the book was to end on their significant (though merely suggested) reunion. Ralph's central experience—his return to the past—proves just as painful as Aurora's European experience, and like hers it ends in disappointment and failure.

This is due, as in the case of *The Sacred Fount*, partly to the young man's too impassioned imagination and intellect; partly to his double consciousness; and partly to the fact that, as a particular type of intelligent observer, Ralph is a manipulator of his (and the others') experience. Choosing to live in the past, but without all its elements, he then modifies its development and puts himself outside the pre-ordained situation to live in an unpredictable and unnatural kind of future. This thematic twist, as we have seen, was also dependent on the particular type of center of consciousness created by James.

Leaving this interesting complication aside, we are still confronted with the surprising meaning which the international theme and the peculiar Jamesian motive of the contrast between Europe and America acquire in the book. In *The Sense of the Past* the usual terms are reversed, and consistently so.

We saw that in the beginning the European experience had led Aurora Coyne to accept and prefer America over

Europe. She had warned Ralph against not only a "super-stitious valuation" but the actual experience of Europe. Ralph's experience in the European past is equally nega-tive, and not merely on account of his peculiar situation. In spite of the ecstatic pilgrimage in Book 2 (written, however, as early as 1900), Europe and the past are utterly defeated and explicitly denounced in the novel. The romance turns into nightmare, reveals its inner emptiness and ugliness. Quite contrary to his habit, in Book 4 and still more in the Scenario (both written in 1914–15) James dwelt upon the mean and sordid aspects of Europe and the past. One has only to think of the hardly disguised greediness of the Mid-mores for Ralph's money, of which his cousin Perry openly avails himself; of their Tory meanness and their far from spotless past; of their closed society and their stuffiness, in which Ralph feels smothered from the start. One can think of their treatment of Nan, kept away in Drydown, of their discussion about European marriages, of Sir Cantopher, of Molly's suspicious limitations. In the Scenario James made it clear that Ralph's charm depended on his 1910 refine-ment, his cleanliness, his perfect teeth, the material advan-tages of his civilization. The material and spiritual condi-tions of the Europeans were in marked contrast: generosity and disinterestedness, physical and moral cleanliness are to be found, among the Midmores, only in Nan, the one who was "modern." It is to Nan that Ralph reveals "how poor a world she is stuck fast in compared with all the wonders and splendours that he is straining back to, and of which he now sees only the ripeness, richness, attraction and civilisation, the virtual perfection without a flaw" (pp. 337–38).

The European past betrays a sense of narrowness, dirt-iness, and suffocation. Ralph's experience in it is useful to him in purely negative terms. If the past, as Sartre main-tains, is an exponential value—its value depending on the value we attribute to it—then here the exponent is zero and the value nil. In any case it is absurd, painful and chilling to stir the ghosts of the past and the possible, here as in "The

Jolly Corner," except that the past and the possible are here represented by Europe and not by America.

A tentative explanation may be suggested for this reversal, by relating the book to its time and its position in the James canon. An explanation is offered by Oscar Cargill: James wanted to react to the contemporary vogue of historical fiction, to the superficial exploitation of historical themes in contemporary novels. He wanted to oppose a widespread romantic veneration for the past. In fact his novel avoids all concessions to a mannered representation of the past, and seems in an almost antithetical position to Adams's in *The Education of Henry Adams* (1906).[28] Although one cannot say with Stephen Spender that James (being "a sincere admirer of H. G. Wells's scientific romances") was imagining his own time machine, his attempt is in some ways similar to Mark Twain's attempt in *A Connecticut Yankee in King Arthur's Court* (1889), as Edmund Wilson remarked with an insight marred only by his insistence on the supposed ambiguity of the book.[29]

It may be true, as Osborn Andreas remarks, that James wanted to explore "a beguiling but unsound escape mechanism"—the romantic view of the past. One might also

[28] Cargill, *The Novels of Henry James*, chapter on *The Sense of the Past*, passim. Osborn Andreas sees it not as a historical novel but as a "story of contemporary people living in a contemporary world" (*Henry James and the Expanding Horizon* [Seattle, 1948], p. 104).

[29] Spender, *The Destructive Element* p. 105; Wilson, "The Ambiguity of Henry James": "Here the Jamesian ambiguity serves an admirable artistic purpose. Is it the English of the past who are ghosts or the American himself who is only a dream?—will the moment come when *they* will vanish or will he himself cease to exist? And, as before, there is a question of James's own asking at the bottom of the ambiguity: Which is real—America or Europe?—a question which was apparently to be answered by the obstinate survival of the American in the teeth of the specters who would drag him back. (It is curious, by the way, to compare *The Sense of the Past* with Mark Twain's *Connecticut Yankee:* the two books have a good deal in common)" (in *The Triple Thinkers* [New York, 1948], p. 114). The second part of the quotation seems more relevant than the first: there is no ground for the suspicion that the American may be "only a dream."

accept the archetypal meaning which Northrop Frye attributed to the story: a variation on the theme of the pilgrim's perilous journey in the monster's belly or in the labyrinth, from which he is rescued thanks to Ariadne's sacrifice.[30] Europe and the past as nightmare, unsound escape mechanism, dark labyrinth; the present as safety but requiring a sacrifice. It is all very well. Yet the most convincing explanation is perhaps to be found in James's own human and artistic evolution. In the last novel of the major phase, *The Golden Bowl,* James had already reached a fairly balanced definition of the complex relation between Europe and America. America still carried the day on the moral level, as the place of salvation away from European corruption and as peaceful retreat in spite of its dreadful social barrenness.[31] In view of the anti-American position of many of his later tales,[32] the rediscovery of America in *The American Scene* (1907) was already a sign of partial reconciliation, even allowing for numberless elements of irritation and the nightmarish quality

[30] Andreas, *Henry James and the Expanding Horizon,* p. 104; Northrop Frye, *Anatomy of Criticism* (Princeton, N.J., 1957), p. 190: "in the most complex and elusive of the later stories of Henry James, *The Sense of the Past,* the same theme [of the perilous journey in the labyrinth or the monster's belly] is used, the labyrinthine underworld being in this case a period of past time from which the hero is released by the sacrifice of a heroine, an Ariadne figure. In this story, as in many folktales, the motif of the two brothers connected by sympathetic magic of some sort is also employed." In this case the first statement seems more relevant than the second.

[31] This is the view held, among others, by Leon Edel, *Henry James: The Master,* pp. 209–23, Laurence Holland, *The Expense of Vision,* pp. 331–407, and Dorothea Krook, *The Ordeal of Consciousness in Henry James,* pp. 232–324. For a contrasting view, see R. P. Blackmur's introduction to the Dell edition of *The Golden Bowl* (New York, 1963), and Quentin Anderson, *The Imperial Self: An Essay in American Literary and Cultural History* (New York, 1971), pp. 166–200. On the whole question, see Ruth Bernard Yeazell's valuable study *Language and Knowledge in the Late Novels of Henry James* (Chicago, 1976).

[32] It is analyzed by Leon Edel in his introduction to the *Complete Tales,* XII, 7–9.

of the landscape. The reconciliation was achieved in the pages of the unfinished Autobiography—the youthful idyll of a lost America of the heart cheerfully revisited and recaptured. *The Ivory Tower* confronted the most complex and peculiar American reality, from which James had so far kept at a safe distance: the grim reality of wealth and money analyzed in the country where it is produced and where it conditions the mind and the soul of man.

Back in Europe, like a true artist James found himself, as he grew old, more and more interested in the present, and indeed the future. Now, the future, for him as well as for many others before and after him, was the image of America, which was vindicated in a book called ironically *The Sense of the Past*. To use a felicitous expression of Howells (in *Venetian Life*), James too seemed to realize, after the early enthusiasms, that "in fact, the Past is everywhere like the cake in the proverb: you cannot enjoy and have it." *Everywhere*: here, in particular, in Europe. Having courted the past for so long, James found that he did not enjoy it any more. He no longer cherished it; he denied and disowned it; he seemed to reject its call, to denounce its sirenlike voice and its subtle deception. On the eve of his death he was not afraid to reverse a lifelong allegiance; he could not conceal his recognition of the value of the present, the here and now, of America. The celebration of this new view was entrusted to a book which, according to Lyon N. Richardson, makes us "sadly aware of our loss of a complete masterpiece. It would surely have been, we feel, the greatest of ghost stories, with a thrill, a *frisson*, entirely new to literature. . . . we have the extraordinary effect, not of a ghost from the past who haunts the present, but of a ghost from the present who goes to haunt the past, and who . . . comes to yearn with a passionate anguish of home-sickness to get back to the humane, familiar modern period out of the strangeness and horror of an age that is not his own."[33]

[33] Richardson, introduction to *Henry James: Representative Selections* (New York, 1941), p. xlix. According to E. Gomez—and his early per-

We might for a moment see in it James's final recognition. That on the eve of his death, while turning over the pages of *The Sense of the Past,* James decided to become a British citizen paradoxically confirms this view. Confronted with American isolationism at the beginning of World War I, James wanted to testify to his deeply felt involvement in the cause of Europe. But this was also his first great gesture of hope and engagement in the present, of confidence in the future.

---

ceptions are indeed startling—James was here reaching out toward something Jamesian beyond James, "something so difficult that one holds one's breath still at the terrifying risk of the experiment . . . . it might have been the pattern of a story which could have given James's final word on the civilized American." Gomez writes of "an equally acute and imperative sense of the Present, a sense of the present becoming more articulate and pressing just as the past dominates, for it becomes thus a sense of the Future. . . . The whole thing," he concludes, "was so difficult as to be perhaps just within James's powers" ("Two Unfinished Novels," pp. 3–4).

VI. *The Ivory Tower* and the Nightmare of the Present

1

BOTH OF JAMES'S unfinished novels are experimental, in subject matter as well as technique. *The Ivory Tower* represents his final and almost baffled attempt to grapple with the American theme and at the same time the final stage of his refining subject matter out of existence by the operation of experimental technique. The American theme is here preeminent, but it is confronted and conveyed in terms of absence rather than presence, and this is borne out on the level of technique. The two aspects are, as usual, strictly interwoven and mutually dependent. Yet it would be hard to envisage a further development on those lines: the form of the novel reaches here what seems its utmost limit of abstraction and then breaks off.[1]

The Ivory Tower was, to begin with, a belated outcome of James's two final visits to America in 1904–5 and 1910–11 and of the "shock of recognition" that inspired his magnificent *The American Scene*. Many coincidences and points of contact have been noted in these two works.[2] In spite of James's disillusionment with America (and with the New York Edition of his novels and tales), in August 1908 he had written to Howells

[1] To read through James's work chronologically, as Robert Marks has written, "is to note a perpetual outgrowing of stages and phases, an artistic evolution that culminated only in the very 'last words' left incomplete by his death." At seventy "he had not yet exhausted his capacity for innovation and was still continuing to improve his quality, to refine further his literary methods and thought" (*James's Later Novels,* p. 131).

[2] See, among others, Donald D. Mull, *Henry James's "Sublime Economy": Money as Symbolic Center in the Fiction* (Middletown, Conn., 1973), pp. 166–70; Peter Buitenhuis, *The Grasping Imagination: The American Writings of Henry James* (Toronto, 1970), pp. 239–40; Matthiessen, *Henry James: The Major Phase,* chap. 5.

that he might want "very much to go back for a certain thoroughly practical and special 'artistic' reason"; four months later he wrote that he had "fortunately broken ground on an American novel." This novel *may* be the one referred to as "The K. B. Case" in the *Notebooks*, although no mention is made there of an "American novel."[3] The original "Katrina B. Subject" was indeed envisaged as an international subject, and as such was developed in the so-called *Mrs. Max* entries of 1909–10.

Most of the names found here were to be used in *The Ivory Tower*, and James was clear in his intention of dealing with the story in a dramatic way, much (though not completely) in the way of *The Outcry*: "I come back, I come back yet again and again, to my only seeing it in a dramatic way—as I can only see everything and anything now." Here he spoke also of *The Other House* as giving him "at every step a precedent, a support, a divine little light to walk by." And here, too, he saw the principle of the limited point of view and the indirect approach as working hand in hand with the scenic method: "we have these facts, as we have others, given us by Cissy Foy as she gives them to Davy Bradham."[4] Yet his subject was an American woman suddenly thrown upon the world by the death of the husband she had nursed for ten years, who was to "decide for adventure" abroad against her mother-in-law's wishes. In Europe Nan was to be accompanied by her friend Cissy Foy and "approached" by Horton, who was presumably after her money. There is no mention of a possible American locale, and it is clear that Nan's money and her consequent wish for freedom, experience, and initiation would have worked as a trap for her as with Isabel Archer and so many early Jamesian heroines. The preliminary setup of characters, however, foreshadows to some extent that of *The*

[3] *Letters*, II, 103 (17 August 1908) and 119 (New Year's Eve 1908); *Notebooks*, pp. 343–44, (1909); and Cargill, *The Novels of Henry James*, p. 463 (for the contrary opinion).

[4] *Notebooks*, pp. 348–69. There are references, too, to the general ugliness of the American world, and to the "crude atmospheric optimism" of a New York April afternoon (p. 359).

Ivory Tower: Nan would give some of her traits to Rosanna; Cissy and Horton seem here already linked in a kind of unspoken conspiracy and share quite a few of their later characteristics (Cissy is "archi-modern; she is the Europeanized American girl").[5] In his final outline of the action, James worked it out according to a "binary system" of relations among characters, which we shall find resumed and developed in *The Ivory Tower*.

Even if superficial, these links are of a certain interest. However, *Mrs. Max* was dropped after just a few pages. When the real work on *The Ivory Tower* was begun in London in 1914 the conception had notably altered and deepened. James was writing his autobiographical reminiscences at the time and had published no fiction for three years. But he was still, as he wrote in his beautiful letter of 31 March 1914 to Henry Adams, "that queer monster, the artist, an obstinate finality, an inexhaustible sensibility. Hence the reactions—appearances, memories, many things, go on playing upon it with consequences that I note and 'enjoy' (grim word!) noting. It all takes doing—and I *do*."[6] In his later days, after so many years of dodging and evading, he was to tackle in fiction no less a subject than America. And it was to be a long novel—his final coming to terms in a fictional way with his country.

Out of the projected ten Books, he managed to complete the first three and the beginning of the fourth (a total of 267 pages), plus a full Scenario of the novel. The Scenario is in fact an unparalleled sequence of working notes by a master-craftsman and a master novelist which leads us straight into an artist's workshop and allows us to participate in his painful struggle with his subject, in his fumbling and groping for solutions, in his moments of triumph or dejection. Ezra Pound called them "the formula for building a novel."[7] They are

---

[5] Ibid., p. 357.

[6] *Letters*, II, 361. His equally celebrated outburst against H. G. Wells ("It is art that *makes* life") is of 10 July 1915 (ibid., II, 490). See chapter 3 above.

[7] Pound also saw them as "a landmark of the history of the novel as written in English" (in terms of form) and as an accumulation of James's

this, and something more: Henry James caught in the act of writing, a transcript of his fictional genius at work. They are interesting in themselves, and in their very elusive relation to the novel itself. Their scrutiny provides a revelation not only of James's later method but of the process of absolute refinement to which he subjected his material. Here we see how his abstract fictional worlds and ways were consciously conceived and nourished, tested and projected, realized and (as it were) canceled in the process. There is no better place to study his stretching of the possibilities of the novel to their breaking point, while always stopping short of the actual break. Going from the Notes to the completed books (and vice versa) is a perfect exercise in fictional hermeneutics. The Notes are there to support and at the same time to *deny* the novel. They provide the scaffolding, the characters and the plot, the time and space relationships, the moral bearing and the thematic links, the development and the purport of the subject. But once all these have been established, tested, and made clear in the Notes, they can be dispensed with in the novel itself. They are clear in the mind of the author and are present behind the pages of the book—but not in the book as such. They are its necessary premises, not its substance. The novel proceeds on the assumption that they are there, but without ever bothering to name or state them, to recall or suggest them. Once the Scenario is drafted, its facts are taken for granted but are not incorporated into the actual book. The novel develops on a detached, higher level, which severs as many links as possible with the underlying structure provided by the Scenario or the Notes. It hovers, as it were, over them, but is free and loose from the drudgery of facts, the constriction of plot, the specification of motives. These have been relegated to the Notes; the author can now proceed unhampered on his cherished level of greater and greater fictional abstraction.

I have dealt at some length with these premonitions of analysis because they seem to me to touch on the essence of

craftsman's knowledge. He wanted them printed at the beginning—to be read at first for excitement (*Literary Essays*, pp. 333–37).

James's later fiction and technique and to account for the exhilarating feeling of void and disconnectedness that they seem
to provoke in the reader. We are in such a rarefied atmosphere
and at such altitude that the feeling of the outer void and
emptiness is always present. The conscious (and often unconscious) process of transition from the Notes to the novel itself
is one of the causes that help to explain the deeper nature
of James's later fiction, which is so dependent on his experimental method. That all this is perfectly visible in a book that
was to deal fully–and deals fully, in its completed part—with
the American theme goes a long way to clarify the particular
nature of James's interest, of his particular concern with
America, and of his treatment of it. It is also a further proof
of the coherence and value of his experimental method, just as
it might raise the suspicion that it is responsible for the sudden
break in composition and the unfinished state of the book. The
subject matter was indeed being stretched to breaking point.
We know, however, that James was writing against failing
health and a strained psychological condition. Furthermore,
when World War I broke out, he felt that the world for which
he had struggled and written was doomed to disappear in
slaughter and destruction. Dealing as he was with a contemporary subject, he felt, as he put it in a revealing letter to Hugh
Walpole, that "the subject-matter of one's effort has become
itself utterly treacherous and false—its relation to reality utterly
given away and smashed. Reality is a world that was to be
capable of *this*—and how represent that horrific capability,
historically latent, historically ahead of it? How on the other
hand *not* represent it either—without putting into play mere
fiddlesticks?"[8]

He had to break off under pressure of the actuality of
the war. He could only go back to writing of a far-off,
purely imaginative, ghostly subject such as that of *The Sense of
the Past*, "as perhaps offering a certain defiance of subject
to the law by which most things now perish in the public
blight."[9] Both novels were left unfinished at his death.

[8] *Letters*, II, 446 (14 February 1915).
[9] Ibid., p. 426 (1 December 1915, to Edith Wharton).

2

First, then, the beautiful scaffolding and the perfect plan. As everything was to be "of the shade of the real," James has a few preliminary skirmishes on the question of names—rescuing some from *Mrs. Max*, testing the subtle significance of others. Horton's surname must not be intrinsically pleasing. The possible Grabham instead of Foy, for Cissy (a name James was dissatisfied with to the very end) is discarded as "too meaningful" and assonant with Bradham. The big, heavy daughter of the billionaire, Rosanna (or possibly Moyra) must have a single-syllable, odd, and ugly surname; from the thumping Chown, James was to revert to the birdlike Gaw. These are minor points, but not so trivial if names have to "fit" their owners, as Pound saw, to be hitched to and expressive of their characteristics (pp. 271–72).[10]

Then the master builder sets to work. It *is* a question of building, raising a structure, constructing an architectural model. In no other place has James so stressed the role of the novelist as architect, mason, and joiner. Each of the books of the novel is envisaged as part of the huge structure, to be resolved in dramatic terms and to serve a specific purpose. James is at this point at the farthest remove from the concept of the organic form in its romantic sense; he is working here to sort out and build in a mechanical, almost scientific way. The strong and symmetrical construction will be a guarantee of order and balance, of tight structure and unified vision. The drama will develop *inside* that structure; the proliferation of aspects and the organic growth of the subject will take place *within* that architectural scaffolding. In this way James's form is functional and "organic" precisely in the architectural sense, while allowing for the display and the growth of his dramatic tensions: "This is exactly what I want, the tight packing *and* the beautiful audible

---

[10] In this chapter, page references in the text are to *The Ivory Tower*, ed. Percy Lubbock (1917; rpt. New York, 1945).

cracking" (p. 278). At the same time, a subtle interplay is set going between the fixity of the outer form and the inner turmoil, the jolts and the overflowing caused by the dramatic principle working from the inside.[11] "Intensities of foreshortening, with alternate vividness of extension: this is the rough label of the process" (p. 326), as James was to write later on. But a closer scrutiny of the process is needed.

The ten books constitute an overall (or macro-) structure that is highly symmetrical and will allow the action to develop and be concluded in an almost circular or concentric way. Each of them has a specific function in the pattern and is organized according to the dramatic principle: "By the blest operation this time of my Dramatic principle, my law of successive Aspects, each treated from its own centre, as, though with qualifications, *The Awkward Age*, I have the great help of flexibility and variety; my persons in turn, or at least the three or four foremost, having control, as it were, of the Act and Aspect, and so making it *his* or making it *hers*" (p. 276).

As we saw in the previous chapters, the dramatic principle aims, on the one hand, at conveying character and meaning through objective action. On the other hand it is linked with and modified by the controlling presence of one of the characters, who is put there to provide his or her view of the facts. Here it is made very clear that it is not only a question of point of view but of "the law of successive Aspects": each character is in turn point of view, central intelligence, and *controlling structural principle*. Later

[11] "Form follows function," as Sullivan had said. And as J. A. Ward has remarked: "What Mark Schorer says of *The Good Soldier* applies as well to James's late novels: 'The mechanical structure . . . is controlled to a degree nothing less than taut, while the structure of meaning is almost blandly open, capable of limitless refraction' " (*The Search for Form: Studies in the Structure of James's Fiction* [Chapel Hill, N.C., 1967], p. 27). To avoid too much linguistic clumsiness and repetition ("was to be," "was meant to be," "would have led to," etc.), the discussion deals hereafter with the plan of the novel as a realized entity of its own. The completed parts will be seen later on.

on in the Notes James speaks of "help by alternations" (p. 349): the new twist of the method whereby the novelist moves consistently and functionally from one controlling presence to another, from one point of view to another, to achieve variety and special effects within the ordered structure of his books. Furthermore, each scene of the book (or "aspect of the Act") tends to be built on the "binary system" that has been hinted at before: two characters are usually paired off in turn for interviews, encounters, or meetings—to have it out, as it were, between them, and react on each other. In these cases one leads while the other follows; one controls while the other is astray; one gives out while the other takes in information, knowledge, and awareness.

Book 1 is meant to present the American characters—the Gaws, the Bradhams, and Cissy Foy—in three successive and separate "aspects," and thus to "present with them the first immediate facts involved," "the first essence of the Situation" (p. 273). They are waiting for the appearance in America of the Europeanized protagonist, Gray (or Graham) Fielder, who will set the action going: he is on the premises but only "learnt so to be," and will appear only in Book 2. Book 1 is Rosanna Gaw's book, or "Aspect," but it takes place, according to the principle of alternation, partly at Mr. Betterman's, partly at the Gaws', and partly at the Bradhams'. The cards are dealt, the scene described, and the main characters defined. Book 2 is Gray's book; it records his appearance on the scene and his three crucial encounters with old Abel Gaw, with his uncle, Mr. Betterman, and with Rosanna. Book 3 is in turn "functional entirely for the encounter of Gray with the two other women"—Cissy Foy and Gussie Bradham—and with Davey Bradham, and for introducing Horton (or Haughty) Vint— Gray's antagonist and the second great spring of the action. This is in part Horton's book (Horton as affected by Gray) and in part Cissy's book, while Book 4 "is to present Gray as face to face with the situation so created for him" (pp. 276–77).

The first three books establish, therefore, the preliminaries of the action, the locale ("The action entirely of American localisation, as goes without saying": Newport and then New York [p. 278]), and the tentative relationships among the characters.[12] These are then analyzed in detail, both in their present state and in their "fundamentals in the past." Gray Fielder has been brought up in Europe and "alienated" from his wealthy uncle, Mr. Betterman, who objected to his mother's marriage and even more to her second marriage in Europe to an Englishman. Gray's alienation has taken the form of his refusal of his uncle's proposal to go back to America; in this decision he has been influenced and confirmed by Rosanna Gaw, who had seen in him "a tremendously initiated and informed little polyglot European" (p. 282). Rosanna's attitude was motivated by hatred of Mr. Betterman, by her infatuation with Europe, and by her growing disgust with "the dreadful American money-world of which she figures as the embodiment or expression in the eventual situation" (p. 286). Her role has been to bring Gray back to America to his dying uncle (Mr. Betterman, a financier who has improved with the years and through suffering) out of a sense of responsibility: "the sense of what she may perhaps have deprived him of in the way of a great material advantage" (p. 288). Being the daughter of a hardened billionaire, Mr. Gaw, and hating every dollar of his, she is going to restore Gray to his rightful inheritance. In a very Jamesian way she will replenish Gray's emptiness. And she succeeds, because Gray's utter lack of interest in money, of business knowledge, and of American connections is an irresistible asset in the eyes of his uncle. He becomes then almost as replete with money as Rosanna, who is left an equally vast inheritance by her dying father.

This is the first "relation," in James's terminology, and the first "joint" of the action. The second is between Gray and Horton, who in the past has saved Gray's life and who is quite

---

[12] James thought for a moment of perhaps treating himself "to some happy and helpful mise-en-scène or exploitation of my memory of (say) California," and "for dear 'amusement's' sake, to decorate the thing with a bit of a picture of some American Somewhere that is not either Newport or N.Y." He thought also of Boston as a possible setting (p. 278).

the opposite of Gray's "utter queer and helpless and unbusiness-like, unfinancial type." "He had made Gray think a lot about the wonderful American world that he himself long ago cut so loose from, and of which Horty is all redolent and reverberant" (p. 290). Back in America with money, Gray will entrust its administration to Horton, who will gradually (and predictably) steal most of it from him. This, as we shall see, is the main line and development of the story, its thematic center and its specific moral concern. But a third relation (and "joint") springs immediately into action: Horton's relation with Cissy Foy—"the poor Girl, and the 'exceptionally clever,' in a society of the rich, living her life with them, and more or less by their bounty" (p. 298). James warned himself of the risk of repeating the figure of Char-lotte Stant in *The Golden Bowl* (with the Bradhams standing a bit for the Assinghams in that novel), just as he was aware of the danger of repeating the Merton Densher–Kate Croy relationship in *The Wings of the Dove*: Cissy Foy is in love with Horton, "so far as she, by her conviction and theory, has allowed herself to go in that direction for a man without money . . . and he [is] in love with her under the interdict of a parity of attitude on the whole 'interested' ques-tion" (p. 300–301).

Given "the frankness of their recognition, on either side, that in a world of money they can't *not* go in for it, and that accordingly so long as neither has it, they can't go in for each other" (p. 301), their mutual relationship becomes a beautiful threefold relationship with Gray (a fourth relation or "joint"): "They give each other rope and yet at the same time remain tied" (p. 303). Horton has proposed to Rosanna and has been rejected by her; Cissy strikes Gray "as the creature, in all this world, the most European and the most capable of, as it were, understanding him intellectually, entering into his tastes . . . the being, up and down the place, with whom he is going to be able to *communicate*" (pp. 303–4). Gray cannot communicate intellectually or aestheti-cally with Rosanna, and he is drawn to Cissy. The binary relations begin to cross and multiply, and new parallelisms are established. Cissy is also drawn to Gray, but after a "moment or season of exhilaration" he may begin to be affected by the same terror as Rosanna: is Cissy making up to him on account of his money?

One has to stop for a moment, as James does here in the notes. Once the complex relations among characters have been established and worked out, the action itself is set going, the novel moves forward, the adventure is on the way. Plot, one might say, depends on the determination of relationships. As James puts it: "What I want is to get my right firm *joints*, each working on its own hinge, and forming together the play of my machine: they *are* the machine, and when each of them is settled and determined it will work as I want it" (p. 304). We move straight into Book 4 and the following (unwritten) books, straight into Gray's own adventure, the center of the novel, both structurally and thematically. James devotes beautiful pages to the growing tangles of the central situation, to its crucial developments and to its gradual unraveling. As in *The Sense of the Past*, the protagonist plunges into a completely new world (here it is America, and New York in particular), develops a growing malaise, and goes through an agonizing experience. Just as he is beginning to have a glimpse of Horton's dealings (James calls this "the Joint that is in a sense the climax of the Joints" [p. 313]), he begins to wonder about Cissy's attitude. She in turn begins to doubt him, "to think him really perhaps capable of strange and unnatural things" (p. 308), such as giving his money away. Horton in the meantime is getting more and more "monied" and "splendid." Does not this imply that Cissy would naturally go back to him, back to Horton, who is now getting rich, away from Gray who is being depleted? In this way "she helps him [Gray] to his solution about as much as Horton does": and the solution becomes, as so often in James, a question of acquired awareness and achieved knowledge, of apprehension and vision.

The central part of the novel was to deal primarily with

Gray's inner adventure and with his process of vision. Books 4 to 8 were to be all Gray's "Aspects," all seen from his point of view and controlling center: "I make my march between IV and VIII inclusive all a matter of what appears to Gray," we read toward the end of the Notes (p. 349). These books were to be much more "conscience" than "action," to avail themselves more of an indirect than of a direct "dramatic" presentation. They are centered, as in so many other Jamesian cases, on the question of "seeing". "A tremendous Joint is formed . . . when the first definite question begins to glimmer upon Gray . . . as to what Horton is really doing with him" (p. 313). "He sees—well what I see him see"; but then, of course, "a Joint here, a Joint of the Joint . . . is Horton's vision of his vision" (p. 314) and Cissy's vision of Horton's improvement. Seeing what *she* sees is for Gray a confirmation of what he himself begins to see about Horton, and a crucial moment of inner pride: "She has them, each on his side, there in her balance" (p. 316). This gives dramatic quality to Gray's apprehension: "The fascination of seeing what will come of it—that is of the situation, the state of vigilance, the wavering equilibrium, at work, or at play, in the young woman. . . . He really enjoys getting so detached from it as to be able to have it before him for observation and wonder as he does, and I must make the point very much of how this fairly soothes and relieves him, begins to glimmer upon him exactly *through* that consciousness as something like the sort of issue he has been worrying about and longing for" (pp. 317–18).

Gray's central adventure is that acquisition of knowledge about his—and *their*—situation, and this involves a greater amount of "illustrational play," of "going 'behind' " Gray. As James himself noted in some preliminary remarks on Books 3 and 4 (partially reported and discussed by Peter Buitenhuis), he wanted to see his characters from the outside, without dealing with their real "consciousness"—except with "Gray's very own when I truly go for it." There was no "going behind" the characters who were dealt with altogether as seen by the others, in action (including Rosanna in Books 1 and 2: "I give her appearances and aspects and semblances and motions there, but at no point speak as from myself for what is actually beneath; and this I keep up for all the rest of the business.").[13] Everything was to be done "on the Rosanna-Davey lines", on the "Horton-Cissy and Cissy-Horton lines," or the Cissy-Davey lines (the "binary system" of interviews and encounters).[14] But in the case of Gray's central adventure James had "to go for it," and this involved "going behind" him extensively in the central books. "The state of mind and vision and feeling, the state of dazzlement . . . is a part of the very essence of my subject" (p. 312), James wrote, and Gray was to become at this point "another of the 'intelligent,' another exposed and assaulted, active and passive 'mind' engaged in an adventure and interesting in *itself* by so being" (p. 340). Gray was to become one of James's typical intelligent and detached observers—"he really enjoys getting so detached from it as to be able to have it before him for observation and wonder" (p. 317)—whose adventure is essentially of the mind and requires, therefore, more illustration of conscience than external drama.

Gray's immersion in New York in the central books is also an immersion in the vagaries of human conduct and the mysteries of conscience. Structurally, thematically, and psychologically his is a plunge into a new world, both in a social and in a moral sense, and a painful acquisition of awareness. The denouement was to mark his "solution" of the case, his reappearance on the surface after an experience of dazzlement, doubt, and discovery often verging on estrangement. Books 8 to 10 provide the denouement in a minutely

[13] Quoted in Buitenhuis, *The Grasping Imagination,* pp. 240–41 (the MS Preliminary Remarks are in the Houghton Library at Harvard).

[14] Ibid., p. 241. Buitenhuis seems to misinterpret James's principle of "binary" scenes—scenes where one character reacts to another—as "lines of dialogue." James speaks of the "degree to which my planned compactness . . . must restrict altogether the larger illustrational play" (*The Ivory Tower,* p. 326)—"restrict," and not, of course, "abolish" or "cancel."

detailed sequence of dramatic scenes and "aspects," which were to correspond structurally as much as possible to the first three books, even if James's "rich indirectness" had by now gathered momentum. Gray's discovery that Horton and Cissy are "together," that she "takes up" with him, was simply the beginning of the solution.[15] James discussed at great length the various possibilities: an open discovery of their "treachery" by Cissy; Gray's direct confrontation of Horton; conversely, his forbearing, abstaining, and standing off; an outright confession by Horton, and so on. But James finally decided that he wanted "the *determination of suspicion* not to come at once; I want it to hang back and wait for a big 'crystallisation,' a falling together of many things" (p. 345). This was to come indirectly to Gray in an interview with Rosanna—in Book (or "Act") 8 of the drama, a climax of effects to be then measured out according to the familiar succession and alternation of "binary" scenes (Gray and Horton, Gray and Cissy). Scenes between Cissy and Gray, Cissy and Horton were to provide the substance of Book 9, which becomes Cissy's book, primarily, but also Horton's and Gray's, "twisting out, that is, some admirable way of her being participant in, 'present at,' what here happens between them as to their own affair" (p. 350). This had been partially the case with Book 3; for similar reasons of symmetry Book 10, like Book 1, was to be essentially Rosanna's book.

James did not expatiate, however, on the conclusion of the story. He tended rather to emphasize its symmetrical disposition and its cyclical development. The action, he wrote,

[15] In a doctoral dissertation, *The Ivory Tower: America Reconsidered,* discussed at the University of Venice in 1975, Maria Teresa Carlevaris draws this convincing diagram of the structure of the novel and of the coinciding adventure of the protagonist (numbers refer to books, arrows to the movement of the action):

1–3   4–7   8–10

"represents and embraces the sequences of a Year" (p. 352), a year that he later stretched to fifteen or sixteen months. He delineated with care a symbolic development from the summer in Newport of his "exposition" through the winter in New York of the central books to the conclusion in the late summer and autumn of the next year in Newport again (or possibly Lenox: Books 9 to 10). He thought of ending on an indian summer note, back where he had begun: "This brings me round and makes the circle whole" (p. 354), he wrote, and also: "It gives me the central mass of the thing for my hero's own embrace and makes beginning and end sort of confront each other over it" (p. 351). It is clear that the exposition and the conclusion in a summer resort were to enclose and seal off the dreadful winter experience in New York as if within brackets. This confirms the relevance of the diagram sketched in footnote 15.[16]

Yet one has to note, first, that James was in this way clearly changing metaphors, working definitions, and structural patterns. This kind of circular development of the action is rather an outcome of the organic growth of the material. It is indeed an example of organic form, which tends to break from within the very principle and the buildup of the scientific and mechanical scaffolding, the tightly balanced structure that James had begun and proceeded with for quite a while. There is little doubt that the symmetry

[16] See note 15 above. Books 1–3 are expository and preliminary (Newport: the left arc), on the outside of the central circle, which is then gradually entered. The revolution inside the inner circle is completed (books 4–7, winter in New York) in thematic and symbolic terms of experience and rejection; a slow emergence from the inner circle follows (summer and autumn in Lenox: right arc, books 8–10); a release, and almost back to where we started. The outside circle is *not* complete: Gray is not where he was at the beginning and will probably go back to Europe (see below). See Buitenhuis, *The Grasping Imagination*, where the shift to the organic form and the cyclical pattern is stressed: "Another organic factor in the novel was to be in the time scheme. . . . He planned to make the temporal cycle concentric with the cycle of adventures of Gray from his arrival in the United States until his departure" (p. 141).

of disposition tends to give way here to a cyclical pattern and to a circular definition of the events. It is as if, as the Notes grow, the original tight scaffolding opens up under the pressure of its inner springs. James knew perfectly well and noted that "in closer quarters and the intimacy of composition, prenoted arrangements, proportions and relations, do most uncommonly insist on making themselves different by shifts and variations, always improving, which impose themselves as one goes and keep the door open always to something *more* right and *more* related" (p. 350). This happened in the completed part of the novel, and it would probably have increased, according to the final indications of the Notes, if he had written the whole of it.

Secondly, if the tight and symmetrical scaffolding tends to open up, the circular movement is not perfectly closed: it remains open, too (as shown again in the diagram of note 15). It is not simply a question of the novel being obviously unfinished, but of the conclusion being left undecided, problematical, practically suspended (as are the Notes themselves). This ties in very well with James's typical inspiration, but also with the particular thematic concern of the novel—his final grappling with the theme of America. This thematic concern was to remain by definition and by practice open and problematic. It stands and indeed thrives here not so much on steady views and definitions as on fascinating but shaky and open grounds, on tentative and elusive rather than full details; on the tension of emptiness and voids, on absence more than presence. Here indeed James is brought round in his thematic development, which is closely related to and dependent on his particular form and technique.

3

The novel reverses James's lifelong pattern and fictional scheme. Not only is it wholly set in America; it avails itself of a typical American situation, to which a "European" (born

in America, Gray has lived all his life in Europe) is
exposed and has to react. Something of the kind, but in the
vein of comedy, had happened in *The Europeans* (1878). In *The
Ivory Tower* the seriousness of purpose and attitude is motivated
by James's belated wish to "do" America in fiction, to recon-
sider his abandoned country, to confront its tumultuous
experience and expansion. He was attracted just as much
as he was repelled, according to the ambivalence inherent in
his late vision of America.

In intention, at least, as we read in the Notes, "my whole
action does, can only, take place in the last actuality. . . . Therefore it's a question of all the intensest modernity of every
American description" (p. 355); "I want to keep the whole
thing, so far as my poor little 'documented' state permits,
on the lines of absolutely current New York practice" (p. 353).
Much in the way of his creator, Gray Fielder goes back to
America with curiosity and expectation, almost as a "passionate
pilgrim." Horton calls him romantic; "it wasn't at all
in readiness for the worst that he had come to America—he had
come on the contrary to indulge, by God's help, in apprecia-
tions, comparisons, observations, reflections and other luxuries,
that were to minister, fond old prejudice aiding, to life at
the high pitch" (p. 255). And "if he had come back at last
for impressions, for emotions, for the sake of the rush upon
him of the characteristic, these things he was getting in a
measure beyond his dream" (p. 74). He has much in common—
and the comparison deserves a closer scrutiny—with Spencer
Brydon in "The Jolly Corner" (1908). Like him, Gray goes
back in a way to what he might have been had he
stayed in America, to see or realize himself in the forsaken
country of his birth:[17] and like him, his expectation of wonder
and his dazzlement will turn into a malaise (if not, as in the

---

[17] Cf. "If he made the sufficient surrender he might absolutely himself
be assimilated—and that was truly an experience he couldn't but want to
have" (*The Ivory Tower*, p. 76) and also "I revel in everything, I already
wallow, behold: I move as in a dream, I assure you, and I only fear to
wake up" (p. 83; see also p. 160). For parallels with "The Jolly Corner"
see *The Complete Tales*, XII, 193–44, 197, and passim.

tale, into horror and nightmare) and a gradual rejection. Before entering the nightmarish experience of meeting his ghostly alter ego, Spencer Brydon is confronted by a world where "there are no reasons *but* of dollars," by "the comparatively harsh actuality of the Avenue." Gray Fielder's expectation will not and cannot possibly be realized because waiting for him in America are only the remnants of two rapacious old financiers and the last betrayed and impoverished specimens of that once so charming creature—the American girl. In America he will also find social and moral corruption: a complete reversal of James's early view of American innocence versus European corruption.

The novel opens on the lovely summer atmosphere of Newport—already used as a setting in some early works, fondly revisited in *The American Scene*, and almost reminiscent, according to S. Gorley Putt, of pre-1914 Balbec in Proust.[18] But as for the people: Abel Gaw is the retired businessman with nothing to retire to, who has dispossessed himself "of every faculty except the calculating" and thinks in figures. He is there, perched "like a ruffled hawk, motionless but for his single tremor, with his beak, which had pecked so many hearts out, visibly sharper than ever" (p. 6), shamelessly spying on his former associate and sharer in the spoils Frank Betterman, who had swindled him. Gaw is waiting for him to die, and will die himself when hearing that the other is improving. As his daughter Rosanna puts it in an agonized crescendo: " 'He's not dying of anything you said or did, or of anyone's act or words. He's just dying of twenty millions. . . . He's dying, at any rate,' she explained, 'of his having wished to have to do with it on that sort of scale. Having to do with it consists, you know, of the things you do *for* it—which are mostly very awful; and there are all kinds of consequences that

---

[18] *Henry James: A Reader's Guide* p. 403. *Du Côté de chez Swann* had been given to James by Edith Wharton in 1914 (Leon Edel, *The Master*, p. 496). James had written of Newport in an 1870 essay, collected in *Portraits of Places* (New York, 1883), chap. 23, in *The American Scene*, chap. 6, and in *The Autobiography* (1913–17), passim.

they eventually have. You pay by these consequences for what you have done, and my father has been for a long time paying. . . . The effect has been to dry up his life. . . . There's nothing at last left for him to pay *with*' " (pp. 140–41).

Gaw and Betterman are both shriveled specimens of financial obsession and sharp business practice; they are two perfect examples of callousness and moral insensibility. Betterman is "business" even at his dying hour because he cannot be anything else. Though partially improved and changed, he is alone, with no family or children left, with only his money to show at the end—that and a wish to "buy" his unknown nephew ("without a flaw") much in the way of Adam Verver buying Prince Amerigo in *The Golden Bowl*. These were the figures James evoked when he finally yielded to the temptation of portraying the American businessman in fiction—the only male type of recognizable features and status, for him, in the country.[19]

Rosanna Gaw, on the other hand, who has brought about Gray's return to America after having advised him in the past to stay in Europe, is no longer the "heiress of all the ages," "the plant of pure America growth," the frail carrier of culture so much cherished by James in his early fiction, from Daisy Miller to Isabel Archer. She is only the plump and clumsy heiress of twenty millions, psychologically uncertain and

[19] See *The American Scene*, p. 345 (but contrast pp. 348–52, headed "The Return of the Male") and passim; *Notebooks*, p. 129 (on the divorce of the American woman from the American male "immersed in the ferocity of business, with no time for any but the most sordid interests, purely commercial"); and his 1898 essay "The Question of the Opportunities," now in *The American Essays of Henry James*, ed. Leon Edel (New York, 1956), where we read that "the typical American figure is above all that of the 'business man,' " who "is often an obscure, but not less often an epic, hero" and remains, "*the* magnificent theme *en disponibilité*" (pp. 200, 202–3). See also Michael Millgate, *American Social Fiction: James to Cozzens* (New York, 1964), pp. 1–17, who discusses James's fictional businessmen—Newman in *The American*, Mr. Dosson in *The Reverberator*, Verver in *The Golden Bowl*, Jim Pocock in *The Ambassadors*, the two in *The Ivory Tower*, and some minor figures in the tales. They are all *retired* businessmen.

isolated. If her father "could sit with screwed-up eyes for hours the case was as flagrant in her aimless shiftings, her incurable restless revolutions" (p. 20). Nothing has been done to educate her, socially, aestheticlly, or intellectually: she is only "*morally* elephantine," a late example of the decay of the American girl that James had been watching with growing concern. In 1906–7, soon after his return to England, he had devoted two series of essays, under the titles "The Speech of American Women" and "The Manners of American Women," to an analysis and a deprecation of their impoverished state. The address he gave to the graduating class at Bryn Mawr in 1905, "The Question of our Speech," contained a plea for their resurrection, for their resuming their cultural and social role. In *The American Scene* he spoke of the "exposed maiden" and let her voice directly her anguish at her deprived and betrayed state: "falsely beguiled, pitilessly forsaken, thrust forth in my ignorance and folly, what do I know, helpless chit as I can but be, about manners or tone, about proportion and perspective, about modesty or mystery, about a condition of things that involves, for the interest and the grace of life, other forms of existence than this poor little mine—pathetically broken reed as it is, just to find itself all waving alone in the wind? . . . Haven't I, however, as it is, been too long abandoned and too *much* betrayed? Isn't it too late, and am I not, don't you think, practically lost?"[20]

The poor heroine of his tale "Julia Bride" (1908) is practically lost, with her six broken engagements and a mother three times divorced; she has to face "the sense of all the folly and vanity and vulgarity, the lies, the perversities, the falsification of all life in the interest of who could say what wretched frivolity, what preposterous policy, amid which she had been condemned so ignorantly, so pitifully to sit, to walk, to

[20] *The American Scene*, pp. 431–32 (also pp. 163–64 and 344–52); also *The Speech and Manners of American Women; The Question of Our Speech and The Lesson of Balzac* (Boston, 1905).

grope, to flounder, from the very day of her consciousness."[21] In another tale of this period, "Crapy Cornelia" (1909), the protagonist finds himself in the New York world of "breathless renewals and merciless substitutions," but he rejects the "music of the future" and the glossy, moneyed "high modernity" of Mrs. Worthingham in favor of the old reserves of poor Cornelia.[22] The women of James's last tales, as Leon Edel has observed, are of coarser grain, decayed or betrayed specimens of womanhood.[23] In *The Ivory Tower* Rosanna does not communicate with the other characters—the faculty of intimacy is not given her—and she is, moreover, "in the dreadful position . . . of not being able to believe she can be loved for herself" (p. 169). As with Catherine Sloper in *Washington Square*, her money and her family life doom her to suspicion, loneliness, and frustration. She is outside the cultural world of Gray just as she is outside the social world of the Bradhams. She is inhibited and traumatized by her money and her lack of education.

As for Cissy Foy, she has accepted the money world and acts within its premises and its boundaries. She is " 'Gussy's' charming friend, Haughty's charming friend, no end of other people's charming friend" (p. 260–61). A poor girl, she is helped and patronized by the rich, adopts their values and becomes their prisoner. In a sense she is a victim of their careless ways and ambiguous morals: she has to "earn her keep" "by multi-

[21] *Complete Tales,* XII, 154.
[22] Ibid., pp. 335–67.
[23] Introduction to the *Complete Tales,* XII, 9–10. As Christof Wegelin noted in *The Image of Europe in Henry James* (Dallas, 1958), James's American girl "had shamed the hereditary aristocrats of Europe by her natural nobility; in story after story he had endowed her with a 'moral spontaneity' innocent of acquired forms which found its foils and enemies among sophisticates whose very *savoir faire,* gave warning of a moral void. Now, after seeing her at home his trust in her unaided wisdom is shaken. Now he recognizes that he has been guilty of idealizing her: creature of his 'incurable prejudice in favour of grace,' the 'supposedly typical little figure,' he now was to confess, 'is of course pure poetry, and had never been anything else' " (p. 158).

plying herself for everybody else" (p. 44). She is conditioned
by her milieu. With Horton Vint she frankly shares the
recognition that "in a world of money they can't *not* go in for
it," and without it, "they can't go in for each other" (p. 301).
She loathes the American girl of whom she herself is a decayed
specimen. James watches her and Horton half in dismay and
half in sympathy. Even more than she is, Horton is expected
and doomed to live up to the money world, to make money in
one way or another. He is to be the future American businessman, such as Gaw and Betterman were in the past, and he is
to be involved in the same kind of malpractice as his predecessors. "The dream of my life has been to be admired, *really*
admired, admired for all he's worth, by some awfully rich
man"(p. 163), he admits; and to some extent he foreshadows
his destiny. He openly considers the possibility of Cissy's
falling in love with Gray; he himself has proposed to Rosanna,
has been rejected, but still "the woman whom he would give
truly one of his limbs to commend himself to is Rosanna, who
perfectly knows it and for whom he serves as the very
compendium and symbol of that danger of her being approached only on that ground, the ground of her wealth, which
is, by all the mistrusts and terrors it creates, the deep note
of her character and situation" (p. 301). He will eventually
betray Gray's trust and rob him of his fortune; but here his
and Cissy's behavior will allow for qualifications.[24]

As for the Bradhams, Gussy, with her "insolence of ease"
is "the vulgar rich woman able to afford herself all luxuries" in
some "inferior and desecrating use of them" (p. 45); there are
"abysses of New York financial history" of which Davey is a

---

[24] The motif of the unfaithful steward is central in James's very last
tale, "A Round of Visits" (1910), where the protagonist, Mark Monteith,
has been cheated of his money and wanders through the labyrinth of
New York to look for sympathy, only to be confronted by a friend who in
his turn is a swindler and commits suicide. The motif of treachery had
been also present in some very early tales such as "The Impressions of a
Cousin" (1883), "A Light Man" (1869), and "Guest's Confession"
(1872). See Edel, *The Master*, p. 505.

natural depository, and he is "beyond, he is outside of, all
moral judgments, all scandalised states" (p. 333). James rightly
wondered in his Notes: "Don't I really see the Bradhams thus
as *predatory*? Predatory on the very rich" (p. 332). They are
society people whose values are superficial and strictly related
to the use of the money-power and the money-prestige. To
complete the picture, there is Mr. Crick, the lawyer, almost
ludicrous in his totally "unfurnished state," in his being
reduced to the pure dryness of money: "it was with the substance of the desert . . . that the abyss of Mr. Crick's functional
efficiency was filled" (p. 241). He is "of such a common
commonness" as to be devoid of personal identity; the business
function has completely sapped and shaped his character.
"The enormous preponderance of money. Money is their life"
(p. 111), as Betterman sums it up for all of them.

To these people and to this world is Gray Fielder brought
back from Europe: and quite properly Rosanna is made to
face with alarm his "possible immediate question: 'Have you
brought me over then to live with *these—*?' " (p. 60).[25] This is
the burden of Gray's experience in America—his turning from
the expectation of wonder to dazzlement and disillusionment,
his going through the recognition of a new world tainted by
deception and subtle corruption. But the point is that he might
like, after all, what should upset him, that he may be pleased
with the final outcome of his adventure. He wasn't really there
to stay; he found what he might have expected and wished for
deep within him, and his belated discovery of the swindle
practiced on him is, after all, a release from his burden, a final
recapturing of his freedom. This seems to be the moral bearing
of the tale, its deep-buried thematic line, its saving grace. It

[25] Rosanna had previously stated that her motive was "to make up to
a person for the wrong I once did him" (p. 14), but she is then rightly
worried by the fact that "without her having thought of it enough in
advance, she had hauled him over to complications and relations" (p. 23).
By being instrumental in making Gray inherit money, Rosanna acts as
Ralph Touchett does in relation to Isabel Archer, and has to face similar
consequences.

ties in with the structural scheme that has been previously discussed, with the nature of the contenders and with James's complex view of life and literature.

Gray comes to America with the expectation that "things should prove different, should positively glare with opposition" (p. 75). As James wrote in his Notes: "I have felt my instinct to make him definitely and frankly as complete a case as possible of the sort of thing that will make him an anomaly and an outsider alike in the New York world of business, the N.Y. world of ferocious acquisition, and the world there of enormities of expediture and extravagance, so that the real suppression for him of anything that shall count in the American air as a money-making, or even as a wage-earning, or as a pecuniarily picking-up character, strikes me as wanted for my emphasis of his entire difference of sensibility and of association" (p. 336).

He is a "very special" and "exceptional" case, an "out and out non-producer," a "non-accumulator of material gain," a "deviation" from the American mode of money-getting: "I absolutely require the utterness of his difference to *be* a sort of virtual determinant in this relation" (p. 339), James wrote. Just because of his difference, Gray is at first delighted with America, with the people and their social ways, even with the sounds of American speech or the lack of consideration and social bluntness of his uncle's nurses. He feels faced with "some presented quarto page, vast and fair" (p. 86); "it's really worth a great pilgrimage [he tells his uncle] to see anything so splendid" (p. 102).

Gray is chosen as an heir by his uncle because he is so "different from *anything*" (p. 104)—because he knows nothing of "the market and the. hustle" (p. 113). "The question isn't of your doing, but simply of your being" (p. 115), he is told: "we require the difference that you'll make" (p. 110). Owing to his nature, Gray is even too willing to stress this difference, to remain a nondoer as he was in Europe. Here lies his trial, and partly his guilt. On the one hand, ignorant of the business ways of America as he is, Gray will prove an easy victim of the money interest and of human greed. He plunges into the American world with complete "innocence" and will come out of it with no more money than he had before the inheritance. The world of rapacious acquisition has no difficulty in stripping him of his wealth. The possession of money, as in so many other Jamesian stories, proves a subtle snare, not a way to freedom but to imprisonment, a means of betrayal. In the end Gray will be happy to come out of the circle of corruption and betrayal. But his is a special case indeed. Gray is at least partially responsible for his betrayal; he is far too willing to lose what he has gained, and by no means as blameless as he might at first appear.

His life in Europe is sheltered and secluded. In America he chooses—physically and metaphorically—to stay in an ivory tower: an ivory tower of wealth and ease, of detachment and noninvolvement, while someone else must do his work for him, perhaps even dirty his hands for him. Gray's handing over his business interests to Horton is motivated by a wish to repay him for having formerly saved his life. But his first interview with Horton, though conducted on a bantering tone, strikes deep truths. "I want to work off on you, Vinty, every blest thing that you'll let me" (p. 199), Gray tells him; "I *can't* stand the expense, and yet I don't for a moment deny I should immensely enjoy the convenience" (p. 202). Horton inquires: "I *must* be just the person, it strikes you, to save you all the trouble and secure you all the enjoyment?" (p. 199). And, with even greater precision later on: "Don't I, 'gad, take the thing straight over from you . . . when I see you, up in the blue, behind your parapet, just gracefully lean over and call down to where I mount guard at your door in the dust and comparative darkness? . . . you want me to take *all* the trouble for you simply, in order that you may have all the fun" (p. 216). Soon after, there is a talk of monarchs who "could still be irresponsible, thanks to their ministers' not being" (p. 252). Gray will not open the letter that presumably might tell him of the nefarious origin of his inherited wealth (though he does not destroy it, either). He wavers, as it were, between the profit and the loss, and so becomes partially responsible for it.

There is no doubt that Gray is a victim of a swindle, in particular as far as the Horton-Cissy relation is concerned. He is bound to be horrified by the way in which he can see the money principle at work in Cissy's wavering between him and Horton, when she begins to see that Horton *is* making money and becoming rich.[26] But it is clear that Gray's detachment, or indeed entrenchment in the ivory tower, is a form of escape from responsibility, of moral weakness and shared guilt.[27] Gray is in a way Horton's "secret sharer." James's first idea, as he himself noted, was that Horton's theft was "accepted and condoned by Gray as a manner of washing his own hands of the use of the damnosa hereditas. . . . Vulgar theft I don't want, but I want something to which Horty is *led on and encouraged* by Gray's whole attitude and state of

[26] "No better, no more vivid illustration of the force of the money-power and money-prestige rises there before him, innumerably as other examples assault him from all round" than when "he finds her believing in Horton just at the time and in proportion as he has found himself ceasing to believe, so far as the latter's disinterestedness is concerned" (p. 317). Cissy strikes Horton as wondering not *how* he is going to be rich, "*how*, at such a rate, has it come on," but *if* he is going to get rich, though James also speaks of "her wonderment as to the character of his methods" (p. 302). Horton, in turn, sees Gray once as "a sort of 'happy Hamlet' " (p. 191) and then as "resembling the man from Assisi" (p. 249).

[27] According to Adeline Tintner, "In *The Ivory Tower* James reverses the situation [of *The Sense of the Past*] by submerging a man of traditional training in the society of the future, America, from which he escapes figuratively and literally through the aid of an ivory tower". (The Museum World," in *Twentieth Century Views: A Collection of Critical Essays on Henry James*, ed. Leon Edel [Englewood Cliffs, N.J., 1963], p. 54). And see Matthiessen: "It certainly did not occur to him that Graham Fielder might feel himself equally trapped, that the resources of sensibility, that the manifold delight in personal relations might come to seem both inadequate and excessive in a society whose decay was no longer hidden beneath the surface" (*The Major Phase*, p. 149). I believe, however, that it *did* occur to James. See also Buitenhuis, *The Grasping Imagination*, pp. 256–57, and Marks, *James's Later Novels*, pp. 146–52, where Gray is seen as a "last example in James of a failure of integrity in thinking," as reverting to a selfish self and as guilty of a subtle perversion of life: "He is an extreme instance of the ravages of culture-hauntedness" (p. 146). Marks's is the most cogent case *against* Gray.

mind face to face with the impression he gets over there of so many of the black and merciless things that are behind the great possessions" (p. 295, my italics). This is, however, one side of the story—the first envisaged motivation of Gray's "covering" of Horton when he learns of his theft: "this being, he feels in his wrought-up condition after what he has learnt about the history of the money, the most congruous way of his ceasing himself to be concerned with it and of resigning it to its natural associations" (p. 296). Rosanna would have put to him that her resources, too, "that should enable her to do immense things . . . are so dishonoured and stained and blackened at their very roots, that it seems to her that they carry their curse with them" (p. 309); and this would have confirmed Gray in his decision to spare Horton and leave everything to him. Gray would thus have acted the part of the betrayed benefactor (partly in the manner of Milly Theale in her relation to Kate Croy and Merton Densher) who washes his hands of the tainted money he did not want to touch.

But the subtle and final point is that the power of money to corrupt is inescapable. It taints by its very presence; no ivory tower is sufficient to ward off the curse. Guilty of escapism and moral weakness for his selfish detachment and seclusion there, Gray not only condones but in a way shares Horton's guilt. James himself spoke first of "this huge constituted and accepted eccentricity of Gray's holdings-off" (p. 323), and then, even more clearly: "It has been my idea that this [Horton's] 'bad' figures in a degree to Gray as after a fashion his own creation, the creation, that is, of the enormous and fantastic opportunity and temptation he has held out—even though these wouldn't have operated in the least, or couldn't, without predispositions in Horton's very genius" (p. 341). "The beauty is in the complexity of the question" (p. 342), James noted. Gray is thus caught not only in the world of rapacious acquisition but in his hidden, secret share of guilt. There can be no triumph for him, there-fore, either in his act of generosity to Horton or in his envisaged return to Europe.[28] There can only be a recognition, perhaps, of achieved humanity; the value, as so often in James, is in the experience and the adventure, not in its possible outcome. If, moreover, in his later work neither Europe nor America is shown as triumphant over each other, here too the blame cannot be wholly placed on America and its business world. A subtle link is established between that world of ruthless acquisition and "the excess of 'culture' " and detachment that leads the "European" to his practical and spiritual defeat.

The fact is—and here James's mastery is indeed superb—that two voids are here evoked, defined, and made to meet. But no real clash, no real dramatic confrontation, is possible between two voids. These tend rather to balance, to remain in a suspended state, as was significantly the case with the novel and with its possible solutions. Absence rather than presence is the informing idea and guiding line of the book.

4

When James wrote of the "enormous difficulty of pretending to show various things here as with a business vision, in my

[28] "He *can*, he could go back to Europe on a sufficient basis: this fact to be kept in mind both as mitigating the prodigy of his climax in N.Y." (his letting Horton off [p. 339]). I do not share Matthiessen's view: "Perhaps James would also have been able to imagine here a solution for both Rosanna's and Fielder's problems in a free and growing life of culture that had put aside the curse of great wealth" (*The Major Phase*, p. 129). Nor do I accept Buitenhuis's idea that Gray "might choose Cissy," after all (*The Grasping Imagination*, p. 250), or the suggestion that Cissy might renounce Horton (See Cargill, *The Novels of Henry James*, p. 472). The most probable solution for Gray seems to me to be "back to Europe." And cf. Marks, *James's Later Novels*, pp. 155–57, for whom Gray "muffs" his chance in America and runs away from the life surrounding him, so that his final regression to Europe is to an ignobly peaceful and quiet and sterile existence. He is betrayed by himself, rather than victimized by the others; this makes *The Ivory Tower* an equivocal and double-edged novel of the greatest interest (p. 152).

total absence of business initiation; so that of course my idea
has been from the first *not* to show them with a business
vision, but in some other way altogether" (p. 293), he expressed a familiar attitude. He had spoken elsewhere of his
total lack of knowledge of the business world, and "often
bewailed" to Edith Wharton "his total inability to use the
'material,' financial and industrial, of modern American life.
Wall Street, and everything connected with the big business
world, remained an impenetrable mystery to him."[29] As he
had done in other novels, he chose the indirect method to
suggest what he could not evoke or describe directly, to cover
up, or make up for, his ignorance of the facts. As in the case
of the revolutionary world in *The Princess Casamassima*, however, in *The Ivory Tower* he tried to make that very absence
part of his fictional scheme and impact, to use it as a kind of
ominous, hovering, pervasive presence.[30] In the first place,
as usual, he wrote not of business practice and the business
mentality in action, but of their consequences; not of money-
getting, but of the effects and ravages of money. Secondly—
and here is the interesting twist—he had come to see the
American business world as, by its very nature, a huge void
and an enormous emptiness. His way of dealing in fiction with
that world, and the American world in general, was, therefore,
to name that void and to evoke that emptiness, to make them
felt and dreaded. Being full of money—a quantitative, not
a qualitative value—and nothing else, the American world
was by definition void and empty. The task of the novelist
dealing with the American theme could not be better fulfilled
than by his sketching and evoking that emptiness, by his

---

[29] Edith Wharton, *A Backward Glance* (New York, 1934), p. 176. Also
Matthiessen, *The Major Phase,* pp. 89–90; Bradford A. Book, "Henry
James and the Economic Motif," *Nineteenth Century Fiction,* 8 (1953), 141–
50; Millgate, *American Social Fiction,* pp. 13–14.

[30] As Pound shrewdly noted, James (like Hardy) did not ignore "the
undertow"—he "definitely isolated it" in *The Ivory Tower.* "James took his
scene mainly above the level of monetary pressure" (Ezra Pound, *Guide to
Kulchur* [New York, 1968], p. 288).

creating that impression and feeling of void. This seems particularly true of *The Ivory Tower*.

Relevant quotations have already been scattered throughout the previous analysis. We shall recall here that to say that Abel Gaw "was surrounded by the desert was almost to flatter the void into which he invited one to step" (p. 4). He has dispossessed himself of every faculty (except, we remember, the calculating); "the extent of his vacancy" (p. 19) is detailed by James in a list of all the things he does not do. Rosanna is almost as empty of social grace (but not of moral seriousness); we hear of her "envy and admiration of possibilities, to say nothing of actualities" (p. 45). Betterman, being business, cannot be anything else. Mr. Crick has no recognizable physical feature, and intercourse with him is "deprived of the flicker of anything"(p. 245). At the funeral of his uncle, when confronted by the New York business world, Gray is "conscious of a kind of a generalised or, as they seemed to be calling it, standardised face, as of sharpness without edge" (p. 248). Nothing much is said of New York in winter, but the crucial events of Book 8 were to occur "in the empty town, the New York of a more or less torrid mid-August" (p. 256). Newport, speaking for a moment of the setting, as we know from *The American Scene*, was an oasis of past associations and fond memories, a sort of neutral ground between past and present, Europe and America, in spite of its inhabitants and now ugly mansions. In the Notes, when speaking of his drama not being of fools or vulgarians, James added significantly: "it's only circumferentially and surroundedly so—these being *enormously implied and with the effect of their hovering and pressing upon the whole business from without*, but seen and felt by us only with that *rich indirectness*" (p. 340, my italics). This is a perfect description not only of his method but of the fact that the void is perhaps more pressing that the fullness of signs, that the implications are more relevant than the direct statements. That absence, in one word, is felt and effective because it is absence.

This, in a different and complementary way, is also true

of Gray, the antagonist and the European. He, too, is defined
and characterized above all in terms of absence; his adventure
is confined within a circle where one void meets another.
His, if anything, is a triumph of negation. There is no need
to recapitulate here the numberless hints and indications. It
is sufficient to recall the almost obsessive way in which
his lack of anything that he may have to show for himself is
stressed in page after page. He is described as detached and
as an outsider, a nonproducer and a nonaccumulator, as
someone who "doesn't know anything about anything" in
America, as a "blank" who is only supposed to be and not
to do. The "great fact" about him, for his uncle, is that he is
"out of it all," that he has no knowledge of business and of
the American world, that he is " not fit, in the smallest degree,
for the use, for the care, for even the most rudimentary
comprehension, of a fortune." He is liked and made to inherit
because he is "clear, to the last degree, not only of the financial
brain, but of any sort of faint germ of the money-sense whatever" (p.212). Two voids meet here, just as two voids meet
when, confronted with the "quarto page" of "all the candid
clearness" of America, Gray feels in the presence "of a volume
of which the leaves would be turned for him one by one and
with no more trouble on his own part than when a friendly
service beside him at the piano, where he so often sat, relieved
him, from sheet to sheet, of touching his score" (p. 86).

This image is repeated for Ralph Pendrel in *The Sense
of the Past*,[31] and the negative implications of Gray's retreat or
regression into the ivory tower of detachment and solipsism
have already been emphasized. His "negative" attitude is
of paramount importance in his relation with Horton, Cissy,
and, indeed, Rosanna—especially in his "encouragement"

[31] See Robert L. Gale, *The Caught Image: Figurative Language in the Fiction
of Henry James* (Chapel Hill, N.C., 1964), pp. 139–40. As for the "candid
clearness" of America, it also involves "the so universally and stupidly
applied American law that every man's face without exception shall be
scraped as clean, as *glabre*, as a fish's". (*The Ivory Tower*, p. 176). But Cissy
and Horton cannot decide whether Gray wears a moustache.

of Horton's theft. Forbearing, standing off, abstaining, letting
go, not putting "anything to a real and direct test"—these are
Gray's qualifying activities. He will succeed only in getting
rid of the inheritance, in going back to his former life and
self. The confrontation (if such a definition can hold) is
between two kinds of equally questionable voids, between one
kind of absence and another.

This development is worth noticing, because it seems to
represent the final issue of a lifelong Jamesian motive and
concern. His rejection of America, on fictional as well as
personal grounds, had started with a painful recognition of its
total lack of signs, of its emptiness and void. The well-known
and much abused passage in his *Hawthorne* (1879) sums up
this attitude: "No State. . . . No sovereign, no court, no personal loyalty, no aristocracy, no church, no clergy, no army,
no diplomatic service, no country, no palaces, no castles,
nor manors, nor old country houses, nor parsonages, nor
thatched cottages," etc. etc.[32] What interests us here is that
that definition is reached by a long list of *negative* items; it is
qualified through negation and determined in terms of
absence. Now, this application of the negative qualification—or of the "negative imagination," as it has been called in
another context—is much more common in James's fiction
than it would seem at first. It runs through his work as a subtle
hidden thread; it proves to be a recurring feature and acts

[32] *Hawthorne,* ed. Tony Tanner, p. 55. This is taken almost verbatim
from an early *Notebook* entry (p. 14). Other loci classici where James
writes of the emptiness of America are in various letters (see, e.g., *Letters,*
I, 22–23 [13 October 1869] and 36–37 [14 January 1874]; II, 297–98 [23
February 1913], etc.), in his *Autobiography,* and in more than a few short
stories. James was originally dismayed by the lack of signs in America
because he deemed them essential for the realistic writer or the novelist
of manners. His *Hawthorne,* with its attack on romance and the allegorical
method, ought to be read in close connection with, and as a counterpart to,
his essays on the French realists collected in *French Poets and Novelists*
(1878). By going to England, where the historical and social signs were
available in great (even too great) profusion, James thought he could
do for the Anglo-American novel what Balzac and Flaubert had done for
the French novel.

as a deep motivation. It involves the definition of his characters as well as the action of his plots. Absense and negation are in James powerful and characterizing motives. One could easily list the places where the lack of items, qualities, and features, the lack of anything to show, the absence of all connections acts as the motivating force, as strong attraction, as a pivot of the action. In *The American Scene* the "lack of signs" in the South will reappear as the only recognizable and qualifying sign. And I shall only quote for our purposes from that long and revealing central sequence in *The Portrait of a Lady* where it is made very clear that Isabel is attracted to Osmond for negative reasons, for his lack of everything, for his emptiness:

"Who and what is then Mr. Gilbert Osmond?" [asks Caspar Goodwood; and Isabel:] "Who and what? Nobody and nothing. . . . He's not a business. . . . He's not rich; he's not known for anything in particular. . . . He comes from nowhere. . . . He has no profession." [He doesn't know America and has done "nothing at all]."

. . . . .

"There is nothing *of* him [Mrs. Touchett insists later on]. "He has no money; he has no name; he has no importance."

. . . . .

"Mr. Osmond has never scrambled nor struggled [Isabel maintains to Ralph]—he has cared for no worldly prize. . . . Your mother . . . is horrified at my contenting myself with a person who has none of his [Lord Warburton's] great advantages—no property, no title, no honours, no houses, nor lands, nor position, nor reputation, nor brilliant belongings of any sort. *It's the total absence of all these things that pleases me.*"[33]

To go back to our novel: its distinguishing trait lies in the fact that *both* contending parties are qualified by emptiness and void. The attraction exercised by "absence" works on Gray in his relation to America and in Betterman's relation to Gray; in Gray with Horton (his lack of money), just as in Horton with Gray (his lack of knowledge). Absence and emptiness, in *The Ivory Tower*, involve both America and Europe.

[33] *The Portrait of a Lady* (New York, 1908), II, 46–47, 54–55, 73–74 (my italics). Note the almost perfect coincidence, from a stylistic point of view, with the *Hawthorne* passage quoted above.

Hence its sense of eeriness (almost similar to that of *The Sense of the Past*) and abstraction, in spite of—because of?—its American theme. But all this, to come to my conclusion, is paralleled and brought about by the concomitant abstracting process of technique. We saw that the principle of a "rich indirectness" is applied to the delineation of the characters and their relations. We also noted that the transition from the Scenario to the novel is characterized by a process of abstraction, by a gradual blurring or exclusion of facts and features. What is stated in the Scenario is taken for granted, subsumed, considered as given; it is only partially transferred into actual narration. As early as 1918 Enrique Gomez had written of the "progressive devouring of the novel by the rapacious 'scenario.' "[34] Not only the scaffolding, but the story line and all actions between characters tend gradually to disappear. We are given only hints and guesses. As James puts it in the novel itself: "The general hush that was so thick about them pushed upward and still further upward the fine flower of the inferential" (p. 216). "The fine flower of the inferential": it is a perfect description of James's technique in *The Ivory Tower*, his unmistakable mark.

Theme and technique were to touch and to coincide in the crucial Gray-Horton relation. Gray, as we saw, was not going to put "anything to a real and direct test" between them. But when James writes that "the extent to which i's are not dotted between them, are left consciously undotted . . . —the way, I say, in which the standing-off from sharp or supreme clearance is, and confirms itself as being, a note of my hero's action in the matter, throws upon one the most interesting work" (pp. 322–23), he is describing both his "action" (or lack of action) and his technique in the novel. All i's are here consciously, purposefully left undotted. *The Ivory Tower*, in its completed parts, is a triumph of not-telling, the crowning pitch of the "unsaid." James is so aware of it, that more than once he openly acknowledges his method.

Rosanna'a refusal of Horton's proposal happens (if this

[34] Gomez, in his review of James's unfinished novels, *Egoist*, 5 (1918), 3.

is the right word for a total absence of action) *without* his proposing and *without* her refusing; it is simply a question of her feeling that he would propose, and of his recognition that he would be "checked." As James writes, "It stuck to her somehow that they had touched still more than if they had loved, held each other still closer than if they had embraced. . . . the fact that might most have affected, not to say concerned, her had remained the least expressed" (p. 58). There could not be a better description of this impalpable meeting of minds, of this light touching of souls, feelings and impressions, perceptions and surmises, that in the novel substitute for action. As for Cissy and Horton: "they were far beyond any stage of association at which their capacity for interest in the contribution of either to what was between them should depend upon verbal proof. It depended in fact as little on any other sort, such for instance as searching eyes might invoke; she hadn't to look at her friend to follow him further—she but looked off to those spaces where his own vision played, and it was by pressing him close *there* that she followed" (pp. 160–61).

"Verbal proof" is dispensed with as much as possible. These people meet only, in accordance with their state of "absence," where their visions play, not on any ground of action, still less in the flesh. Now, the crucial point is not only that the novel records these brushings and meetings in the void; it does so by renouncing its very nature, by refusing to tell and describe, to state and define. The novel becomes an exercise in abstraction and abstractness. "Here have I been with you half an hour without you practically telling me anything!" Horton tells Gray—and for Gray this becomes "a piece of information of the greatest relevance" (p. 221). There is not so much a distrust in verbal communication, as no need or willingness for it. Encounters between characters are characterized by silences, minimal gestures and subliminal looks, mere attitudes of mind and suggested hints, rarely (except perhaps in the Gray-Betterman interview) by open statement and direct avowals. The play is indeed the play

of the inferential; implications submerge facts. The movements of hands and eyes, the smallest gestures express and
convey the meaning and carry the process forward. Reticence,
on the very level of language itself, is the prevailing mode of
expression. People talk but do not converse—their utterances
brush but do not meet. A "rich indirectness" pervades every
aspect of language. A mere flicker of the eyes or the trace
of a smile releases more energy and carries more meaning
than statements and definitions. Passages such as these are
even too frequent: "So that after all perhaps his caring so little
what went on in any world not subject to his direct intelligence
might have had the qualification that he [Gaw] guessed
she [Rosanna] could imagine, and that to see her, or at least
to feel her, imagine was like the sense of an odd draught about
him when doors and windows were closed" (p. 11). "Only
here he was for her clothed in the right interest of it, not bare
of that grace as he fancied her guessing herself in his eyes"
(p. 131).

They are not only a product of James's later manner or of
his tiredness. They reveal an attitude of mind as well as a
stubborn linguistic and fictional purpose. It is a functional
triumph of what James called "the silent exhibition," where
even lapses of speech are relevant and meaningful. These
winding, suspended sentences fill in the void while suggesting
its presence, while making it felt. In this connection even
the use of images and metaphors serves a purpose not so
much of concrete reference as of abstraction and removal
from reality. Those metaphors and symbols (like the ivory
tower that Gray prefers to the cigar case) or those episodes
(like Gray's envisaged gift of pearls to Cissy) that tend to
bring the level of expression down to a factual level are the
least effective of all. James's figurative language becomes
here a coat and a patina designed to blur the contours rather
than to make them stand out.[35] We are in a state of suspension,

[35] For the linguistic and stylistic question, see, among others, Newton
Arvin, "Henry James and the Almighty Dollar," *Hound & Horn*, 7 (1934),
437; R. W. Short, "The Sentence Structure of Henry James," *American*

of hovering and void that involves form as well as subject matter, where technique and attitude, style and thematic concern meet and are mutually dependent. Because the emptiness is there—social as well as existential—and James had found his way of suggesting and expressing it *in its own terms*. He had grasped the deeply abstract nature of his crucial confrontation and his theme, he had realized that to tackle America in fiction one had to rely, fictionally, on absence rather than presence, and he had worked beautifully on that assumption and final awareness. He has rescued the American theme from oblivion and from his own fear of impotence by using those very aspects he thought would deny it. He had made an asset of his "ignorance" and turned America's "lack of signs" into fictional material. His stylistic abstraction was, then, perfectly in keeping with his theme, was indeed a way of embodying and expressing it.

Thus Robert Marks is right in observing that the "last fine tracings of his pen in essence are refinements of the ideas, the techniques and the style he had previously brought to extreme advancement."[36] It is only in this sense—of a strenuous refinement—that we can accept the view that in *The Ivory Tower* James succeeded in portraying contemporary America. It is arguable that for a full-fledged, realistic analysis and description of its business world and its corruption one might—and probably should—go to Dreiser's *The Financier* (1912) and *The Titan* (1914). Maxwell Geismar has no doubt about it. But this is missing the real point, and even Edmund Wilson's enthusiasm for the brilliant human quality of the observation in this novel is misleading.[37] As Jan W. Dietrichson has noted, "James's art expresses society obliquely rather than directly. . . . he succeeded in conveying to his

Literature, 18 (1946–47), 77; and, for a comprehensive analysis, Seymour Chatman, *The Later Style of Henry James* (Oxford, 1972). Cf. also Putt, *Henry James: A Reader's Guide,* p. 407, and, for a statistical analysis, Tuomi Laitinen, *Aspects of Henry James's Style* (Helsinki, 1975).

[36] *James Later Novels,* p. 132.

[37] Geismar, *Henry James and the Jacobites,* pp. 418–22; Wilson, "The Ambiguity of Henry James," in *The Question of Henry James,* p. 188.

readers the 'feel' of the society or social group on which he focused his attention.[38]

Ezra Pound was paradoxically nearer the mark when he stressed the circumstantial precision and at the same time the elusive quality of "James's drawing of *moeurs contemporaines*."[39] Pound was, presumably, already thinking of the "compression" of the Jamesian novel that he would attempt in *Hugh Selwyn Mauberley* (1920). But he realized the abstract quality which the Jamesian novel was approaching or to which it would lead. James had faced and surveyed the abyss of emptiness stretching before him. By stretching his stylistic and formal abstraction as well, he was balancing his perception of that void with his best possible way of expressing it. No wonder, then, that the novel would break in the process.

[38] *The Image of Money in the American Novel of the Gilded Age* (Oslo, 1969), p. 64.

[39] *Literary Essays:* "James's drawing of *moeurs contemporaines* was so circumstantial, so concerned with the setting, with detail, nuance, social aroma, that his transcripts were 'out of date' almost before his books had gone into a second edition; out of date, that is, in the sense that his interpretations of society could never serve as a guide to such supposititious utilitarian members of the next generation as might desire to use them" (p. 339).

Looking Forward

JAMES'S experimentation with the novel, as discussed in this study, begun and ended on the theme of America. From *The Bostonians* to *The Ivory Tower*, a thirty-year-long process of development led from "solidity of specification" to the highest form of fictional abstraction; from James's break with his country to his final coming to terms with it; from a desire to "compete with life" in its fullness to the triumph of the unsaid and the unstated.[1] This development marks the transition from the assuredness of nineteenth-century fiction to the exhilarating uncertainties and adventures of the twentieth-century novel. But it is marked, in turn, by James's stubborn adherence to the principle of experimentation, which makes of him one of the fathers of literary Modernism.

In *The Bostonians* and *The Princess Casamassima*, in *The Reverberator* and *The Tragic Muse*, James had attempted to portray his time with keen awareness and a full display of the social, historical, and psychological forces at work in the contemporary world. His adoption of the pictorial and illustrative method of presentation coincided with a battle for realism. And in historical as well as Jamesian terms, a battle

[1] The steps of Jame's gradual reconciliation with America may be traced from his *William Wetmore Story and his Friends* (1903) through his 1906 encounter with Hamlin Garland (recorded in Garland's *Roadside Meetings*, [New York, 1930]); his conception of the New York Edition of his novels and tales (1907–9) as a kind of homage to his city and to his country (see Edel, *The Master*, pp. 316–17 and 321); his troubled vision of *The American Scene* (1907) and his idyllic reconstruction of a lost past in his unfinished *Autobiography*, up to his revealing letter of 19 February 1912 to W. D. Howells—extolling Howells's American inspiration (*Letters*, II, 221–26)—and to his two unfinished novels. See my essay "Henry James e l'America," *Annali di Ca' Foscari*, 11, no. 2 (1972), 443–62.

for realism at that time was as much an act of experimentation, a step in the direction of literary Modernism, as the later refinements of technique.

Working on the assumption that fiction was one of the fine arts, which required an awareness of social contrasts as an avowed counterpart to the moral dilemmas of the individual, was one of the distinguishing traits of the end-of-century novel, to which James contributed more than anyone else in the Anglo-American world. All the conquests of realism—as defined for instance in that textbook of Modernism, *The Modern Tradition*, such as objectivity, historical and naturalistic determinism, and so on[2]—are present in James's novels of the 1880s. Moreover, his joining forces, even if temporarily, with the naturalistic movement gave him a touch of the avant-garde. Contemporary fiction, with all its subjective dimension, grew out of that awareness as well (witness James Joyce).

James's experimental achievements in technique, however, were of even greater importance for the contemporary novel and marked him out as one of its fathers. Not only did he partake, in the 1890s, of the general trend to renew the novel from within; he forged most of the tools and provided the means of its renewal. It is not so much that he contributed in a decisive way to the "Art of Life" and to the autonomy of art, to "the purification or fiction" or the idea of the "objective artifact."[3] Nor is it only, in general terms, that he discovered, developed, and applied in a consistent way the fictional principle of the limited point of view—though one could hardly underestimate its importance. It is rather James's combination of the scenic method *with* the limited point of view that marked him out as a significant experimental novelist and a father of Modernism.

[2] See *The Modern Tradition: Backgrounds of Modern Literature*, ed. Richard Ellman and Charles Feidelson, Jr. (New York, 1965), pp. 229–99. See also *Documents of Modern Literary Realism*, ed. George J. Becker (Princeton, N.J., 1963).

[3] See "under-sections," so named in *The Modern Tradition*, pp. 121–31, 132–54, 182–92, and passim.

With his open experimentation in *The Spoils of Poynton* and *What Maisie Knew*, as well as in *The Awkward Age*, James supplied the twentieth-century novel with the structural and formal principles of the rhythmic juxtaposition of scenes and the skillful montage of significant moments. The author restricts his outlook on the world, chooses an angle of vision or a limited perspective, while exercising the firmest control of that particular point of view. He aims at a maximum of objective rendering while fully allowing for the play of the subjective vision. One aspect qualifies the other and makes it possible.

In one of his severest experimental attempts James provided the means of overcoming the curse of the novelist—the split between the objective experience and the subjective view, the world and the self, the scene and the viewer, the stage and the beholder. Such was James's mastery and assurance that he put forward the highest and most consistent plea for fiction as "rival creation," for the novel as providing an autonomous world of its own that is almost opposed to the actual world. The novel becomes self-contained and self-sufficient; it defies the world, it aims at a totally independent existence of its own. Yet a subjective presence is needed to make it possible, to sustain its structure and its pretentions.

It is again a mark of James's greatness and experimental importance that he realized not only the full implications but the destructive potential of that subjective presence. The center of consciousness, the limited point of view, allows and indeed calls for suspense and surprise, ambivalence and ambiguity, whose devious ways, whose subtle dangers and exalting possibilities James was among the first to discover and explore. But the "field of consciousness" of which James became a master, the awareness and the preponderance of the self, are secret and unexpected threats to the fictional worlds for which they are responsible or accountable.[4] That

[4] See ibid., "Self-Consciousness," pp. 690–765, for that contemporary heritage.

subjective presence threatened at each moment to distort or disrupt the universe of the novel. The very principle of "rival creation" is not only called in question but shattered.

Under the burden of ambiguity, undermined by the very uncertainties of that subjective presence, the novel so majestically raised and reared breaks down, crumbles, and collapses. James was among the first not only to realize the fact but to capitalize on it. By a great leap of the historical imagination, in *The Sacred Fount* he managed to make full use of the realization. This most daring of his experimental attempts links James in more than one way with the contemporary phenomenon of the antinovel and the *nouveau roman*. Just as he had contributed to the "solidity of specification" of the realistic novel, he offered startling examples of the reflexive novel, of the novel turning on itself. He who had previously aimed at the perfection' and self-sufficiency of fiction was one of the earliest to realize the hubris, the dangers and the consequences of that claim. He had elaborated the most ambitious technical, formal, and epistemological scaffolding for the novel, but foresaw its inevitable collapse. He had trusted the viewer and the subjective self, only to witness its destructive implications. The perfect palace of thought could, and indeed did, crumble like a house of cards. No sooner had James provided the novel with the tightest possible structure than he questioned the grounds and the very possibility of its existence.

In *The Whole Family, The Sense of the Past,* and *The Ivory Tower* we see James's method at work to enhance, but at the same time to check and jeopardize, the possibilities of the novel. In *The Whole Family* the outcome is an almost immediate and irrevocable standstill. In *The Sense of the Past* the question of not-knowing, ignoring and having at every moment to guess and to foresee, becomes the distinguishing trait, the curse and the frustration of the narrator. James discovers the outer bounds of his cherished "field of consciousness"—what has been called the next world, the next step of consciousness, the dubious borderland between the self, the unconscious, and the superconscious. He deals in elusive states of mind, and bafflement is the answer. But it is also an exalting adventure, of the mind as well as of the contemporary novel. In *The Ivory Tower* a similar position is complicated by James's stretching of the possibilities of the novel to breaking point. The leap is here into the unsaid and the unstated as modes of being and expression—as providing the very theme and substance of the novel. Not only has the outer objective world been refined out of existence, but statements of facts or expressions of feeling are equally dispensed with. "Verbal proof" is dispensed with; we witness a triumph of the "silent exhibition." We are led to, and left in, a state of absolute suspension, of hovering and void. The void has taken over, has become the subject and form of fiction.

Thus James's experimental dealings with the novel also mark the passage from presence to absence, from the full picture to the total void, from solidity to solution and dissolution, from realism to abstraction. He foresaw and enacted the transition; he embodied the crucial development. Negation becomes in later James a different and stranger form of affirmation, just as absence is recognized as a subtler form of presence. Negation involves the subject matter as well as the verbal substance of the novel; absence gradually verges on an existential condition. Moving away from the models of Titian and Tintoretto, James reaches toward Mondrian or the blank canvas at which we stare to discover its equally oppressive fullness. These terms and these fictional attitudes, more than anything else, seem to me to mark James's role and pretentions not only as a father of literary Modernism but even as a great-uncle of postmodernism.

He lurks in the background of Samuel Beckett or William Gass just as he is a presence and a driving force alongside or behind some of the best efforts of the twentieth-century novel—Marcel Proust and Thomas Mann, James Joyce and Virginia Woolf. It is the totality of James's outlook and the sum of his indications, his exploring and reaching out in all directions, that counts. It is his affirming *and* questioning at the same time that is so fruitful. To sum up: James's experimentation seems so important because it involves, in a thirty-year-long process, both the total structuring and the total dissolution of the novel form. It is a capsule embodiment of a century-long historical and literary process. Everything is there, in such a short stretch of time and relatively few novels: the fullness of the pictorial method and the urge to realism; the scenic fracturing of plot combined with the subjective reconstruction of the intelligent observer; the dramatic form combined with the field of consciousness; the highest bid for fictional creativity and the standstill of narrative impotence.

The difficulty and the exaltation, as always with James, is that the two sides of the question, the two aspects of his experimentation and his Modernism, work together and must be kept simultaneously in mind. He pushes as far forward as possible and at the same time he accepts all checks and balances in his untiring search toward the outer limits of fiction. Just as we stress his final indications leading to fictional dissolution, we must constantly remember that his is also the greatest effort in the direction of structural cohesiveness, symmetry, and control in the novel. In an age of Structuralism, James provides most of the premises and quite a few illustrations of a structural theory of narrative. He is a presence behind or inside much contemporary theorizing, from Todorov to Genette. He provides a solid ground and convincing samples on which to build, test, and exemplify structural theories and practices. It seems so delightful and so significant that while providing that solid ground he also showed the constant danger of its dissolution and the exhilarating possibilities of total refinement.

In a well-known image in the Preface to *The American*,[5] James had spoken of the balloon of experience that the novelist—the realistic, traditional, and responsible novelist—must keep tied to the earth, while the writer of romances was at liberty to cut the cable that bound it to the ground, to

[5] *The Art of the Novel*, pp. 33–34.

let it float "at large and unrelated" in the air of further and further refinement and abstraction. Not in the sense in which he intended it, but from the point of view of contemporary fiction, James did both.

Index

Index